Biomedical Policy
and Mental Health

Biomedical Policy and Mental Health

Donna R. Kemp

PRAEGER

Westport, Connecticut
London

Library of Congress Cataloging-in-Publication Data

Kemp, Donna R.
  Biomedical policy and mental health / Donna R. Kemp.
      p. cm.
  Includes bibliographical references and index.
  ISBN 0–275–94812–9 (alk. paper)
  1. Mental health policy—United States.   2. Biological psychiatry—
Research—United States.   3. Mental health services—United States.
I. Title.
  [DNLM: 1. Mental Disorders—diagnosis.   2. Mental Disorders—
therapy.   3. Mental Health Services—United States.   4. Health
Policy—United States.   WM 100 K3156 1994]
  RA790.5.K39   1994
  362.2′0973—dc20
  DNLM/DLC
  for Library of Congress   93–43788

British Library Cataloguing in Publication Data is available.

First published in 1994

Praeger Publishers, 88 Post Road West, Westport, CT 06881
An imprint of Greenwood Publishing Group, Inc.

Printed in the United States of America

The paper used in this book complies with the
Permanent Paper Standard issued by the National
Information Standards Organization (Z39.48–1984).

10 9 8 7 6 5 4 3 2 1

To my family: April, Sadie, Sam, and Sara

Contents

Preface

This book presents an overview of the relationship between biomedical policy and mental health. It explores the policy issues of a broad array of biomedical research and technology which impact mental health policy, and it examines how the very conducting of biomedical research and the use of its technology have implications for the mental health of people. There are both negative and positive consequences possible for mental health policy and for the mental health of human beings as the result of biomedical research and technology.

This book does not attempt to provide an in-depth analysis of any particular biomedical research or technology, nor does it explore in detail the public policy or ethics debate of biomedical decision making. Various research and technology are used to illustrate the effects of biomedical research and technology on mental health policy and the various implications of biomedical research and technology for the mental health of people. This book aims to highlight the significance of biomedical research and technology on mental health policy, and to point out the need to recognize the mental health consequences of the use of biomedical research and technology on all people exposed to those processes. This book does not attempt to cover all issues relating to biomedical policy and mental health, but instead to illustrate the wide array of issues raised by the crossover of biomedical policy and mental health policy.

Acknowledgment for assistance with this project goes to Jim Haehn, Dean, College of Behavioral and Social Sciences; Irv Schiffman, Chair, Department of Political Science, California State University, Chico; and Elaine Wangberg, Dean of the Graduate School, for assistance with funding for word processing and to Kathie Pendo and the California State University, Chico word processing staff for the final word processing of the manuscript.

Biomedical Policy
and Mental Health

1

Mental Health Policy and Definition

Most of what are defined as mental illnesses are classified as behavioral abnormalities. Some deny that mental illness can be considered a disease. Others view mental illness as including disease, disability, and abnormal behavior (Wing, 1978). There are those who believe that "mental health" and "physical health" are artificial distinctions, and that there is only one health (Sagan, 1987). Yet mental health policy in the United States continues to segregate physical and mental health policy. Mental health policy itself is increasingly fragmented and segregated. Historically, persons with mental illness, mental retardation, or substance abuse problems were grouped together. Recent trends, however, have separated legislation, funding, and services for the three populations. There are those like Finch (1985) who believe that this has been to the detriment of mental health.

INCIDENCE AND COSTS

Mental health problems may include psychiatric illness, substance abuse, emotional disorders, and developmental disorders. Estimates of mental illness are based on definitions developed by the American Psychiatric Association in the *Diagnostic and Statistical Manual of Mental Disorders-IIIR* (1987), which is currently being revised as the *DSM-IV*, and the federally funded Epidemiological Catchment Area (ECA) Surveys conducted during the 1980s (Regier et al., 1984).

The National Institute of Mental Health (NIMH) (1986) has found that 18.7 percent (29.4 million) of adult Americans have a diagnosable mental illness at some point during a given six-month period and 2.1 to 2.6 percent of this adult population at any time is suffering from a serious mental illness (SMI) (NIMH, 1992). Thirty percent of all Americans will have an episode of significant mental illness during their lifetime (Freedman, 1984; Robins et al., 1984). There is uncertainty as to whether mental illness is increasing or not, as there are no consistently applied measures of mental illness in the United States. Twenty-five percent of all hospital inpatient days are for mental disorders (Kiesler and Sibulkin, 1987), but many cases of mental illness never come to medical attention. As many as 25 percent of general medical visits are occasioned by mental health problems, which are not always recognized by either the patient or physician. Only when the most serious symptoms are present, such as hallucinations, do nonpsychiatric physicians tend to recognize mental disorders (Kiesler and Sibulkin, 1987). This raises public policy questions involving expenditure of Medicare and Medicaid funds for ineffective and inefficient treatment occurring from misdiagnosis.

According to the National Institute of Mental Health (1986), the most prevalent mental disorders in the United States (8.3 percent of all adults) are anxiety and somatoform disorders including phobias, panic disorders, and obsessive compulsive disorders. The next most prevalent problems (6 percent) are affective disorders, including bipolar disorders, depression, and manic episodes. In addition, almost one out of every one thousand adults (.9 percent) are diagnosed as schizophrenic. Prevalence varies by age, sex, social class, and urban versus rural status. The most prevalent mental health problems for men are alcohol abuse and dependence, phobias, and drug abuse (drug abuse is the second most common problem for women age 18 to 24). For women the major disorders are phobias, major depression, and dysthymia (neurotic depression). For men and women over 65, cognitive impairment is the most prevalent problem. People in urban areas have a higher risk (32.2 percent lifetime prevalence) as compared to people living in small towns and rural areas (27.5 percent lifetime prevalence) (Robins et al., 1984). A study by the National Institute of Mental Health (1986) indicates that mental illnesses may cost the United States $185 billion each year.

The National Institute of Mental Health (1986), in their door-to-door survey of three communities (Baltimore, New Haven, and St. Louis), found alcoholism to be the most common single disorder, with a six-month prevalence of 5 percent and a lifetime prevalence of 12 to 16 percent. This means that more than one of every ten Americans will be affected by alcoholism. In addition, another 2 percent of adults have problems with drug abuse or dependence. The National Institute of Mental Health (1990) reported that 6.2 percent of all patients admitted to mental hospitals have a principal diagnosis of alcohol-related disorders, with the lowest rates in state hospitals and the highest in veterans' administration centers. In addition, 3 percent of admitted persons have a drug-related primary diagnosis, with the lowest rates in state hospitals and the highest in general hospitals with psychiatric units.

According to the National Institute of Mental Health (1990), more than 12 percent of U.S. children and adolescents (7.5 million) suffer from mental disorders, often for life. This results in $1.5 billion in treatment costs each year. Yet insurance coverage is limited for mental disorders. Children with autism are less likely than other children to be covered by private health insurance. Less than one fifth of afflicted children receive appropriate treatment. Many of those treated fail to recover because their disorders are inadequately understood. The lost lifetime productivity of those unable to work consistently or to live independently adds to the cost.

The Institute of Medicine of the National Academy of Sciences Commissioned a study of children who were dependents of employees of a large company to compare the treatment costs of children's mental disorders and physical disorders. From 1984 through 1986, insurance data showed that $2.7 million (16 percent) of $16.7 million spent on hospital care was for mental disorders. About $1 million (23 percent) of $4.9 million spent on outpatient care was for mental disorders. These figures did not include hospitalization costs which went beyond insurance reimbursement or outpatient care by private practice psychologists, social workers, and counselors (NIMH, 1990).

Costs for mental disorders in children and adolescents appear in the mental health, physical health, education, welfare, and juvenile justice systems. In the 1986-87 school year, 384,680 children with serious emotional disorders were receiving special education and associated services. The average cost per student ranged from $4,500 in self-contained special education classes to $6,204 in private school placements contracted with public education funds. In 1985 there were more than 49,000 young people in juvenile facilities and thousands more in adult facilities. It is estimated that as many as half of them have at least one mental disorder. In 1984 the average annual cost of care varied by state from $15,200 to $66,100 (NIMH, 1990).

Suicide rates are rising in the United States, and suicide is the third leading cause of death among teenagers and young adults. Twenty percent of suicides are committed by persons under age 25. The actual suicide rate may be as much as three times as high as the reported rate (Sagan, 1987). The suicide rate among Native Americans is two and a half times higher than for the general population and even higher among youth. This contributes to the fact that Native Americans have a shorter life span than any other population group in the United States (American Indian Policy Review Commission, 1977).

Mental retardation is a developmental disability. The American Association on Mental Deficiency (AAMD) defines mental retardation as "significantly sub-average general functioning existing concurrently with deficits in adaptive behavior and manifested during the developmental period" (Grossman, 1973:5). Under this definition, approximately 3 percent of the U.S. population is afflicted with mental retardation (Stedman, 1971:5). Stroud (Stroud and Sutton, 1988) believes mental retardation is better served by schools, sheltered workshops, residential services, and support services than other developmental disabilities.

In the United States, persons with mental retardation have often been cared for in institutions for the mentally ill. However, over time the mental retardation field has moved away from mental health. Now mental retardation is usually included under developmental disabilities, which are defined as chronic and severe disabilities which are attributable to either severe mental or physical conditions, are manifested before a person is 22, are likely to continue indefinitely, and result in substantial functional limitations in several areas of activity (42 USC, Section 6102). Thus mental retardation is placed with epilepsy, cerebral palsy, and autism.

The term *developmental disability* covers a range of conditions which are defined as "a severe, chronic disability which is attributable to mental or physical impairment or combination of mental and physical impairments, is manifested by age 22, is likely to continue indefinitely, and results in substantial limitations in three or more areas of major life activity" (Grossman, 1983:168).

Biomedically, mental retardation implies a distortion or pathology in the central nervous system, particularly in the higher centers of the brain, which causes behavioral and specifically intellectual dysfunction. The pathology may extend to other systems as well, resulting in wide variations of multiple disability (Plog and Santomous, 1980). Mental retardation has been classified by severity by the AAMD as mild, moderate, severe, and profound. The AAMD definition contains three criteria: significantly subaverage general intellectual functioning, concurrent deficits in adaptive behavior, and onset during the developmental period (Grossman, 1983). Mental retardation has existed among humans throughout their existence, but national interest through medical technology and research did not occur until the 1950s. It is suspected that a high percentage of cases of mental retardation exist prior to birth, and modern technology has been developed to a level that it can detect signs of fetal abnormalities.

The United States has an aging population. This means that the society can expect to be faced with more chronic cases of mental disorder. This will contribute to a growing focus on providing for long-term care for the chronically mentally ill. Many of the needs of the elderly will be mental health needs.

In spite of the extensive prevalence and high cost of mental illness, mental health policy has continually been relegated to a second-class position. Policies addressing physical ill health have consistently been established with entitlements, while many mental health programs have relied upon annual legislative renewal. Mental health programs must rely on general fund appropriations, subjecting the programs every year to the politics of assembling of executive budgets and to the competition of legislative apportionment of general funds which are inadequate to meet the demands made upon them.

CURRENT POLICY ISSUES

Kiesler (1980) has seen mental health policy as a "nonfield" or at best undeveloped. His definition of national mental health policy is "The de facto or de jure aggregate of laws, practices, social structures, or actions occurring within our society, the intent of which is improved mental health of individuals or groups.'' (p. 106)

De jure policy is intentional and usually legislated as statutory law. De facto policy is the net outcome of overall practices regardless of whether the outcome is intended or not. Over the last 30 years, national and state de jure mental health policy has been based on deinstitutionalization of large state institutions and outpatient care through community mental health services. By the end of the 1970s, there was growing concern over whether deinstitutionalization had occurred successfully, whether community mental health systems had failed, and whether mental health systems had ever been funded adequately (Kemp, 1991).

Many professionals and researchers believed there was increasing evidence of a ''revolving door'' cycle in community hospital psychiatric units, emergency rooms, and state hospitals, with recidivism rates running from 14 to 40 percent within a six-month period. This would indicate that deinstitutionalized persons and others, who would at an earlier time have received long-term care, now were involved in episodic county hospital visits (DeRisi and Vega, 1983). Kiesler and Sibulkin (1987), however, concluded that there was no ''revolving door'' because the national readmission rate to hospitals had not changed over the last 15 years. Kiesler (1982) noted that despite deinstitutionalization, the national rate of hospitalization had actually increased, but Keisler and Sibulkin (1987) found that most of the increase in the number of people and the rate of people hospitalized was accounted for by the increased risk associated with the demographics of the ''baby boom'' cohort, who were in the age range of onset for schizophrenia and other disorders. Their research indicated that our de facto policy is inpatient care, and the most frequent inpatient site has become the general hospital, where the most episodes occur in those hospitals without a separate psychiatric unit. The 60 percent increase in mental hospitalization over the last 15 years is due to treatment in those general hospitals without psychiatric units. Although the cost of inpatient care has risen at all sites and most sharply in general hospitals, total costs have been held in check because the length of stay has decreased. Although most of that recent decrease has occurred in state mental hospitals and veterans' facilities, those facilities continue to have the longest stays. Inpatient days in all hospitals for mental disorders have declined from 50 percent 35 years ago to 25 percent in the mid-1980s.

Kiesler (1982:359) also concluded that there were no studies showing hospitalization to have a ''positive impact on the average patient which exceeded that of the alternative care.'' He found that patients of alternative care were less likely to be hospitalized, and the best predictor of hospitalization was prior hospitalization. Kiesler and Sibulkin (1987) found that alternative care outside of hospitals was more effective and less costly, and that aftercare, in general, delayed rehospitalization. They also found Gordon Paul's (Paul and Lentz, 1977) "social learning" approach to be the most effective form of hospital treatment for severely disturbed persons.

Funding issues have remained critical. With an intergovernmental system, each level of government has tried to place more costs on another level of government. Medicaid reimbursement has focused on institutional care. When many mentally disabled were in effect transinstitutionalized into nursing homes and large group homes, states sought ways to receive federal funds for these facilities. Medicaid, however, has sought to contain costs by defining who is eligible for reimbursement in nursing homes.

Because the federal government controlled expenditures for the mentally disabled in nursing homes, states moved people with mental illness or mental retardation from nursing homes. This, in effect, created a second deinstitutionalization as people previously transinstitutionalized from the state institutions to nursing homes were moved again. This movement was promoted primarily because of funding rather than the desire to enhance the living or service needs of the clientele. The U.S. Omnibus Reconciliation Act of 1987 (OBRA, P.L. 100-203) required screening of new and current nursing home patients for mental illness and developmental disabilities to prevent further movement of these populations into nursing homes.

The 1980s saw growing fiscal retrenchment in the states. Researchers in California found several trends in reviewing the public mental health services of 11 California counties from 1978 to 1983. These included a greater focus on the more severely disabled; an increase in the utilization of hospital care, residential treatment, day treatment, and case management services; and a decrease in traditional outpatient services. They found that although the severely mentally ill were receiving a high priority for service, the service systems still did not meet their needs for long-term maintenance and support services (Surber et al., 1986). Through the 1980s and into the 1990s, there have been growing problems with providing an adequate mental health budget (Kemp, 1991). Inadequate resources were being made available. This has also been the case in most other states (Torrey, Erdman, Wolfe, and Flynn, 1990).

Mental health services in the United States account for approximately $20 billion per year in public funds, plus many more dollars in insurance and private personal expenditures. Mental health care is being scrutinized increasingly. Insurers, the states, and the federal government are focused on cost containment. Limitations on inpatient care and outpatient care are not uncommon. Insurance companies often have lifetime limits on expenditures. Co-payments and deductibles are also used widely. Increases in out-of-pocket expenses often result in reductions in use of services, and a reduction in the use of mental health services is more likely to occur than a reduction in the use of physical health services (Scheffler, 1987).

Inpatient costs remain the most costly, with data on some health insurance plans showing that 4 to 5 percent of inpatient users may account for 20 to 40 percent of costs (Scheffler, 1987). Soon hospital mental health care providers will be reimbursed, like hospitals receiving Medicare for physical health care, by Diagnostic Related Groups (DRGs). Categories for this prospective payment system have been under development. Mental health coverage was proposed in the 1993 Clinton administration national health legislation, but mental health coverage is not as extensive as the physical health coverage in that proposal.

During the 1980s research emerged as the National Institute of Mental Health's primary mission, and that research is increasingly biomedical. Research has become more focused on such areas as classification and diagnosis, psychopharmacologic drugs, genetic studies of adopted twins, new treatments for affective disorders, and new behavioral approaches to managing disorders. This research approach has been reinforced by the training that NIMH has supported of basic and clinical researchers in biology, psychology, and the social sciences. New specializations have been encouraged such as mental health economics, mental health epidemiology and statistics, mental health systems planning, and program evaluation. A greater emphasis has been placed on the rigor of research proposals, and interdisciplinary research is growing as biomedical and behavioral sciences are combined. For instance, behavioral neurochemistry studies explore how behavior affects neurochemical responses, which are then explored for how they affect subsequent behavior. In the mid-1980s, NIMH established an agenda which focused on the homeless mentally ill, children and adolescents, the elderly, and violence and made research on schizophrenia and prevention research a priority (Frazier and Parron, 1987).

By 1993 there had been massive dehospitalization, but numerous hospitals remained open; a substantial amount of traninstitutionalization had occurred, particularly to nursing homes, but a second deinstitutionalization was under way to transfer mentally disabled out of nursing homes; there was a significant number of mentally disabled among the homeless population; the availability and quality of services varied across the country and many mentally ill received no or inadequate services; a full range of quality community services, widely available, had not been established; there were growing concerns over the inability to treat mentally ill persons under the provisions of established civil rights protections; funding was still focused on inpatient services; there were growing funding problems at the federal and state levels; and research was increasingly biomedically focused.

The Medical Model and Other Approaches

In recent times mental health service delivery has followed a medical model, with psychiatrists as the dominant profession. This model is disease oriented and emphasizes illness. The focus is on finding and treating the cause of the emotional and behavioral dysfunction. The approach is based on diagnosis, treatment, and cure. Traditionally the focus has been inpatient (in the past long-term, in the present short term), with the emphasis on medication and intrapersonal needs and with little attention or resources for interpersonal and environmental needs with a psychosocial focus.

In the 1980s the emphasis in mental health policy was on trying to improve coordination and to develop a wider base of service and support systems for the chronically mentally ill. Some of the approaches being tried were case management, multidisciplinary treatment teams, community support systems, integrated services, substate mental health authorities, and funding through pooling of resources or capitation (Dill and Rochefort, 1989). Many of these service and support systems have also been used widely in the mental retardation field and often have been applied there first.

The mental health approach to people with less serious emotional disorders has focused on outpatient treatment and modalities such as family systems psychotherapy and employee assistance programs, which have a nonmedical, interpersonal, and environmental approach. A variety of professionals have become active in this area, including psychologists, clinical social workers, and family counselors. The orientation of many of these professionals is away from the medical model, but they often must pay at least lip service to that model when third-party payors require diagnosis using the *Diagnostic and Statistical Manual of Mental Disorders* (*DSM-IIIR*) (1987) for reimbursement.

Substance abuse, which also has broken away from mental health, has retained a medical model focus, with alcoholism being defined as a disease under the most accepted model. Inpatient treatment remains a primary and often medicalized treatment approach. Alcoholics Anonymous (AA), established in the 1940s, has operated with an outpatient, interpersonal, and environmental approach. And in recent years outpatient treatment social models have been increasing.

Care and treatment of persons with mental retardation has moved away from the medical model. Families and educators have become dominant in the field. The service delivery model is psychoeducational and is based on developmental theories. The focus is on lifetime habilitation, continuous development, and support of the individual rather than cure. The service delivery model is focused on community services, the most normal setting and approach, and a continuum of care. The field is seen as separate from mental health and is focused on developmental, educational, and social models increasingly organized with social services or physical disabilities. But for all groups with mental disabilities, problems of stigmatization and discrimination remain.

Stigmatization and Discrimination

People with mental illness, mental retardation, and substance abuse problems are all stigmatized; they are perceived as significantly different in a negative way (White and Wolfensberger, 1969). This is evident in the resistance of neighborhoods to group homes for any of these groups. However, mental retardation is received more sympathetically because it is viewed as an accident of nature, usually non-dangerous, and beyond the person's control. The perception of it also is highly associated with children rather than adults (although most persons with mental retardation are adults). Mental illness and substance abuse are seen as volitional, and mental illness is also perceived as associated with violence. Both are perceived to be associated with adults, who are seen as responsible for their actions (although many children and adolescents are found in these populations).

Parents of the mentally ill and substance abusers have often been blamed for causing or being a part of the problem. Families of people with mental retardation often are more involved because they frequently deal with the disorder very early, in infancy and early childhood; families of substance abusers and mentally ill persons often do not face symptoms until adolescence or early adulthood, when it may take longer to identify and face the problem. Substance abusers and the mentally ill may have cyclical patterns in which at times everything seems all right, so these conditions tend to reestablish hope. Support systems and services are much more readily available early on for children with developmental disabilities, while services may be difficult to find for children or adolescents with mental illness or substance abuse problems. Support systems for family members are most available for people with developmental disabilities and substance abuse problems, especially alcoholics, and are more difficult to find for family members of persons with mental illness. The burden for families of a person with mental retardation seems to relate more to the family's perception for the need for care (Willer, Intagliata, and Atkinson, 1979), while the stress level for a person with a family member with mental illness seems to relate more to the severity of the symptoms (Doll, 1976). How people with mental disabilities are perceived is critical because it affects policy development and resources.

IMPACTS OF BIOMEDICAL RESEARCH AND TECHNOLOGY

The service systems for people with mental retardation, chronic mental illness, or substance abuse problems and people who are emotionally distressed have diverged along with growth in knowledge, clearer definitions of the problems, improved identification and assessment techniques, increased biomedical knowledge of causes, and better approaches to treatment and training.   All of these groups may benefit from the growth in biomedical technology and research, but they may also benefit from viewing each person as a whole person in an environmental context.   Understanding the relationship between physical and mental health components and the importance of psychosocial approaches, as well as biomedical and technological approaches, may enhance individual lives.

Congressional committees have held numerous hearings on a variety of issues related to biotechnology and biomedical research.   Calls were made early to go beyond the commercial, medical, and scientific communities, with the public interest represented by individuals and groups (Randall, Mandelbaum, and Kelly, 1980).   President Carter appointed a Commission for the Study of Ethical Problems in Medicine and Biomedical and Behavioral Research, which transmitted a report to President Reagan in November 1982.   The Commission indicated that new institutional arrangements might be necessary to deal with the distribution of political power over biotechnology (President's Commission, 1982).   In 1983 the House Subcommittee on Investigations and Oversight of the Committee on Science and Technology held hearings on human genetic engineering.

Some scientists have claimed that there is already too much government interference in the research and marketing of biotechnology (Strobel, 1987). The process of regulation in biotechnology is one of the most complex in the federal government.   State and local governments are also involved.   Huber (1987) views the relationships between state/local government and the federal government regarding questions of biotechnology as increasingly complex and confusing.   Numerous laws are in place, and various government agencies address various aspects of regulation across all three levels of government. Attempts have been made to involve the public in various review bodies, institutional biosafety committees, and congressional hearings.   As in many policy areas (including mental health), this results in a complex crazy quilt of regulation and gaps.   Others are concerned that biomedical research and technology are not regulated sufficiently.

Biomedical research is providing information and explanations for many mental disabililties.   This ranges from work on dopamine as it relates to schizophrenia to gene markers for depression.   Financial support for biomedical research will probably continue to grow.   And within psychiatry and the other mental health professions, there is a growing acceptance for using biomedical technology and the findings of biomedical research.   Psychiatry in particular is becoming increasingly medicalized, with psychiatrists focused more on medication and biomedical aspects rather than psychotherapy, and with increased interest in brain chemistry and psychoimmunology research and application.

The mental health issues of biomedical policy making have generally received either no notice or have been raised as peripheral issues to other questions being addressed in biomedical policy.   But certainly biomedical research and technology have many ramifications for mental health and have the potential to bring about change in mental health policy. The mental health policy arena remains confused by lack of clear definitions. Biomedical research may or may not help clarify these definitions.

Further confusion is caused by a lack of consensus on the role of the environment versus biology in the etiology of these problems. Biomedical research is rapidly developing more knowledge about etiology. Whether knowing more about etiology will help clarify policy remains to be seen. Biomedical research is also pointing increasingly to the significance of the mind-body link. Whether this new support for holistic views will lead to holistic policy is in doubt, as political forces support self-definition, separation, and fragmentation. These unresolved issues affect the ability to make meaningful policy choices about prevention, treatment, rehabilitation, habilitation, cure, or maintenance.

DEFINING MENTAL HEALTH

In order to have effective mental health policy, we must be able to define the problem. Over time, definitions have shifted from insanity to mental illness to mental health. The basis of definition has moved from culturally deviant, to possession by evil spirits or the devil, to sickness. The cause has been associated with possession, social and cultural stressors, family dysfunctions, developmental problems, genetics, diseases, and brain dysfunction. Thus sometimes scientific, biomedical focuses have been primary and others times they have not.

The World Health Organization's (WHO) Preamble (1946) defines health as "a state of complete physical, mental, and social well-being." This definition of health includes mental health, but there are those who do not like this definition. C. Van de Vate (1990:1) objects to this definition because "it is impossible to speak of a healthy mentally handicapped person." He views the WHO definition as having no boundaries and particularly no ethical boundaries. He sees it as legitimizing medical practitioners as gatekeepers of happiness through application of medical techniques such as gene technologies and abortion.

Mental illness is perplexing and its definition is influenced by social, cultural, religious, and psychological factors. It has unlimited definitional boundaries. Scholars, psychiatrists, and researchers cannot provide a universally accepted definition (Taube and Goldman, 1989; Toufexis, 1990), and its definition has changed over time.

Eaton (1980:27) felt that before the fifteenth century mental illness seemed to be regarded as an "undifferentiated experience." Treatment consisted mostly of benign neglect. Bizarre behavior was seen as culturally deviant, but not requiring confinement.   There were few references to people with bizarre behaviors.

Foucault (1973) argued that the view of mental illness changed because it represented a threat to the economic Age of Reason, which precipitated a need for control. *Malleus Malificarun* (Witches' Hammer) in 1487 equated mental illness with control by the devil.   This crystallized a major change in the Western view of mental illness and led to the Inquisition.

A penal and social control approach developed toward the mentally ill. This has been countered at times by a more humane view which sees people as sick and requiring protection, not possessed by devils.   But even today, the view of the mentally ill as people possessed by demons remains in rural areas of such countries as Jamaica where the mental health law in 1989 still allowed a person to be arrested for being "insane."

In colonial America, definition and treatment of the mentally ill was based on social class and economics.   The wealthy were locked away by their families in attics and cellars.   They were considered to be a family disgrace and were not acknowledged publicly.   The less wealthy were considered to be paupers and roamed the countryside as wild persons.   If capable of work, a man might be auctioned off as a laborer to a farmer, who would receive a small payment from the town.   Those who attracted too much attention or were violent were considered felons and were pilloried, whipped, or imprisoned in dungeons. Occasionally they were hanged or burned at the stake.   Gradually alms houses, work houses, and houses of correction took custody of the insane (Joint Commission on Mental Illness and Health, 1961).

Dr. Benjamin Rush, the first director of the Pennsylvania Hospital, which was the first U.S. hospital to admit mental patients, believed terror should be used in the treatment of madness because it acted powerfully on the body through the medium of the mind (Deutsch, 1949).   Patients were chained to the walls of cellar prison cells, and attendants carried and used whips.   The Joint Commission on Mental Illness and Health (1961) suggested that fear and punishment of the mentally ill were related to Old Testament views of mental or physical illnesses as visitations of punishment for sins.

Dr. Pinel's humane view and use of moral treatment in Paris in the eighteenth century led to the unchaining of patients, and the violence of patients decreased dramatically (Bockoven, 1956). Moral treatment was environmentally based and behavioral, not medically based and somatic.   The York Retreat approach in England was based on the view that there was a need for seclusion from the stresses of urban society.

In the nineteenth century, the holistic view prevailed in U.S. psychiatric hospitals; all parts of the body were perceived as interdependent. Health and disease were believed to result from the interaction of individuals with their environments. As American medicine became more scientific with pathogenic and bacteriological discoveries, an argument arose over the cause of mental disorder. Dr. John Gray, as editor for the *American Journal for Insanity*, rejected moral treatment and argued that patients were physically ill with a brain disease. This view was accepted eventually along with a generally pessimistic attitude toward cure (Kiesler and Sibulkin, 1987). Managed care became imbued with medical overtones. Drugs became popular to manage difficult patients. Sedatives and hypnotics were used widely. Institutions focused on social control and guarding the public and patients against irrational acts. The emphasis became keeping the mentally ill physically alive. While the ultimate cure was awaited, custodial care was accepted for the interim (Grob, 1983). At the turn of the century, Social Darwinism and a biological focus on heredity led to the eugenics movement, which resulted in the surgical sterilization of many institutionalized mentally ill and mentally retarded persons.

During the first half of the twentieth century, psychiatrists tried to redefine the concepts of mental disease and therapeutic interventions. Psychiatrists were trained in medicine and preferred a therapeutic, not a custodial, role. What appeared to be modern, scientific medicine in other medical specialties made psychiatry appear more backward and less desirable as a specialty. The traditional model had held that there was a sharp distinction between health and disease. Mental disease was seen as being marked by dramatic behavioral and somatic signs. However, by the turn of the century Sigmund Freud in Europe and Adolf Meyer in the United States challenged this view. After World War I most psychiatrists were trained psychoanalytically or in psychodynamic psychiatry. The argument was made that behavior occurred along a developmental continuum. This raised the possibility of psychiatric interventions being able to alter an outcome. Psychiatric involvement with nonpsychotic patients was rationalized by the prevention, early treatment, and continuum concepts. This interest in prevention and early treatment in the community led to child guidance clinics, the mental hygiene movement, and psychoanalytic approaches (Grob, 1983).

World War II accelerated the move to psychodynamic approaches. Psychiatrists during the war were called on to help identify and screen recruits with neuropsychiatric problems. Opponents objected to this activity as contributing to racial and ethnic discrimination and discrimination in civilian life for the people who were rejected in the process. The war also led to the conclusion that prolonged stress associated with warfare led to mental breakdown (after the Vietnam War, this would be called posttraumatic stress syndrome). The conclusion was that the environment played a major role in the etiology of mental problems. This moved the focus back toward social and environmental factors and toward an interest in less severe mental problems referred to as neuroses. Brief therapy in settings near the front were found to be effective, and this also reinforced the movement for prevention, brief psychotherapy, and treatment in the community. This change in focus resulted in a new psychiatric epidemiology. Instead of just focusing on the pattern of mental disease among hospital populations, studies became much broader with an interest in socioenvironmental variables, social class, and many more diagnoses. Social science became much more involved, and definitions were broadened from the narrow medical focus. This change in definition supported increased social activism, which influenced policy changes.

This led to the establishment of the National Institute of Mental Health in 1949, which was grounded in the social basis of mental disorders. Biomedical research was not assigned a high priority. This was reinforced by the limited research base available on the brain and physiological processes relating to mental illness. Much of the research was directed by social scientists, with only 15 percent of the early NIMH research being directed by biological scientists (Grob, 1987).

The family began to be viewed as playing a causative role in mental illness. The term *schizophrenogic mother* was introduced by Fromm-Reichmann (1948) to describe the effects that some mothers appeared to have in predisposing their children to schizophrenia. The concept was a part of a number of related ideas developed in the 1940s and 1950s that suggested that the immediate psychosocial context surrounding the schizophrenic played a causative role in producing schizophrenia. Watzlawick (1968) emphasized that there were different degrees of psychological disturbances brought about by double-binding communication. Only repeated exposure within a relationship required for survival could cause severe pathology. (The term *double-bind* was introduced by Bateson in 1956 to describe the paradox created by an unresolvable sequence of experiences in interpersonal communication.)

Psychoanalytic theory also generated several concepts regarding development of the human being. Freud (1905) developed a six-stage developmental theory from the oral stage to the mature genital stage. Erikson (1959) developed an eight-stage model from basic trust versus basic mistrust to integrity versus despair. Mahler, Pine, and Bergman (1975) focused on the very early phases of development of identity, from the fourth or fifth month, until around the thirtieth month, as the time of separation-individuation.

The self-actualization concept was developed to describe the central motivating tendency in life. The term relates to the innate capacity of humans to grow and develop toward emotional and psychological maturity. Goldstein (1934) believed that self-actualization is the only ultimate organismic motivating factor which drives the individual to develop and perfect his/her capacities to the fullest extent. He believed that it only occurred through mastering conflict with the environment and anxiety. Rogers (1951) believed that it was the one basic tendency of the organism and used the concept to describe the primary goal of normal development. Maslow (1970) viewed self-actualization as the highest level of his hierarchy of human needs. The tendency was thought to be universal, and great reliance was placed on a person's ability to have self-restorative capacities. The concept has been criticized for placing too high a value on the rights of the individual. Thus, it would be more acceptable in some cultures than others. The concept has been attacked based on the view that there is no innate tendency toward growth, but there is a capacity to learn (Butler and Rice, 1963; Dollard and Miller, 1950).

Many behaviorists, orthodox psychotherapists, and some systems theorists view behavior as determined by innate drives, stimulus-response mechanisms, or the needs and constraints of the psychosocial system. Humanistic and existential psychotherapists view people as influenced by their understanding of their life purpose, goals, and intentions (Walrond-Skinner, 1986).

In recent years the pendulum has swung again to a biological focus in definitions. A wide range of mental disorders have been defined, and definitions are focusing increasingly on biological components. The National Institute of Mental Health has also shifted its focus to funding biologically based research. Genetic components are increasingly being explored in schizophrenia, depression, and alcoholism.

However, in Canada an innovative, broad-based definition of mental health was released in 1988 (Health and Welfare Canada, 1988). The definition reflected several themes, including "psychological and social harmony and integration, quality of life and general well-being, self-actualization and growth, effective personal adaptation, and the mutual influences of the individual, the group and the environment" (Lakaski, Wilmot, Lips, and Brown, 1993). The new definition which replaced a traditional one read: "Mental Health is the capacity of the individual, the group and the environment to interact with one another in ways that promote subjective well-being, the optimal development and use of mental abilities (cognitive, affective, and relational), the achievement of individual and collective goals consistent with justice and the attainment and preservation of conditions of fundamental equality" (Health and Welfare Canada, 1988:3).

DEFINING MENTAL DISORDERS

Mental disorders seen in children, adolescents, and adults include psychosis; mood disorders such as depression and anxiety; personality disorders; behavioral problems involving disruptive and antisocial acts; and developmental impairments that limit the ability to think, learn, communicate, and form social attachments. Disabilities are not mutually exclusive. Many people have two or more mental disorders. Autism and severe mental retardation are often seen in the same person, as are alcohol abuse and major depression (NAMHC, 1990).

Studies are showing a relationship between disorders. Depression or anxiety disorders in adolescence may double the risk of later drug abuse or dependence. Studies in the general population show that alcohol, drug abuse, and mental disorders often co-occur (NAMHC, 1990). For example, the peak age for the onset of alcohol abuse or dependence and drug abuse or dependence was identified in 1990 by NIMH as 15 to 19 years. ("Peak Ages . . . ," 1990). Research is needed on the possible reduction of subsequent substance abuse by early treatment of anxiety disorders and depression (NAMHC, 1990). Alcohol, drug abuse, and mental health (ADM) services are usually segregated, and this may cause conflicts over primary diagnosis and who is responsible for treatment of those with a dual diagnosis. This raises the question of whether integrated services are more appropriate.

Epidemiological Studies

The purpose of psychiatric epidemiology is to examine the distribution of psychiatric disorders in the population to determine the causes of mental illness. Some of the most recent information on prevalence comes from the ECA studies done in the 1980s. Those studies included approximately 3,000 adults interviewed in the community and 500 institutionalized adults in each of five research sites: Baltimore, Los Angeles, New Haven, North Carolina, and St. Louis. These 20,000 adults were interviewed to determine the prevalence of specific psychiatric disorders (Regier et al., 1984).

Within the last decade, advances in diagnosis and classification have made it possible to develop more reliable national epidemiologic data. The NIMH-sponsored ECA program is providing a portrait of specific mental disorders in adults for various geographic areas and influencing classification and diagnosis worldwide.

NIMH wants to find out more about variables affecting the responses of informants. Parents with mental disorders such as depression are known to be more likely to report higher levels of psychopathology in their children. Fathers tend to report less disorder than mothers. Parents as a whole are poor in describing their own behavior, especially parenting (NIMH, 1990).

NIMH released a study in 1990 which analyzed data from the NIMH major ECA Survey conducted from 1980 to 1984. That study found that the peak ages at which serious mental disorders develop are childhood and adolescence. There are more than seven million adolescents and children who have mental illness. Only one in three receives any treatment, and only one in five gets appropriate treatment.

In fiscal year 1989 NIMH began to develop procedures for a multisite epidemiologic and services study of mental disorders among children and adolescents ages 9 through 17. That three-year project was to develop a Common Core Battery and other survey procedures to be used in larger field trials (NIMH, 1990). Previous studies have relied on clinician's judgments about what groups of symptoms constitute specific disorders and analysis of data on large samples of children and adolescents receiving care. Recently the

NIMH Diagnostic Interview Schedule for Children (DISC) has also been used. The new Common Core Battery will include a structured psychiatric interview, a measure of impairment, data on services, and assessment of demographic psychosocial and behavioral risk factors.

Assessment of children under age seven or eight is especially difficult because they have limited cognitive and language skills. They do not reliably report their feelings, memories, self-perceptions or behavior. Information is also needed about special populations such as children in foster care and those exposed to community-wide catastrophic events (NAMHC, 1990).

There is also insufficient information on the relationship between symptoms and impairment. Some people with multiple symptoms have minimal impairment, while others with few symptoms have significant impairment. It also remains difficult to predict the length of a disorder or the possibility of spontaneous remission.

Lewis Judd, MD, NIMH Director in 1990, said, "Because of the revolution in the neurosciences, we are now capable of demystifying our most complex organ system—the brain—and of providing solutions for the serious mental illness suffered by millions of children. Reducing the burden of childhood psychiatric disorders may be the most important challenge facing our mental health care system today" ("Peak Ages . . . ," 1990:7). But in order to accomplish this, there must be accurate diagnosis.

There are two systems of diagnosis used widely in the United States: the revised third edition of the *Diagnostic and Statistical Manual of Mental Disorders (DSM-IIIR)* (1987) and the *Manual of the International Statistical Classification of Disease, Injuries, and Causes of Death*, volume 1 (1977), known as the *ICD-9.*

DSM

The first edition of the *DSM* appeared in 1952. It was developed primarily by and for psychiatrists and presented a psychobiological approach to emotional disorders. The second edition was published in 1958 and established a focus on mental illness that emphasized neurosis, psychosis, and personality disorder.

The third edition, published in 1980, was a collaborative venture of the American Psychiatric Association. It sought to provide a detailed description of all categories of mental illness. For each disorder a description usually contained a list of essential features and a clinical sketch; a summary of characteristics usually associated with the disorder; information on the typical onset and course of the disorder, the impairment caused, and potential complications; information on known predisposing factors and frequency of occurrence of the disorder; information on similar disorders to assist differential diagnosis; and diagnostic criteria for the disorder (*DSM-III*, 1980). It was atheoretical and did not elucidate causes of mental disorder. Its primary function was description. It was more detailed and used less highly charged language than its predecessor. The term *neurosis* was no longer recommended for diagnostic use, and the term *depressive neurosis* became *dysthymic disorder*. Homosexuality was no longer classified as an emotional illness, but there was a diagnosis for homosexuals who were uncomfortable with their sexual orientation: egodystonic homosexuality. Schizophrenia was defined more narrowly, and mood disorder and adjustment disorder were broadened to encompass more symptoms. *DSM-III* (1980) provided five axes for diagnosis: Axis I, with clinical psychiatric syndromes and other conditions and which encompassed most of the disorders, with the exception of personality disorders and specific developmental disorders; Axis II, with categories that generally were presumed to be long-standing and developmental and were not generally viewed as mental illnesses for insurance purposes; Axis III which included physical disorders or conditions mentioned in a client's records or self-reported; Axis IV, for assessing severity of psychosocial stressors involving pressure or disruption in a client's life; and Axis V, for rating the highest level of adaptive functioning of the client related to the quality of a client's social and occupational performance. Diagnoses were divided into 17 broad categories, with each subdivided into specific diagnoses. Categories included disorders usually first evident in infancy, childhood, or adolescence; organic mental disorders; substance abuse disorders; schizophrenic disorders; paranoid disorders; psychotic disorders not elsewhere classified; affective disorders; anxiety disorders; somatoform disorders; dissociative disorders; psychosexual disorders; factitious disorders; disorders of impulse control not elsewhere classified; adjustment disorders; psychological factors affecting physical conditions; personality disorders; and conditions not attributable to a mental disorder.

The *DSM-III* was a radical, new method for identifying psychiatric illness and was used to challenge the pervasive criticism that psychiatric diagnoses were invalid and unreliable. The developers of the *DSM-III* claimed that it was guided by scientific evidence and principles. Its success has led to its being known as the "psychiatric Bible," and its bestseller status has generated profits for establishing the American Psychiatric Association Press (Kirk and Kutchins, 1992). However, the *DSM-III* has been challenged.

Kirk and Kutchins (1992) argue that the *DSM-III* was not a triumph of science, but was the result of a small group of researchers who interpreted their findings about psychiatric reliability to promote their beliefs about mental illness and to challenge the Freudian view. By focusing on reliability, these researchers were able to gain political advantage within the American Psychiatric Association and were able to reform the official diagnostic manual. Kirk and Kutchins argue that the *DMS-III* did not resolve the problem of diagnostic unreliability and that the manual's success has come from the political context in which it was created and from the management of received science.

As the *DSM-IIIR* shows, one method of developing definitions is through professional judgments based on guidelines established by professional organizations. The *DSM-IIIR* is currently being revised as the *DSM-IV*. Other methods which have been illustrated previously are grounded in philosophy and science (both biomedical and social sciences). However, definitions also are established by government agency definitions influenced by political considerations and legal definitions established by statutes and court decisions.

IQs—Assessing Intelligence and Psychological Testing

Scores on intelligence tests have played an important role in defining mental retardation. Intelligence tests examine a sample of behavior and assign a score based on that sample. How this is done is largely dependent on the test author's conception of intelligence. Typically 13 kinds of behaviors are sampled by tests: abstract reasoning, analogies, comprehension, detail recognition, discrimination, general information, generalization, induction, memory, motor behavior, pattern completion, sequencing, and vocabulary (Salvia and Ysseldyke, 1981). Widely used intelligence tests are the Stanford-Binet, the Wechsler Adult Intelligence Scale, and the Wechsler Intelligence Scale for Children. The Stanford-Binet emphasizes verbal ability, while the Wechsler scales focus on verbal ability and performance or problem solving ability.

Intelligence tests are controversial. First of all, there is no accepted definition or explanation of intelligence even though there are many theories. It is unclear exactly what intelligence tests measure. There has been a long-term problem of intelligence tests having both culture and gender bias, and no single test score accurately reflects intelligence.

Because of problems with I.Q. tests, including overrepresentation of minorities, the American Association on Mental Deficiency expanded its definition of mental retardation to include deficits in adaptive behavior as a diagnostic criterion. This was defined by Heber (1961:61) as "the effectiveness with which the individual copes with the natural and social demands of his environment." Well over 100 instruments are available for assessing adaptive behavior. Two common instruments are the Vineland Adaptive Behavior Scales and the AAMD Adaptive Behavior Scale.

There are large numbers of tests which have been developed to diagnose various psychological conditions. Among these are projective tests like the Thematic Apperception Test (TAT) and the Rorschach; tests for detecting cognitive dysfunction, which include the Bender Visual Motor Gestalt Test and the Goldstein-Scheerer tests, and personality tests like the Minnesota Multiphasic Personality Inventory (MMPI) and the California Psychological Inventory. One of the criticisms of using tests to determine pathology is that the examiner always finds some pathology to report (Szasz, 1970).

I.Q. and psychological tests should be used only with the understanding that test scores may change over time, tests are descriptive and not explanatory measures, the standard deviations and the means of each test have a direct bearing on the interpretation of that test, and tests vary as to their technical adequacy, which depends upon the reference group upon which the test has been normed and the reliably and validity of the instrument.

New Disorders

Every day new biological research is defining and redefining mental disorders. This has a significant impact on the constant need to refine and change mental health policy and services; new disorders are being defined constantly. For example, doctors in Denmark have warned that a preoccupation with computers can reveal a dormant psychosis. Psychiatrists Eva Jensen and Erik Simonsen and psychologist Bent Brok said that one 18-year-old who spent 12 to 16 hours a day at his home computer and neglected friends so merged with it that he began to think in computer programming language, suffered insomnia and anxiety, and finally was unable to tell the real world from his programs. He was hospitalized for a psychosis. The Danish computer trade recognizes this problem. It is estimated that 5,000 young people, mostly boys age 12 to 18, are overly preoccupied with their computer, often sleeping until afternoon, sitting before their screen until four in the morning, and substituting computer for human contact. This is an example of a technology-caused mental disorder. There is also growing interest in using computers for diagnosing patients, and there are efforts to develop forms of computer-assisted therapy (Plutchek and Toksoy, 1991).

For policy makers to set priorities for research and services and to distribute resources, it is necessary to understand the scope of the problem in relationship to types of disorders, prevalence, and distribution. This requires agreement among mental health professionals about how to classify disorders and what criteria and assessment tools should be used to diagnose individuals. But classification is in constant flux as research continues.

RESEARCH AND MENTAL DISORDERS

Interdisciplinary research is being conducted on early brain growth and the emergence of cognitive functions. This research includes studies of frontal lobe development and the relationship between tissue growth and behavioral function. Growth curves are being examined as predictors and indicators of disorders and of central nervous system integrity. This could lead to identification and treatment of children at risk for thought disorders. Brain imaging techniques such as Position Emission Tomography (PET), and Magnetic Resonance Imaging (MRI) scans allow researchers to examine brain structure, electrical activity, and metabolism. These techniques have shown specific patterns of brain pathology in schizophrenia and autism. The National Association of Mental Health Consumers (NAMHC) (1990) hopes these techniques will improve diagnostic precision and indicate new ways to correct abnormal brain functioning.

The assumption that many mental disorders reflect deviations from normal development underlies much of today's research. The age of onset of some serious mental disorders may be related to maturation of the brain. Research in neurobiology is being used to prove this. Studies indicate that different neurotransmitters (chemical transmitters) in the brain are activated at different stages of development. The brain's norepinephrine and serotonin systems involved with mood states develop in the early years. The dopamine system matures slowly until the teen years. That system is implicated in psychotic conditions, including schizophrenia. The different rate of development of brain systems may be related to the different ages at which symptoms appear (NAMHC, 1990).

Through developmental cognitive research, systematic observations and measurements are made of perception, movement, and coordination and some aspects of higher-order cognition. This research has helped clarify the causes of developmental disorders of language and learning. Language disorders often co-exist with attention-deficit hyperactivity disorders. Language and learning disorders are significant components of autism and Tourette's disorder.

Neurobiological research is showing how neurotransmitters affect the brain's early differentiation and growth. Such research is also looking at how molecular mechanisms affect the enviroment's impact on brain circuitry and function. These same neurotransmitter systems appear to be involved in regulation of sleep, emotion, and cognition. This could explain sleep disturbances associated with some mental disorders and night terrors (NAMHC, 1990).

Dopamine has been implicated in attention-deficit hyperactivity disorder, Tourette's disorder, and schizophrenia. Rat studies of destruction of brain pathways that use the neurotransmitter dopamine show results of profound inactivity. But the same destruction in newborn rats causes hyperactivity. Under stimulants the newborns become calmer, while the adults become more active. Such studies are expected to lead to more knowledge about the biological origins of mental disorders (NAMHC, 1990) and are redefining those disorders.

Major advances have been made in mental health research over the last two decades. A scientific base has been developed which allows for diagnosing and treating a number of mental disorders. This research includes knowledge about human development; interaction of biological, psychological, and social forces and their relationship to mental health or illness; and biological and psychosocial approaches to prevention and treatment. This mental health research is constantly redefining the definitions of mental disorders.

An example of current multidisciplinary mental health research is research on child development, which is important for identification of why in some children the process goes awry and results in mental disorder. Research examines biological, social, and psychological factors from prenatal life through young adulthood. Technological advances in the biological sciences, including neuroscience, are bringing about a greater appreciation of biological and genetic factors in the understanding of normal and abnormal behavior and maturation. Research shows that enviromental influences, including the family, are also very powerful in determining development including adaptability to the biological endowment. In times of economic problems, parents and children may experience high anxiety, stress, or depression. These may contribute to behavioral problems and disorders. In the past two decades, progress has been made in developing techniques to measure environmental influences (NAMHC, 1990).

This type of research shows the importance of looking at a full spectrum of influences when breakthroughs occur in biological sciences. Many mental health problems are complex and require multiple approaches to reach a solution. Research also affects how a disorder is viewed and may lead to its inclusion in *DSM*.

Premenstrual Syndrome

Premenstrual Syndrome (PMS) was originally thought to be all in the mind and was often considered to be a pseudodisease of the "weaker sex." Research has resulted in the acknowledgment of PMS as a bona fide physically based disease with a mental health component. Linkage has been made between PMS and the hormones estrogen and progesterone. The biologically based disease consists of a series of symptoms in a cycle which must appear in a consistent pattern over at least two or three months. Women are symptom free at least two or three weeks per month. Some 180 symptoms have been described that fall into four categories: pain, water retention, emotional/psychological, and miscellaneous (including nausea, vomiting, food cravings, fatigue, and poor concentration). Emotional/psychological symptoms include anxiety, tension, depression, irritability, withdrawal, and low self-esteem.

It is estimated that 20 to 30 percent of women have PMS. Dr. Leslie Hartley Gise, associate professor of psychiatry at Mount Sinai School of Medicine in New York, says that less than 5 percent of women have PMS severe enough to interfere with functioning (Sperling, 1988). Therapy aimed at particular symptoms can be effective, including sedatives for anxiety. A well-balanced diet seems to have a positive effect, and in some cases vitamin B_6 appears to help. In some cases birth control pills help, while in other cases symptoms may worsen. Stress, both psychological and social, can worsen the symptoms. Dr. Elizabeth Connell of Emory University says that "simply realizing she's not crazy does a lot for a woman" (Sperling, 1988:40).

PMS is a good example of how a definition can impact the view of a disorder. The recognition of PMS as a physiological condition with a mental component has led to research into the relationship between the disorder and violence. Dr. Katharina Dalton of the Premenstrual Syndrome Clinic at University College Hospital, London, believes that although PMS will cause only a small minority of women to be violent, it may be responsible for many violent acts. She has found that 46 percent of women admitted to psychiatric hospitals are in their eight-day paramenstruum. Also, 53 percent of women attempting suicide are suffering premenstrual tension. In addition, of 156 female prison inmates, 49 percent were sentenced for crimes committed during their paramenstruum. This research has led Dr. Dalton to conclude that there should be a "hormonal influence" defense included in the insanity definition (Restak, 1988:290). This would be a variant of a temporary insanity plea. Thus changing definitions may also lead to changes in the law. Late luteal phase dysphoric disorder (PMS) is currently listed in *DSM-IIIR* under proposed diagnostic categories needing further study. In *DMS-IV*, it appears that PMS will be included as a diagnostic category. There has been considerable political controversy to its inclusion, with opposition by some women's groups.

DEFINITIONS OR LABELS

There are concerns about labeling adults by placing them in a diagnostic classification. The use of definitions raises concerns about labeling. During the twentieth century, identification of, and early intervention in, children's emotional or behavioral problems has been thought to be vital for preventing the development of more pervasive problems of adjustment in later years (Escalona, 1974; Hobbs, 1975; Stringer, 1973). Preschool screening for identifying later behavioral and emotional problems is one approach that has been taken, but questions have been raised over the possibility of labeling children, both through early screening programs and through delivery of therapeutic services in schools (Children's Defense Fund, 1977; Coleman, 1978).

Some mental health providers dislike attaching labels to the people that they work with, but insurance companies generally will not pay for counseling or psychotherapy services unless a diagnosis is supplied. Not all diagnostic categories are viewed as illnesses. But most health insurances will not reimburse for those categories which are not viewed as illness. Thus they tend to exclude such issues as parent-child problems or occupational problems.

Human services agencies tend to classify clients not only for reimbursement purposes but to demonstrate accountability and to justify their role to other funding sources.

The stigma which may become associated with diagnostic labels may lead to new definitions and regroupings of diagnostic categories, as in the case of mental retardation, which is now included in the term *developmental disability*.

Legal Definitions and Issues

Legal processes have increasingly established definitions in the mental health field.   However, these are not always clear.   P.L. 94-142, which mandates education for handicapped children, has been defined to include a proper evaluation and the preparation of an individualized education program (IEP).   The IEP describes the specially designed instruction for the child and the related services to be received.   Multiple, nondiscriminatory tests must be used to evaluate a child.   Court cases have been used extensively to define every aspect of the law and its implementation, including addressing the use of standardized intelligence tests; the length of the schooling year (based on the issue of regression recoupment, which involves difficulty in recouping lost skills after regression over the summer); and what related services must be provided, including those that are "medical" in nature such as catheterization and psychotherapy (both required) (Vitello, 1981).

Mental Disability and the Law.   In 1990 a trial was held in Wisconsin involving a second-degree sexual assault on a 27-year-old woman who was mentally ill with a multiple personality disorder.   Wisconsin law forbids sexual contact with people suffering from a mental illness or deficiency so severe that they cannot understand the consequences of their behavior.   The trial raised issues about mental diagnosis, sexual consent, and legal protections of mentally ill persons.   The woman, who was abused as a child (as are 97 percent of people with multiple personality disorder), testified that she had told the accused about her many personalities.   On a date, the accused asked the woman to switch into a fun-loving personality and had sex with her.   Later when the woman, through other personalities, recognized what had occurred, she reported her sexual assault to the police. ("Woman's 'Attacked' Personality . . . ," 1990). This case shows that by defining accurately a mental disability, special protections for mentally disabled people can be written into the law and upheld.

Technology has increased the ability to claim mental disability as a legal defense in criminal actions.   Position Emission Tomography's (PET) ability to analyze the brain's active and inactive areas increases the possibility of detection of brain defects.   An example of use of this technology is a 1989 case in which a defense attorney claimed a convicted killer should not face the death penalty because of a mental defect revealed in a PET scan.   The scan done at the

University of California Irvine Medical Center showed brain damage and evidence of brain shrinkage. The scan's results were considered relevant on the grounds of criminal responsibility ("Lawyer . . . ," 1989).

Sexual Offenders. Although upbringing plays a role in whether a person acts on sadistic or pedophiliac impulses, researchers also acknowledge that impulses to sex crimes must be very powerful because so many offenders are repeaters despite guilt, a desire to change, and therapy. In a separate study of a rare kind of rapist, abnormalities were found in the part of the brain that allows the conscience to control instinctive emotions. The men were loners who committed their crimes during sudden brain seizures without anger or motive ("Lawyer . . . ," 1989).

In 1989 studies were reported on subtle brain damage of sex offenders during a session on the biological roots of instinctive behavior at the annual meeting of the American Association for the Advancement of Science. Ron Langevan, senior research psychologist at the University of Toronto's Clarke Institute of Psychiatry, reported that 40 percent of sadists and half of the child molesters in a study of 400 men had abnormalities in portions of the temporal lobes. The temporal lobes are involved in memories, recognizing patterns, and triggering sexual fantasies to arouse the limbic system, the more primitive part of the brain which helps regulate emotions. The researchers believed the findings could not be used for a defense because the perpetrators still had the capability to recognize and control urges and there were other factors such as substance abuse and family abuse.

These are but a few examples of how biomedical science impacts public policy making and the law by determining who is mentally ill, what protections are required, and what level of responsibility people with mental disabilities can be held to.

Some Public Policy Consequences of Definition

In the mid-1980s approximately 140,000 babies (4 percent) were being born per year with physical abnormalities, mental retardation, or learning problems. Those numbers were double the approximately 70,000 in the 1950s. Some specialists believed the increase might be more apparent than real because of increased medical access and improved diagnosis. Concern remained, however, that there would be major social and economic effects. Since the 1975 legislation which mandated special education and training for the disabled, there has been a 15 percent increase in the number of children in special education. By the mid-1980s federal outlays for those special services rose to over $1 billion per year. The huge outlays involved point up the need for accurate definition and diagnosis. A continuing problem, however, is that what constitutes a serious defect cannot be measured precisely.

In addition, there is much pressure to expand definitions. For example, the classification of learning disabled is included in special education, and now there is interest group pressure to include that classification under developmental disability which would expand access to rights and services.

The case of lead poisoning is a good example of the public policy problems we face when we define a problem and then change the definition. Lead poisoning can have serious consequences involving behavioral and mental problems. The Centers for Disease Control (CDC) uses a blood lead guideline of 25 micrograms per deciliter, but new guidelines were expected to bring that level to 10 micrograms. Dropping the level would bring 10 times as many children under testing. Screening costs rose from $4 million to $8 million in 1991. The Bush Administration proposed doubling the budget for screening to $15 million, but that would obviously not cover a 10-fold increase in screening caused by a definitional change. The American Public Health Association, the American Academy of Pediatrics, and other groups lobbied Congress for $39 million for fiscal year (FY) 1992. While experts seemed to agree on the health effects of lead poisoning and there was little difficulty in defining the problem, there was little agreement on implementation of a massive lead abatement program to resolve the problem. Issues raised over implementation involved insurance, worker protection and certification, and cost (Murphy, 1991).

Like so many policy areas, it seems that even if we are able to define the problem, establish a working definition of the level of the problem to be addressed, and identify effective ways to resolve the problem, we are still far from being able to correct the problem and terminate the policy.

2

Mental Health and Reproductive Technology and Research

Technology and research have increased the capabilities of the health community, and certain technological developments have spurred improvements in infant care and strengthened efforts such as fetal research, prenatal intervention, and human reproductive intervention. These technological advances inevitably have been accompanied by change, and while they have allowed for improvements in some forms of health care, they have also sparked controversy.

One area of controversy concerns where we put our resources. Henefin (1988) raises the issue of why we focus so much attention on reproductive technologies when as a society we do not solve fundamental problems of allocation of medical care and social services, find ways to prevent infertility, provide adequate prenatal care, and find families for many homeless children. There are also those who believe it makes no sense to put resources into learning how to diagnose relatively rare diseases to prevent those births when so many potentially healthy babies are disabled for known and preventable reasons related to poverty and extreme youth or age of the mother (Hubbard, 1988).

Another issue of concern is why we use so much technology. One view of why we are so heavily involved with technologies is that availability and economic investments in them encourage their use. Caroline Whitbeck (1988) believes that because of the large number of births each year, there are financial incentives to promote the use of technologies with high fixed costs during pregnancy and birth without sufficient regard for the biological (and, perhaps, emotional) vulnerability of infants, the emotional vulnerability of birthing women, and the importance of the mother-infant bond. Whitbeck also raises the issue of inappropriately high levels of care and asks, ''When is it reasonable and/or responsible to simply accept some impairment (such as infertility) and get on with the rest of one's life?'' She also asks, "What kinds of support do people need in order to face new decisions?'' (p. 56).

We also overuse technology because of our fear in American society of loss and death. The possible death of a young woman in a stage of life which people think of as safe from health problems increases the resistance to the idea of risk and possible death, which, although statistically small, remains a part of childbirth. Science is looked to for absolute safety; thus the overuse of technology is driven by psychological needs and fears rather than the value of the technology in a particular case. This attitude may be as much the patient's as the medical provider's—a pervasive societal value. For the professional, "Giving up the illusion that technology offers certainty and perfect safety means we let into our professional lives a lot of painful emotions. It means being willing to share the sadness and rage of a woman who will never be able to bear a child and to experience the grief of a family facing death" (Sarah, 1988:71). Thus emotional needs are a major driving force of the use of technology.

As Littleton (1988) points out, women and men have a constitutional right to procreative choice, which includes the choice to become a parent (*Skinner v. Oklahoma*, 316 U.S. 535, 1942; *Cleveland Board of Education v. LaFleur*, 414 U.S. 632, 1974; and the right to raise a child (*Stanley v. Illinois*, 405 U.S. 645, 651, 1972). But how this right to procreative choice relates to reproductive technologies remains unclear, and perhaps one of the most unclear elements is the relationship of mental health to the use or denial of use of technologies. There are those like Schuker (1988) who support the maximizing of voluntary choice. She believes advocates of social control are expressing their own prejudices and psychological needs by dominating and controlling others. But others fear the outcomes of reproductive technologies and wish to see them controlled or, in some cases, forbidden. Whitbeck (1988) believes that it is not surprising that women-centered critiques of reproductive technologies have led the way in considering not only biological risks, but risks to human relationships, because in our society the care and tending of relationships has been left to women.

The development and use of technologies may include the desire to relieve psychological pain and stress, but it must be recognized that these same technologies may also cause stress and emotional pain. The mental health components of the development and use of these technologies need to be addressed in any public policy which is developed.

INFERTILITY AND MENTAL HEALTH

The average probability of conception in a given menstrual cycle is estimated to be 0.15 to 0.2 (Cramer et al., 1979). After one year, almost 85 percent of couples will conceive. This results in the definition of infertility as "one year of unprotected intercourse without conception" (Glass, 1985:575). Even when there is conception, half of all zygotes terminate spontaneously and about half become pre-embryos, which travel to implant in the uterus. Typically only one makes this journey at a time. In natural development only about one in four zygotes will actually develop to birth (Grobstein, 1988:77).

As many as 70,000 American women per year might seek infertility treatments (D'Adamo, 1988) out of the 5 to 12 million Americans who are infertile. While only 1 percent of teens are infertile, 25 percent of those over 30 are infertile (Schwann, 1988).   Studies differ, but generally infertility is diagnosed in 40 percent women, 40 percent men, and 20 percent both or unexplained. Some of the causes of infertility are delayed childbirth, use of birth control pills and intrauterine devices (IUDs), sexually transmitted diseases, and environmental toxins. Dr. William Keye's (1982) study of the causes of infertility presented by women at the University of Utah Medical Center led to his view that iatrogenic (doctor-caused) infertility is common. Technology has played its role through surgery, widespread use of IUDs, and the use of the drug diethylstilbestrol (DES), a synthetic hormone, to prevent miscarriage. DES is associated with impaired fertility in the daughters of the users. How much do societal attitudes toward women also contribute to this situation? We do not know, but women's complaints are often dismissed as psychosomatic (Wiesner, 1979).   Such dismissals can lead to failure to diagnose pelvic inflammatory disease (PID), which may lead to infertility. Refusals to respond to complaints of pain with IUDs can lead to infections or perforations causing infertility. We also know little about the psychological damage which may occur along with the physical damage.

Sterilization has surpassed the Pill as the most common method of birth control. In 1982, 9.7 million couples (33 percent) used sterilization. Over three million men and 6.4 million women had been sterilized. Sterilizations are generally considered irreversible; even procedures done based on the possibility of reversal are done only with the emphasis that the sterilization may be permanent. This voluntary use of technology, which often is emotionally driven, may lead to new problems. With growing numbers of divorces and remarriages, more people are seeking to regain their fertility to have children with new spouses. For people who often sought sterilization to relieve the emotional stress of imperfect birth control methods and the fear of pregnancy, there is often an inability to imagine the emotional need to have a child with a future partner. With professional commercial sperm banks and cryopreservation techniques, males now may store semen prior to undergoing a vasectomy, as a kind of "fertility insurance," but it is not known how many men are counseled about this option or have the resources to afford it.

Thus emotional needs lead to the use of technology to prevent birth and later may lead to the desire for more technology to relieve the technologically caused infertility. This leads to the question of whether public and private insurances should cover sterilizations and later cover procedures to reverse those sterilizations.

In February 1984, Dr. Shenan Silber performed surgery in which he, by microsurgery, reversed the sterilization of a woman and removed one ovary and fallopian tube for transplant to her identical twin sister, who had no fallopian tubes or ovaries. The donor had been sterilized, but after her husband's death she had remarried and wanted to have children. The use of technology to remedy that situation was not unusual, but the dual procedure was. That procedure was only available to identical twins because of possible organ rejection. But safer methods of immunosuppression could expand the surgery ("Woman Gives . . .," 1984).

This is but one example of growing technologies to reverse voluntary sterilizations and to establish reproductive capacity in nonfertile women. This particular type of procedure raises issues concerning the emotional vulnerability of family members in situations which allow the removal of some part of their body to be used for a relative. How much psychological pressure is exerted on the potential donor, and what happens to family relationships when there are refusals? What happens emotionally to individuals and to family relationships if a woman gives up one ovary only later to become sterile because of a problem with the remaining ovary? We lack answers to these kinds of questions.

Couples facing infertility problems also face mental health problems. Men and women face infertility differently. Women tend to view it as disastrous and are more likely to become depressed. Eighteen percent of infertile women are clinically depressed. A counselor and educator, who has herself experienced the problem, says that the infertile label becomes your central label. "After a while you feel like you don't deserve to be parents, you feel bad about yourselves. Everyone has their doubts, but infertility makes mountains out of molehills. . . . You spend a huge amount of time thinking, why? You even start to wonder if you're being punished for past sins. . . . baby boomers are brought up to believe if they just work hard enough they'll get it, so it really feels like a personal failure" (Lowman, 1990:1B). Wives experience anger, guilt, and a wish to make reparations, while husbands suffer transient impotence, loss of self-esteem, and withdrawal (Berger, Doody, Eisen, and Shuber, 1986).

A study of 59 couples attending an infertility clinic found that it was easier for females to talk about the problem with people outside the marriage, while most males reacted negatively to talking with others. The intensity of the initial disappointment was significantly greater for females than males. Women experienced more stress and envy from childlessness and took longer to come to terms with the problem (Brand, 1989). Callan and Hennessey (1988), in a study of 53 infertile women and 24 mothers who later experienced infertility, revealed that infertile women who had never borne a child reported less satisfaction with their lives. They rated life less interesting, less rewarding, emptier, more lonely, and they were less content. In contrast, "men have no freedom to express their disappointment, so they tend to detach themselves. . . . They'll think it's too bad, but they are more likely to find a substitute activity." Many men feel more of a loss of their wife, that she isn't the same person (Lowman, 1990:1B).

A 1985-86 study of 22 couples in New York State found that reproductively normal husbands of infertile wives empathized with their wives' emotional distress. However, reproductively normal wives of infertile husbands also considered themselves to be physiologically infertile (Greil, Leitko, and Porter, 1988). Male infertility was seen as more damaging to masculinity, so women sometimes took on the social stigma (Miall, 1986). Humphrey and Humphrey (1987) suggested that the infertile husband might be in particular need of emotional support from his wife and that careful appraisal of the marriage was warranted before artificial insemination by donor (AID) treatment, because AID introduces another male into the relationship.

Corea (1988) argued that when women were given the message that reproduction was their prime function, a "barren" woman might feel threatened emotionally with loss of love, abandonment, rejection, isolation, and social humiliation. Is it any wonder then that so many women submit to difficult procedures to try to reproduce? In addition to their own psychological needs, pressure from husband or family and the authority of medical personnel may appeal to unconscious fears and the formation of the belief that nothing is too much to go through for procreation.

Dennerstein and Morse (1988) suggest that the very diagnosis of infertility is likely to cause stress; in addition, the many investigations and procedures associated with in vitro fertilization (IVF) compound distress. Mental, sexual, marital, and social adjustment may be affected. They advise clinicians involved in reproductive technology to incorporate consideration of psychological aspects of infertility into every aspect of the investigation and treatment program. This finding supports the need for counseling in infertility treatment. One research study of four couples over a seven-month period found that positive scores, on most of the seven psychological measures used, decreased at a seven-month follow-up period. The authors concluded that this suggested that the investigative procedures of the infertility clinic provoked distress (Edelman, Connolly, and Robson, 1989). Women and men who have already suffered emotional trauma from infertility may not only have their emotional pain ignored, but they may be subjected to more psychological stress through reproductive technologies.

REPRODUCTIVE TECHNOLOGIES AND MENTAL HEALTH ISSUES

An early approach to infertility was artificial insemination. It is still the most widely used form of reproduction-aiding technology. Approximately 30,000 to 60,000 procedures are performed annually, resulting in 6,000 to 10,000 live births (Mascola and Guinan, 1986). The sperm may be the husband's or a donor's, but more mental health issues are raised relating to the use of donors.

Sperm banks may use selection criteria for donors to rule out mental and physical disease. Perhaps the most well-known mental selection criteria were used by the Repository for Germinal Choice, which was set up in 1979 in Southern California to make available the sperm of Nobel Prize winners and other creative and intelligent people. The first baby conceived with sperm from the bank was a baby girl born in April 1982 to a woman who was described as having a high I.Q. Founder Robert Graham had made a fortune from pioneering techniques to develop shatter-proof plastic eyeglass lenses. He established the repository to bring a few more creative, intelligent people into the world who otherwise might not be born. Nobel Laureate William Shockley, 1956 physics winner, said he contributed to the sperm bank, but donors' names generally were not disclosed. ("Sperm Bank . . .," 1982). Selecting sperm donors based on intellectual attributes raises for some people the specters of "master races" and eugenics fears.

Brand (1987) contends that a thorough examination should be made of underlying motives for a decision by patients to use AID. In such a situation, an external factor, semen of an anonymous donor, is introduced to a complex dyadic system that is susceptible to emotional stress. One research study of psychological indications for AID among 835 couples between 1978 and 1985 showed a negative psychological indication for 26 couples and a doubtful indication for 143 couples. Negative indications were most often psychotic symptomatology. A doubtful indication was given if the conviction and reflection of one or both partners was insufficient, if the personality of one or both partners presented some "neurotic" aspects, or if the stability of the couple's relationship was undergoing crisis (Micioni, Jeker, Zeeb, and Canpana, 1987). If decisions to administer AID are based on psychological assessment, this raises issues about the validity of the assessments and whether they are reliable across social and socioeconomic lines.

A more complex technique, in vitro fertilization made its public appearance on July 25, 1978 when Lesley and John Brown of Bristol, England, made history by becoming the parents of the world's first "test-tube baby," a girl, Louise. Prior to her birth, Mr. Brown was unemployed. After her birth the Browns became celebrities and obtained considerable wealth from TV appearances and paid interviews. Lesley Brown, the mother, did not know how much of an experiment she was. She imagined that hundreds of children had already been born through the method. She did not remember being told the method had ever worked, and she never asked about it (Brown and Brown, 1979). In October 1982, the Browns paid Drs. Patrick Steptoe and Robert Edwards approximately $3,200 for a second procedure for another pregnancy; this time no doubt with greater knowledge of the process.

The issue of consent in reproductive procedures remains difficult. Even when people are given good information, they tend to hear what they want to (selective perception) and ignore what is painful or difficult. The in vitro fertilization population is especially emotionally vulnerable. If they are desperate enough, no risk is too great. Their psychological condition may cause them to discount risks and misunderstand or ignore clinic success rates. This also makes them vulnerable to unscrupulous practitioners (Shannon, 1988).

One of the problems for people interested in using in vitro fertilization is obtaining accurate information on success rates. Many fertility centers report inflated figures or report success rates of 20 to 30 percent, based upon national averages and not on the record of that particular clinic (Shevory, 1990).

IVF involves removal of eggs from a woman's ovaries, fertilization outside her body, and reimplantation. Removal of the ova clearly involves some physical and psychological risk. The Office of Technology Assessment (OTA) (1987) emphasizes the emotional and physical effects of the medical and surgical procedures and states that the drug clomiphene citrate may prolong the menstrual cycle, raising false hopes of pregnancy. Other drugs may cause mood swings, hot flashes, acne, nausea, and weight gain. While the ova are in the lab, test cells from the blastomeres can be examined for abnormal genes by using molecular probes. Preimplantation diagnosis can be used to select which embryo(s) to bring to term. (This also raises the issue of sex selection, which will be addressed later.) The ova are maintained in culture in the lab for a few days until they reach the 8- to 16-cell stage. When the fertilized egg is placed in the uterus, there are risks of perforation or infection of the uterus. The highest risk comes after a pregnancy is established if an ectopic pregnancy occurs. In addition to risk to the woman, the egg can be damaged at several points during the process.

Monash University Clinic in Australia has found a 13 percent rate of pregnancy with in vitro fertilization when only one embryo is transferred. If three embryos are transferred, the rate of pregnancy increases to 35 percent (McBain and Trounson, 1984). This increases the risk of multiple births and raises questions about the impact of multiple births. The first quadruple birth from these techniques occurred in 1984 in Australia. Some IVF practitioners feel that they must transfer to the uterus all available pre-embryos rather than freeze or discard those above the optimum number (Grobstein, 1988).

Since the best success rate occurs with multiple embryos, clients have to be emotionally prepared for twins, triplets, or other multiple births. As the number of fetuses rises, there are increased risks of low birth weight and premature delivery. This means increased risk of physical and mental disability. In addition, in cases of several fetuses, the issue of selectively terminating some to enhance the chances of others has been raised. Little is known of the mental health consequences of these decisions for parents and surviving siblings.

The first legal conflict in the United States over in vitro embryos raised mental health issues. *Del Zio v. Presbyterian Hospital* (1974 Civ. 3588, S.D. N.Y., 1978) concerned the first in vitro fertilization procedure in the United States. A doctor in a New York hospital removed an egg from Doris Del Zio. Her husband took it to a second hospital, where it was placed in an incubator. This hospital had not given permission for the procedure, so the department chair of Ob/Gyn removed the fertilized ovum from the incubator, which destroyed it. Mrs. Del Zio was unable to produce another egg (Andrews, 1984). The Del Zios sued the hospital not only for destruction of the embryo (improper conversion of property) but for emotional distress. The property claim was not recognized, but the mental anguish claim was, and the jury made an award of $50,000 for emotional distress. The chief of Ob/Gyn, Presbyterian Hospital, and Columbia University paid the award. There are nearly limitless possibilities for emotional distress cases arising out of mental health issues involved in reproductive technology cases.

A second case, the Rios case in Australia in 1984, raised a different set of mental health issues. Mr. and Mrs. Rios unsuccessfully tried in vitro fertilization in Australia in 1981. Two fertilized ova were frozen and left in Australia. When the couple died in a plane crash in 1983, a committee was established by Parliament to consider legal, ethical, and social issues of in vitro fertilization. The Waller Committee released a report of 60 recommendations in August 1984. Among the recommendations were that couples be informed adequately about the process of cryopreservation and that an agreement be made regarding disposition of embryos before they were frozen. This would allow the couple to determine knowledgeably the outcome for the embryos. However, the committee also recommended that unclaimed embryos be placed in a pool to be offered to anonymous recipients, and only where there was no interested party should embryos be discarded.

As for the couples' embryos that had been left in legal limbo in Melbourne, a committee recommended in September 1984 that the embryos be destroyed. State officials accepted the recommendation but said that nothing would be done for three months in order to allow for public comment. In October the Upper House of the Victoria State Parliament attached a special amendment to another bill, clearing the way for the embryos to be put up for adoption and implanted in a surrogate. Although the embryos were offered to a couple, their fate is unknown. Because of poor technology at the time, they probably did not survive (Saharelli, 1985).

Wurmbrand (1986) argues that the respect due embryos is great enough to provide the state with a compelling interest in protecting them. So the state could require that all frozen embryos be implanted in a donor, including an anonymous donor. Cases like the Rios case leave unanswered questions about the feelings of any other relatives of the couple and what the mental health outcomes would be for any children born of the ova. What rights would they have had to know their origins or to contact their genetic relatives?

When adoption issues are increasingly about open adoption and the right to find one's birth parents, how could policy realistically focus on establishing anonymous recipients for embryos? This approach also leaves unanswered the question of the right to control one's genetic inheritance and the mental health issues that might result from inability to control that inheritance. What are the emotional costs of having unknown children out there somewhere? One of three rights-based arguments to give control of embryos or fetuses to mothers is that there is a psychological burden for mothers of having children in the world that they cannot account for (Tushnet, 1984). The same argument has been made for fathers (Shevory, 1990). Another argument is based on the property right of a woman to her genetic heritage (Tushnet, 1984), a claim which could also be made by fathers. Robertson (1988) argues that the control over disputed embryos should favor the person who wants to discard them because of the psychological and financial burdens of an unwanted child. Although changes in the law could absolve the genetic parents of financial burdens, the psychological trauma issue cannot be resolved by law. On psychological grounds, a case can also be made for the man or woman who wants to retain the embryos and who might suffer great psychological distress upon destruction of the fetus. Shevory (1990) argues that the presumption for disposition of embryos favors women because of their greater contribution to the process, their historical relationship to embryos and children, their lack of equality in reproductive prerogatives, and the ability to subvert implicitly their reproductive prerogatives. The equality and control of prerogatives issues are the most compelling from a mental health viewpoint, as empowerment and control are significant factors in good mental health.

Stored embryos lock a woman and man into a relationship with each other; a relationship that because of divorce or death may no longer exist at the time of the development or birth of the child. The *Davis v. Davis* (Circuit Court, Blount County, Tennessee, 1988) case concerning frozen embryos raises such relationship and mental health issues. The disposition of the Davises' embryos was not determined in advance. When the Davises sought a divorce after seven unsuccessful in vitro fertilization attempts, a dispute arose over seven frozen embryos. The dispute revolved around issues of life and property. Mary Davis won custody of the embryos. Her attorney argued that the embryos were "quasi-property" and that her contribution involving the procedures she had to go through for removal of the ova were greater than were Mr. Davis's in donation of the sperm. While the conflict might be resolved legally with property arguments, the many mental health issues obviously were not resolved by the court, and there may be many years of relationship problems. In addition, there is a certain irony, along with the mental health issues, that women who have struggled to remove themselves from paternal property rights to themselves and their children are establishing maternal property rights to children.

Among the issues involved in cryopreservation of pre-embryos are the likely rate of abnormalities caused in offspring and the psychological and social impacts of extended time periods when an embryo is left in suspended animation. This includes the mental health effects of an embryo being born after the genetic parents have died of old age. When IVF began, there was much concern about birth defects, but hundreds of births with the procedure have brought reassurance. Generally, IVF babies are believed to be no different than other babies genetically or developmentally. Two studies of 72 IVF children born in Australia found their psychosocial early childhood development to be normal (Mushin, Beruieda-Hanson, and Spensley, 1986; Yovich et al., 1986). As in other pregnancies, there is a risk of a major congenital malformation of about 2 percent, and a risk of chromosome problems proportional to maternal age (Andrews et al., 1985). There are, however, some studies indicating problems. An Australian register of 15 IVF programs reported major birth defects in 1,094 births (2.1 percent) compared to 1.5 percent in the general population. This was believed to be a statistically significant increase (Saunders, Matthews, and Lancaster, 1987). Some work which has been done with excess human embryos has shown that a substantial minority are not normal biochemically, genetically, or morphologically (Verlinsky and Pergament, 1986). This could explain low pregnancy success rates.

Another reproductive technique, Gametic Intra-Fallopian Transfer (GIFT), involves secondary oocytes that are obtained by laparoscopy, mixed with sperm, and transferred immediately back to the fallopian tubes. GIFT requires at least one normal tube and the use of laparoscopy. Its major disadvantage is the inability to determine whether fertilization has occurred. Although the success rate of 25 percent is probably greater than the IVF success rate, the patient population is not comparable (McShane, 1988:43).

Technology now allows for embryo lavage techniques, the birth of a baby conceived in one woman's womb and carried to birth in another's without the use of test-tube fertilization. The birth of the first baby using this procedure was announced in February 1982 by Dr. John E. Buster of the UCLA School of Medicine. The hormonal cycles of the donor and the recipient were matched.

Five days after the donor was artificially inseminated, her uterus was flushed out and when a healthy embryo was present it was inserted immediately into the recipient's uterus. The embryo was in the 8- to 10-cell stage, and donors and recipients were matched by blood type, Rh factor, and hair and eye color.

In the fall of 1990, an extension of this procedure, which can extend women's years of giving birth into their forties, fifties, and perhaps even sixties, was reported in the *New England Journal of Medicine*. If a woman has reached menopause and her ovaries are no longer functioning, doctors remove eggs from a younger woman donor and fertilize them with sperm from the older woman's husband. The older woman, who has received hormone treatments to prepare her womb for pregnancy, receives the implanted embryos. The 1990 cost of the procedure was $8,000, plus $1,500 to the egg donor. The mother is not the genetic parent of the baby, but she can have a normal pregnancy and delivery. The research reported the use of the new technique on seven women over age 40. One pregnancy ended in miscarriage and one child was stillborn. Of five successful pregnancies, six children were born, including a set of twins (Sauer, Paulson, and Lobo, 1990).

Menopause usually occurs around age 50, but about 10 percent of women reach menopause at 40. Women who have delayed childbearing for careers or other reasons may wish to have a child in their forties. Pregnancy has been considered riskier for older women because of greater likelihood of high blood pressure, premature labor, and bleeding, but more older women are seeking to become pregnant. Dr. Anne Wentz of Northwestern University, who has a "geriatric infertility practice," states that there is no way to know the effects of carrying and delivering a child on a woman in her fifties and beyond ("Test Tube Fertilization . . .," 1990).

MENTAL HEALTH RESEARCH ON REPRODUCTIVE TECHNOLOGIES

There have been a number of research reports which have focused on the emotional factors and psychological profiles and reactions of primarily women and the IVF process (Alder and Templeton, 1985; Kemeter et al., 1986; Mazure, Delune, and DeCherney, 1988; Shrednick, 1983). The focus of these studies has been examination of women's motivations for participation (Crowe, 1985); psychological evaluation in screening (Freeman et al., 1985; Haseltine et al., 1985; Johnston et al., 1985; Kemeter, Eder, and Springer-Kremser, 1985); comparison of personality characteristics between in vitro fertilization patients and other infertile patients (Given, Jones, and McMillen, 1985); grief reactions following in vitro fertilization (Greenfield, DeCherney, and Diamond, 1988); marital responses (Mikesall and Falk, 1985); and psychological support programs (Shrednick, 1983).

Not much is known about negotiation and marital trade-offs involved in reproductive technology. Mental health problems such as depression and martial conflict may be increased where people lack accurate information regarding the low success rates of procedures. Couples may blame themselves or their partners for what are technological failures. The tendency for males and females to react differently to infertility, reproductive procedures, and procedure failure may add to couple conflict. The cost of IVF treatment may be an additional stress on couples undergoing it. The first attempt is estimated to cost approximately $5,500. Further attempts are somewhat less costly. With a 10 percent chance of success with each attempt, a 50 percent chance of a successful birth might cost $50,000 (D'Adamo, 1988).

There is a growing body of information about how women experience reproductive technology or the emotional or psychological well-being of participants (Sokoloff, 1987). Dr. Barbara Burton (1985), in her study of 12 women in an IVF support group who had been treated in six different IVF programs in Australia, found that women felt the treatment was embarrassing and that they had to leave their pride at the door. To tolerate procedures, sometimes women had to separate emotionally their minds and bodies. This might affect sexuality, as women might have trouble feeling connected enough with their bodies to have sex. Corea (1988) raised the question of how emotionally damaging this might be and related it to reactions of prostitutes who separate mind from body in sexual acts with strangers and people who develop multiple personalities after abuse. Howitz (1989) examined psychological aspects of IVF, including anxiety over acceptance into an IVF program; embarrassment and humiliation due to the infertility problem and treatment procedures; failure of the IVF resulting in intense mourning; physician's control; and the "last choice" aspect of the use of the technology.

Women are often told by physicians that procedures are easy and not painful when they are. Women are reluctant to complain when they believe they are not supposed to be making a fuss. Women are often left with strong emotions (Corea, 1985). It is in the economic interest of IVF clinics to encourage women to keep trying regardless of their feelings. But by suppressing their emotions and leaving them unaddressed, feelings may come out in destructive ways such as depression, self-medication, or physical symptoms.

Husbands may also experience stress. They may need to produce semen by masturbation under time pressure and with a minimum of privacy. In some clinics there are on-site training programs to relieve this anxiety (Edwards and Purdy, 1982). In addition, microsurgical techniques can be used to obtain sperm from the testes of males who have problems with ejaculation or low sperm counts during ejaculation. In some IVF programs there has even been an emphasis on a romantic emotional environment for the couple, with night implantation including the presence of the husband and the wife dressed up for the event (Andrews, 1984).

The most stressful IVF trial is the first one because of the high level of expectation of success (Lorber, 1988). Women during infertility treatment are exposed to high levels of stress, with their hopes being constantly raised and then dashed. Most women who go through IVF programs do not have a baby. Burton (1985:6) described women who felt like failures after unsuccessful IVF treatment: "I just want to sit in a corner and die, but life goes on." "You want to be told it's not your fault you bombed out. You just go home and feel a failure." The women Burton interviewed expressed a need for follow-up and assurances of their lack of responsibility for the outcome.

A study of 37 women undergoing IVF (Reading, Chang, and Kerin, 1989) assessed the women at the start of treatment, at day 8, and after the treatment outcome. Two subjects became pregnant, while 11 had their treatment canceled due to a poor hormonal or follicle response. Women discontinued at midcycle scored higher on an index of grief. No significant effects were found from repeating treatment, and psychological test scores in general remained low. However, on the General Health Questionnaire, 18 percent of the women manifested clinical signs of depression, and scores on the Profile of Mood States and Stress measure increased over time. The women's initial psychological states correlated with their outcomes. Feeling out of control and less able to cope with failure were associated with greater distress posttreatment (Reading, Chang, and Kerin, 1989). This indicates that psychological testing might help identify women who would require more counseling and psychological support during the process.

Another study found a significant relationship between the initial trait anxiety level and the number of cycles necessary for conception. A higher initial level of anxiety correlated with more attempts being necessary. Subjects having early spontaneous abortions also were found initially to show more stress (Demyttenaere, Knoninck, Nijs, and Steeno, 1988). This research indicates the importance of counseling and behavior modification techniques, such as relaxation processes and hypnotherapy, in enhancing the success of the procedure.

A psychological study of couples prior to and five weeks after completing an IVF protocol found that couples tended to be overly optimistic about the likelihood of achieving a pregnancy via IVF. They tended to rate the procedure as moderately stressful, but one third evaluated it as very stressful. Common reactions to hormonal administration were moodiness, fatigue, weight gain, and headaches. Reactions to unsuccessful IVF were sadness, anger, and depression, with reactions significantly more pronounced in wives. Despite failure to conceive, most subjects reported satisfaction at having attempted IVF (Leiblum, Kemmann, and Lane, 1987). Another study found that IVF patients overemphasized the possibility of success. Data on their distress, based on mood ratings, showed high anxiety at points of uncertainty and failure. While couples shared their inaccurate judgments about the possibility of success, they did not necessarily share their distress (Johnston, Shaw, and Bird, 1987).

A study of 59 women attending clinics for IVF or AID treatment and 34 of their partners indicated that both women and men experienced high levels of anxiety, but not depression. Women and men were divided into high and low distress groups and compared regarding their coping strategies. Subjects who were anxious and/or depressed were more likely to engage in avoidance strategies. Assessment of current marital and sexual functioning did not reveal significant levels of problems. No relationship was found between avoidance coping and either marital or sexual functioning (Cook, Golombok, Mason, and Parsons, 1989). However, another study of 86 couples who completed in vitro fertilization without a pregnancy indicated significant effects on marital relationships, sexual functioning, and lifestyle. Sixty-six percent of women and 40 percent of men reported depression. The severity of the depression decreased over time. In addition, 94 percent of women and 64 percent of men reported somatic and psychological symptoms of depression and anxiety. Women suffered disruptive grief reactions when in vitro fertilization failed to render them pregnant. The symptoms of this response mirrored the symptoms of women suffering a pregnancy loss. Research indicated that grief reactions were greatest after the first failed cycle. These researchers also found that unreasonable expectations of success could intensify the grief reaction (Greenfield, DeCherney, and Diamond, 1988). Yet another study showed a different result. Shaw, Johnston, and Shaw (1988) investigated the emotional and relationship problems of 60 couples seeking IVF. The subjects completed a questionnaire while on a waiting list for IVF and embryo transfer treatment at a London hospital. Anxiety was measured using the State-Trait Anxiety Inventory (STAI). The researchers concluded that the female sample did not have significantly higher state or trait anxiety, and the couples showed little evidence of emotional or marital problems.

The type of treatment may influence the psychological effects. An Australian study reported that IVF patients experienced greater anguish from failed fertilization than from failed embryo transfer (Yovich, Stanger, and Kay, 1984). This may be because the failure to fertilize is seen as a male problem. Lorber (1988) suggests that physicians think that male infertility is more anguishing; so they may reinforce this reaction.

Mazure, Delune, and DeCherney (1988) believe it has been difficult to establish objective measures of the anxiety experienced by IVF/embryo transfer participants because these people are a normal population and in order to detect their anxiety a very sensitive measure is required. But measures of major psychopathology or self-reports have usually been used, and may not be adequate instruments. Self-reports require awareness of one's level of anxiety and a willingness to report and measures of major psychopathology may not detect their level of anxiety. Mazure, Delune, and DeCherney used the Taylor Manifest Anxiety Scale and the Marlowe-Crowne Social Desirability Scale with 60 participants, and found a marked pattern of repression. Either consciously or unconsciously, participants were not reporting accurately. This may explain some of the variability in the reported levels of stress in research reports.

Women have been found to have a need to know why attempts have failed. Couples from the beginning, throughout, and at the end of IVF and other reproductive treatments need to receive emotionally supportive therapy, full information, and constant reinforcement regarding the fact of the low success rates of these treatments. But this runs counterproductive to providers, who do not want to discourage women from proceeding with treatment. It also incurs time and expense by requiring medical personnel to take time to talk to women and provide explanations and to expend money on mental health workers for intensive mental health support. However, in some places some types of emotional support are being provided. These include educational talks and counseling (Appleton, 1986); support groups (Leeton, Trounson, and Wood, 1982); and social workers or nurses who are assigned to give psychological support (Harris, 1986; Needleman, 1987).

SURROGACY AND MENTAL HEALTH ISSUES

Gestational mothers may be used where the genetic mother has health or age factors that create risk or where the genetic mother has exposure to toxic substances at work. The first known commercial surrogate mother in Britain gave birth to a girl in January 1985. Mrs. Cotton said she had cuddled and kissed the baby but would have no trouble giving her away: "I'm pleased she's fine, but I shall not want to keep her. The parents will absolutely adore her" ("Lawyer . . .," 1986:1B). Mrs. Cotton had two children from her own marriage and was paid $7,475 to bear the child, the money was to be used to renovate her north London home. A Magistrate's Court issued an order to retain the baby in the hospital until a Juvenile Court hearing ("British Tell Hospital . . .," 1985). The Warnock Commission in England has since recommended that commercial surrogacy be a criminal offense and that the contracts be nonenforceable (Warnock, 1985).

Until the Baby M case, there were only six known cases, including four in the United States, of surrogate mothers attempting to keep babies. All were settled out of court, including one in which the couple allowed the surrogate to adopt the baby. Thus, the New Jersey Supreme Court was the first U.S. court to rule on the enforceability of a surrogate parenting contract (*In re Baby "M,"*

A-39-87, 4, New Jersey Supreme Court, February 3, 1988). The court found parenting contracts invalid. The Baby M case has raised many mental health issues regarding surrogacy.

While the lower court in 1987 had ruled a contract valid between Mary Beth Whitehead and William Stern, given custody to the father, permitted Stern's wife to adopt the infant, and terminated Whitehead's rights (*In re Baby "M,"* No. A-FM 25314-86E, slip op. at 91-92, New Jersey Superior Court, March 31, 1987), the higher court ruled such contracts contrary to public policy and tantamount to baby selling; gave custody to Mr. Stern on the basis of the "best interest of the child," who had lived 18 of her 22 months with the Sterns; and restored Whitehead-Gould's parental rights and her right to maintain a relationship with her daughter. The court also prohibited lower state courts from granting even temporary exclusive custody of an infant to anyone but a natural mother, unless there was a demonstration of her incapability to care for the child.

Before the New Jersey high court, Whitehead-Gould's lawyer had argued that the surrogate's parental rights could be terminated only if she was an unfit mother. The child's court-appointed guardian told the court that the termination of Whitehead-Gould's parental rights was improper. But she said the surrogate should be denied visits with Baby M for five years to give the child more stability and reduce the chance of psychological harm.

Noel Keane (the lawyer who founded the Infertility Center of New York, which had united the couple with the surrogate) said Whitehead had fit the "perfect surrogate profile" as she was married, had children, and didn't want any more ("Court Invalidates . . .," 1988:6A). This raises questions about the validity and reliability of such selection methods. But months later in a letter, Mary Beth Whitehead said, "I felt like I was used for one purpose and I was no longer needed or wanted. After a sleepless night I realized how distraught I was for my child" ("Court Invalidates . . .," 1988:6A). The next morning, she went to the Sterns and made an emotional plea for the baby. Fearing she might be suicidal, the Sterns agreed, but three weeks later they demanded the baby's return. When she refused, they sought a temporary custody order. The Whiteheads then fled New Jersey. They were found by detectives in Florida, and the baby, who had been renamed Sara, was returned to the Sterns until the court determined custody.

In the Baby M case, the judge applied the traditional "best interests of the child" test. Henefin (1988) argues that the best interests of the child must also consider the interests of the birth mother because denial of her interests can lead later to guilt for the child when she/he realizes the role of the court, her/his father, and adoptive mother in terminating her/his birth mother's rights. This is only one future relationship of many in which such a child could be burdened with feelings of guilt for not meeting the needs of one of the involved parties.

In the fall of 1991 an Orange County Superior Court Judge in California gave shared custody of a 16-month-old girl to the child's surrogate mother and the biological father who had contracted for the child. The father, Robert Moschetta, had fathered the child through artificial insemination. He and his wife paid $26,000 through the Surrogacy Center in Los Angeles for Elvira Jordan to be the surrogate mother for the child. After the birth of the baby, Moschetta's marriage failed and Jordan filed for custody. A report by court-appointed experts recommended that Moschetta have sole custody of Marissa with visitation rights for Jordan. But the judge gave Jordan custody of Marissa from 8 A.M. to 4 P.M. Monday through Friday and Moschetta custody the rest of the time. The child was to alternate between homes during vacations and holidays, and the two parents were to share the child-rearing costs. The estranged wife was ruled to have no biological or legal relationship to the baby. The judge expressed sympathy for her but said there was no legal precedent to award her visitation because the biological father objected. The surrogate mother, Jordan, had expressed a desire to include Mrs. Moschetta in the child's life. The court-appointed attorney for the child expressed pleasure with the decision in that it allowed "a full relationship with each parent" ("Surrogate Mother . . .," 1991:5A).

One can only speculate about the mental health consequences of the Moschitta case for the child. Two primary issues involve the shared custody and the adoptive mother's exclusion. Shared custody can be extremely difficult, even when two former spouses remain somewhat congenial. When the parents sharing custody are virtual strangers, it would appear to require two extremely mature individuals to make this situation work without causing major emotional and developmental problems for the child. Certainly a highly emotional cost is being extracted from the woman who wanted to adopt the child. The emphasis was clearly placed on biological origin rather than the capacity for nurturance. Interestingly enough, in this case the surrogate mother was willing to share maternal nurturance while the husband was denying it. The emotional costs for the child are unknown.

There have been some psychological studies of surrogate mothers (Franks, 1981; Parker, 1984, Schuker, 1988). Some surrogate mothers have idealistic feelings of giving the "gift" of a child and are altruistic. The surrogate may have previously enjoyed pregnancy and saw it as an achievement. Some surrogates obtain more pleasure from bearing children than from raising them. Potential conflict may be established when the surrogate fantasizes a couple who will be forever grateful. When this does not occur, she may feel isolated and left out when the new parents' attention is focused on the new baby rather than her. (This may have been the situation in the Baby M case.) Some surrogates are motivated by the desire to make up for a previous abortion or adoption, and they see a controlled placement as healing (Schuker, 1988). Surrogates need support systems and the availability of counseling after release of the baby for adoption. Bereavement should be expected as a natural part of such a process. Rothenberg (1988) has discussed the role health care professionals should play in surrogacy arrangements, including the contract, evaluation, counseling, and informed consent.

In 1992 the California legislature was considering legislation, the Alternative Reproduction Act, which would allow limited fees to be paid to women who agreed to bear children for infertile couples. The Center for Surrogate Parenting in Los Angeles found sponsorship for the bill because it estimated that one fourth of the 5,000 surrogate births which have occurred in the United States in the last 15 years have been in California. The Assembly Judiciary Committee was considering the bill, which would make California the first state to legalize paid surrogate pregnancies. The committee amended the measure to set a limit of $15,000 for surrogacy plus medical and other related costs of the pregnancy. The legislation would permit either artificial insemination or implanting in the surrogate of a third woman's egg and would exempt surrogates and egg donors from state law, which makes it a felony to sell or pay for custody of a human being. Supporters said that it would provide legal protection for both the intended parents and the surrogate mothers. But critics felt it would erode the custody rights of surrogate mothers, who later changed their minds and wanted to keep the babies ("Bill Would Set Guidelines . . .," 1992).

PSYCHOLOGICAL IMPACTS ON CHILDREN

The new reproductive technologies have the potential to affect significantly the psychological attitudes of parents using those technologies and the psychological development of children created through them. Although the question has been raised (Baruch, 1988; Schuker, 1988), we do not know what the impacts of having multiple parents through reproductive technologies will be for individuals' psychological well-being. Will the problems be similar to or different from those for adopted children or blended families with stepparents? What would be the psychological ramification if technology allows parthenogenesis, reproduction from only one genetic parent, which would produce only female children?

Schuker (1988) contends that four psychological principles aid in understanding the psychological affects of the new technologies: (1) The special circumstances of parenting and birth stimulate fantasies in parents and children, which influence the child's personality and identity; (2) human parenting does not require a biological connection, as nonbiological parents can be equally effective nurturers; (3) good parenting involves psychological interaction from birth; and (4) new technologies relieve the psychological pain of infertility. But development is a lifetime process from fertilization to 80 or more years. When genetic engineering procedures are performed, there is no way to predict future results over a lifetime.

Psychoanalytic literature on adoption can provide some indications of psychological issues faced by children with different parenting situations (Blum, 1983; Brinich, 1980; Schechter, 1967). Research indicates that having two sets of parents can lead to beliefs of being specially chosen or beliefs of being abandoned and unworthy. Some parents may take on an idealized fantasy role. But the birth circumstance can become the focus of conflicts and problems. A family pattern of shame, dishonesty, or withholding may appear in which secrecy or untruths hide birth circumstances. Psychological studies of the adopted have shown that if they are raised in secrecy or with a distorted truth, it is hard to build self-identification. "Genealogical bewilderment" is a sense of confused origins that comes from not understanding where one comes from, while "adoption stress" is not being able to cope with the confusion. Such children may be insecure and maladjusted with low self-esteem, lack of trust, and a preoccupation with fantasy (Lipton, 1988:150). A disproportionate number of adopted children have been reported in the caseloads of mental health clinics and residential treatment centers. The knowledge that they were not the first choice, but second to the child their parents might have had biologically, may be damaging to these children (Lifton, 1979).

Adopted children may be overvalued or overprotected, or they may be seen as a disappointment. They may be used to heal the wound of infertility. They may be used to repair a damaged self-view, or they may be rejected due to the parents' projected hostile feelings toward self. Family members also may reject a child for lack of desired familial characteristics (Blum, 1983).

Lifton (1988) sees adoptees as a product of social engineering and the babies of the new reproductive technologies as the product of scientific engineering. She believes being raised by an unrelated family as if actually related, and sharing the destructive byproduct of secrecy, can produce feelings of despair and isolation. Others concur that agreements of confidentiality are harmful and should be overridden in cases where the need of a person born of a gamete or embryo donation overrides the interest of the contracting parties (Robertson, 1988). If we maintain systems with secrecy, who determines when the need of the offspring to know his/her genetic roots overrides the donor's need for confidentiality? What damage occurs to the party whose needs are denied? Bell (1986) believes policies developed to cope with problems in adoptions (right to know, genetic information, etc.) may provide a basis for solving some of the new dilemmas.

Various forms of blended families, such as stepparents and adoption, are now accepted socially. But the situation of children of the new technologies is not identical, as many of these new babies will have a genetic relatedness to at least one parent, and they will be starting out from infancy with the parents; whereas many adoptees will experience time with other care givers before adoption. Even so, lack of knowledge about even one parent may be damaging. "The absence of some part of one's heritage is always felt" (Lifton, 1988:150).

Another issue is the psychological impact of surrogacy. What attitudes will babies born of surrogates have toward those women? Will she be a missing mother? Or will she be someone whose body was borrowed for gestation? If the latter, what view of women will the child have? Will women be perceived as a commodity or convenience? Will surrogate children believe they were nurtured and loved by their biological mother and then relinquished? Will sperm donors and surrogates who take money make the child feel devalued? Will anonymous parents make children feel unborn, as do many adoptees (Lifton, 1988)? The reaction of children to knowing that they were paid for, and that their genetic and birth mother may have been a low-income woman who had them for money, is also unknown. But there is a potential for psychological damage to the child. If adoption policies involving 10-day to six-month waiting periods are used in surrogacy situations, mental health issues concerning bonding are raised.

The mother of even a wanted child pays a price physically, psychologically, and socially, and this results in an intense relationship between the pregnant woman and the unborn child. The interest of neither party can be served without significant consequence to the other. Considerable research has been done on the process of bonding (Greenspan, 1981; Spitz, 1965; Stern, 1985). Any early disruptions or delay may damage this psychological development process. This underlies the significance of clear determinations of who the nurturing parents will be and the avoidance of legal or other entangling delays. Children who cannot integrate their heritage while growing up may act out sorrow and anger as adolescents or adults (Sorosky, Baron, and Pannor, 1978).

The children most at risk for never being able to find their biological origins are those fathered from sperm banks, where records may not only be sealed or not kept but where semen from more than one man may have been mixed. Genetic fathers are protected as sperm donors by state laws in most states. They are not recognized as legal fathers and do not have rights or responsibilities (Back and Snowden, 1988). We do not know the effects of this protection on the mental health of the children born through this process.

Research by Back and Snowden (1988) analyzed the reasons for and against the anonymity surrounding the artificial insemination by donor (ABD) process, using case records of 899 ABD couples and interviews with 57 of them. They concluded that donor anonymity may reinforce negative stereotypes of ABD and other reproductive techniques in general, in addition to violating interpersonal relations and social norms. A study of 22 semen donors in Australia showed that the major motivation for being a donor was a desire to help infertile couples. Other reasons were to evaluate their fertility and to earn money. Almost all donors wanted to know the outcome and said that they thought about their offspring. Eighty-six percent were willing to provide identifying information, and 73 percent of the donors said they would donate even if the children, when 18 years of age, could trace their identity. These findings contradict often stated views of the necessity of anonymity to obtain donors. The researchers concluded that these donors had a psychological bond of some importance with their offspring (Daniels, 1989).

A new issue concerning the father in artificial insemination was raised in 1992, when it was revealed that an infertility doctor may have artificially inseminated up to 75 women with his own sperm without their knowledge. Dr. Cecil Jacobson was charged with 47 counts of fraud and six counts of perjury in Virginia. He was charged with lying to childless couples about using sperm from anonymous donors from a sperm bank to impregnate the women. He supposedly told some parents he could match the husband's physical characteristics and religion from the sperm bank and that the donor would never be identified. The prosecution believed the doctor was guilty of grossly abusing the trust between a physician and a patient. The defense argued that it was not illegal for a doctor to donate sperm for a patient and that fresh sperm was more effective than frozen sperm, frozen samples might not have been tested for AIDS, by mixing his sperm with the defective donor sperm the chances of pregnancy were increased, and patient consent was given. The children born were four to 14 years of age and were biological half-siblings. The doctor was also accused of falsely telling some of the women they were pregnant when they were not, giving them hormones to simulate pregnancy, and claiming to see the fetuses on sonograms. Eventually the women were told they had miscarried or the fetus had been absorbed into their bodies ("Infertility Doctor . . .," 1992).

Concerns were also raised that the half-siblings could meet and marry, but experts emphasized that with the small numbers concerned this would be highly unlikely. Of greater concern are the possible mental health consequences involving the sense of disempowerment and betrayal for the parents and how this will affect their relationships in their marriages and with their children. Also unknown are the affects for the children of learning who their biological father is and what the circumstances of their conception was.

Robertson (1988:193) believes that "psychosocial confusion, even genetic bewilderment, is an acceptable price for the offspring to pay in order to exist." He bases this view on the belief that even if there are more psychological problems and suffering than for an ordinary child, the possibility of life itself outweighs the negatives. This raises the issue of quality of life versus quantity. These children may not have significantly more difficult lives, so the price may be worth paying, but we do not know this. Is any life worth having, no matter what the price?

The new technologies can both extend the biological clock and compress it. A woman could have all her children at once through superovulation and multiple implant, or even twins by separation of the blastomeres at the early two- or four-cell stage. This raises psychological issues concerning birth order and raises issues about older mothers.

Schuker (1988) supports older women becoming parents through reproductive technology, as she sees the issue of mothering as a psychological issue. Nurturing behavior and psychological readiness would be her criteria, not age. Research indicates that the desire to have genetically related children is culturally, not biologically, determined (Hollinger, 1985). Parenting does not depend on biology, but on psychology—the personality, maturity, and ability to nurture and commit, along with financial, community, and emotional support systems. A culture which is accepting of nonbiological parenting supports the psychological adaptiveness to this role for nonbiological parents. The key to good parenting is in having experienced nurturing as a child. Studies have shown that it is inadequately nurtured people who have problems parenting (Spitz, 1965).

Mental health issues of late motherhood have been raised. These include concerns about the ability of older women to deal with disturbed sleep and other rigors of rearing babies, which could add stress and lead to child abuse. However, studies have tended to indicate that child abusers are often young, including teenagers (Egeland, 1979; Taitz, 1980). In addition, there is a long history of older fathers, with anecdotal support concerning the advantages of older fatherhood. One issue about older parenting concerns the mental health consequences of the loss of a parent. Dr. Kamren Mognissi of Wayne State University has stated that "some of them won't live to see their kids get married or even graduate from college. The natural life span for women is around 80 years, but some women die at age 60 or 65" ("Test Tube Fertilization . . .," 1990:2A).

The possible positive effects of older mothers have also been mentioned, including that the mother may be more emotionally developed and will not be as likely to expect the child to fulfill her needs. However, this may not always be true, as indicated by Dr. Phirma Engelstein, associate professor of psychiatry at Albert Einstein College of Medicine, who reported in an in-depth psychological study of eight older unmarried mothers that the women wanted to be in full control of their babies. They wanted the babies to be theirs alone. Their decisions were "a deeply psychologically grounded act" (Dullea, 1981:C1). A common theme for the studied women was a history of abortion, which is a common element in other interviews of single mothers. The Engelstein researchers concluded that abortions were a way to test their system before they were ready to make the decision. The actual decision tended to come at a major crossroads in their lives, such as ending an affair or having a professional disappointment. Some unconsciously prepared their bodies for pregnancy by losing weight or giving up smoking. Others bought homes prior to making the decision. None of the women interviewed sought artificial insemination (Dullea, 1981), but other women have.

Older, unmarried women applying for artificial insemination to the Yale New Haven Medical Center fell into two categories: lesbians and heterosexuals who wanted to avoid child custody battles. Occasionally there was a eugenics issue, but most wanted the thrill of becoming mothers. The center screened applicants for physical, emotional, and financial ability to be single mothers (Dullea, 1981). This raises social policy issues, as selection is being made on judgments of physical and mental fitness and low-income women are being excluded. On the other hand, single parenting requires a higher level of energy, stability, and income because there usually is not a second person to rely upon for support. Potter and Knaub (1988) noted that there has been little research on the increasing prevalence of single motherhood by choice as a parenting alternative. They examined issues raised in choosing single motherhood by artificial insemination by donor, including emotional factors and personality characteristics of the mother, psychological factors related to AID, ethical and legal issues of artificial insemination and single motherhood, and economic concerns of single motherhood.

The issues that have been raised in this chapter concerning mental health and reproductive technology only scratch the surface of the significance of mental health issues in the development and use of reproductive technology. However, even this limited review points out the significance of technological impacts on mental health; the need for mental health criteria in research, data collection, and policy development concerning reproductive techniques; and the need for mental health support in the use of those techniques.

PUBLIC POLICY AND REPRODUCTION

The United States has no formal policy regarding reproductive technology, but some countries such as Australia and Great Britain have established policies. In the United States the government does not support IVF research and provides little support for any infertility research. Instead, research and technology have occurred largely unrestrained in the private sector. Some guidelines have been developed in the private sector. But in spite of much debate over reproductive research and technology, public policy remains in the formative stages.

When looking at the question of public policy and reproduction, various authors have focused on different dimensions. For example, three recent books take somewhat different perspectives. Arthur L. Greil (1991:8), in *Not Yet*

Pregnant: Infertile Couples in Contemporary America, as a sociologist, discusses the experience of infertility as "a window on contemporary American society." He focuses on three tension points within American institutions: the struggle over intimacy within marriage, the growing power of the medical profession, and the question of infertility in terms of its individual meaning to infertile persons.

Greil looks at infertility as not just a medical problem, but as a personal and emotional problem that affects all aspects of a couple's life. He is sensitive to the mental health issues of reproductive policy. He believes the main concerns of the feminist critics may not be put aside easily. His research supports the claim that there is a coercive element to reproductive technology because medicalization and industrialization may make it more difficult, especially for infertile women, to keep from trying every alternative.

Greil thinks that social policy is made whether we do it consciously or whether we do it unconsciously through the decisions of physicians, hospital administrators, and courts. He thinks that policy should be made deliberately and that an acceptable social policy will allow infertile couples the option of using technology. He believes the best policy will not focus on the technologies but will focus on the social context, including the welfare of children, fostering a social definition of parenthood rather than a biogenetic one, promoting more opportunities for women, incorporating more humane values into medical institutions, and providing more social support for individuals and families. He supports regulation regarding reporting of success rates, access to treatment through payment by insurance and other third-party payors, and regulation of the use of particular technologies (for example, by slowing down commercialization through banning the sale of human embryos, eggs, and sperm, outlawing commercial surrogacy, and giving precedence to the rights of the gestational woman).

Andrea L. Bonnicksen (1989), in *In Vitro Fertilization: Building Policy from Laboratories to Legislatures*, as a political scientist, looks at how couples, scientists, physicians, the media, and policy makers view reproductive technology. She says, "The danger lies not in technology itself, but in the subtle value changes that foreclose possibilities once thought perfectly legitimate" (p. 8). She suggests that we are in a stage where we can still observe the values relating to the technology as they emerge. The various publics involved in this policy arena—physicians, patients, policy makers, and the interested public—still have time to ask questions, set limits, and assume responsibility.

Bonnicksen does recognize some of the mental health issues of reproductive technology in regard to how the patients, particularly women, feel about their experiences with the technology. She asks, "In what ways are patients vulnerable to exploitation in the IVF setting? In what ways can they enhance their autonomy within that setting?'' (p. 51). She discusses vulnerability in regard to the jaded patient who experiences lack of control, frustration, diminished self-esteem, and depression. She recognizes the long unrecognized psychological pain, but she also recognizes the less jaded patient, particularly involving a second wave of patients who are less desperate and have more options, which also includes women with strong psychological defenses and some who have a limited commitment to conception. She identifies the range of individuals and the variety of their responses to the technology.

She does not promote any specific policy. Instead, she focuses on the process for establishing policy. She stresses the need for regulatory policy to be enacted incrementally with a clear idea of the specific benefits of the regulation. All regulation should involve agreed upon and stringent criteria. She believes delayed policy is better than sporadic and ill-defined laws which fail to meet their original purpose and result in unintended and unwanted impacts. She feels that public policy cannot be established until the values and practices of the technology are better understood, so she encourages slowing the pace of technology while continuing the debate.

Robert H. Blank (1990), in *Regulating Reproduction*, as a political scientist, looks at the social context and the current state of reproductive technology. In the absence of a national policy for regulation, he explores the various uncoordinated private and public actions (court cases and state laws) aimed at regulation. He also examines some attempts by other countries to deal with the issue. He focuses on national public policy options by displaying a continuum of government involvement (prohibit, discourage, encourage, and mandate). He discusses the constraints on action in the U.S. political system and examines the role of the courts, Congress, the federal bureaucracy, and the public.

Blank focuses on the establishment of a rational reproductive policy. He argues that it is not too early to set social priorities regarding research and application. He believes that it is necessary to clarify social priorities, raise public consciousness, establish public mechanisms to assess and monitor the technological advances on a continuous basis rather than ad hoc, and define and evaluate the potential risks and benefits during the developmental process before there is wide diffusion. He points out how the revolution in reproductive technology is altering societal values, but he also says that it is both undesirable and unlikely that the technologies will be prohibited. He sees the major policy problem as one of protecting the interests of all parties, especially those vulnerable to abuse and exploitation. He also includes impacts on future generations. He suggests the use of technology assessment and forecasting and political feasibility analysis. He also suggests framing a consensual base for reproductive policy using areas of common ground: healthy children, reduction of infertility, minimization of risk or misuse of reproductive intervention, maximization of individual freedom and choice, maintenance of social order, and the best possible existence for future generations.

Although Blank does not specifically focus on mental health issues, his suggestions are adapted easily in relationship to mental health. For example, the definition of healthy children could specifically address their mental health; maximization of individual freedom and choice could also specifically address how this improves the mental health of individuals through their empowerment; and the best possible existence for future generations could include their mental health. Including mental health in the policy process is largely an issue of consciousness raising among professionals and the public.

3

Prevention

Research is leading to the ability to prevent mental disabilities. Prevention often requires a change in parental behavior. Issues of particular concern are the effects of parental use of alcohol or drugs. Another area of concern is job based and other environmental toxins. In addition, other preventive approaches have been taken including sterilization, abatement and surveillance, and early identification and intervention.

EUGENICS

In 1883 Francis Galton, a cousin of Charles Darwin, introduced the concept of eugenics as a science to deal with the influences that improve the inborn qualities of a race. This philosophy originally emphasized the positive aspects of the perfectibility of the human race through selective breeding. Soon, however, the focus became regulating undersirables (Bender, 1977). Two books aimed at showing that deviance was hereditary encouraged the movement: *The Jukes* (Dugdale, 1908) and *The Kallikak Family* (Goddard, 1912). Dugdale (1908) and Goddard (1912) believed that mental deficiency inevitably led to crime, disease, moral degradation, poverty, and sexual promiscuity. Their writings led to what Kanner (1964:21) has called the "eugenic scare." This resulted in negative public policy consequences by supporting the belief that no amount of education or training could reduce or improve mental disability, hurting the viewpoint that mentally handicapped persons could live outside institutions, encouraging the sex segregation of residents and patients in institutions, and encouraging an attempt to keep people with mental disabilities out of society and prevent their reproduction (Evans, 1983).

In 1911 a Committee of the American Breeders' Association proclaimed that people with mental disabilities were thriving and multiplying while leaving a dwindling number of the more intellectually better off. They concluded that these people must be removed from society and their reproduction curtailed.

Goddard (1908) believed all mentally retarded males should be castrated and all mentally retarded females should be given ovariectomies. There was a growing belief that mentally retarded persons were likely to become wards of the state, so attempts should be made to prevent their being born. In 1906 Indiana became the first state with statutes providing for compulsory sterilization of persons referred to as "idiots," "imbeciles," or "mentally defective." Between 1894 and 1944, one Midwest institution recorded 655 castrations (Perske, 1973). By 1926, 23 states had mandatory sterilization laws (Love, 1973). Most of these statutes applied only to individuals in institutions, and ironically at that time residents of most institutions were separated by sex and were thus the least likely to bear children (Kemp, 1978).

In 1927 the U.S. Supreme Court handed down a decision in the case *Buck v. Bell* (584 U.S. 200, 1927). That case concerned an 18-year-old woman whose mother and illegitimate daughter were also labeled mentally retarded. The superintendent of the Virginia institution to which Buck had been committed obtained court approval of a petition to sterilize her. She appealed through her court-appointed guardian on grounds of equal protection and due process (Fourteenth Amendment). The law applied only to mentally retarded persons in institutions and not to those in the community. The Supreme Court decision, set forth by Justice Holmes, sustained the state's authority to compel eugenic sterilization for the promotion of the general welfare. Justice Holmes likened sterilization to the need for compulsory vaccination and made his now famous comment, "Three generation of imbeciles is enough" (*Buck v. Bell*, 584 U.S. 200, 1927).

The third generation, Ms. Buck's daughter, may not have been mentally retarded. She was labeled mentally defective at the age of one month, and at the time of her death of measles in 1932 she had completed the second grade and was considered quite bright by her teachers (Ogg, 1973). The Holmes opinion did specify certain procedural rights regarding sterilization, including notice of a hearing, right to attend the hearing and present evidence, access to a permanent record of the hearing, and the right to appeal. However, the Holmes decision led to 50,000 sterilizations between 1925 and 1955 (Ferster, 1966). Some 35,000 operations were performed on persons with mental retardation under compulsory sterilization statutes (Ogg, 1973).

With the rise of the civil rights movement for persons with mental retardation or mental illness, restrictions began to be placed on sterilizations. By the early 1970s sterilizations had declined to around 400 per year in the United States (Ogg, 1973). Sterilization lost favor as awareness and legal action increased. It became clear that 80 to 90 percent of children with mental retardation were born to apparently normal parents (Brakel and Rock, 1971). The argument for continuing compulsory sterilization was based on the belief that persons with mental retardation were not capable of being adequate parents.

A 1971 survey of state sterilization laws for mentally retarded persons revealed that two states, New Jersey and Texas, had prohibited sterilization; 23 states and Washington, D.C., had no law regarding sterilization; 24 states permitted sterilization; and no information was available for two states, Arizona and New Hampshire (Krishef, 1972). But increasingly, courts were finding compulsory sterilization statutes unconstitutional. For example, an Alabama federal court found that state's statute unconstitutional and issued an order promulgating guidelines for "voluntary" sterilization (*Wyatt v. Aderholt*, 368 F. Supp. 1383 N.D., Ala., 1972). A 1977 survey of large state institutions for persons with mental retardation found that of 44 respondents approximately half of the institutions had written policies regarding sterilization. Authority for sterilization varied, with some states requiring only the consent of the parent/guardian and/or mentally retarded person and others requiring the consent of a court, agency, board, or institution (Kemp, 1978). By the 1990s sterilization of persons with mental disabilities was very difficult to obtain, but concern about parental behaviors was growing.

PARENTAL BEHAVIOR

A fetus develops under complex conditions which may be influenced greatly by parental actions. Although not every fetus experiences devastating maternal behaviors, those that do may have a life of undeserved physical and mental problems. Many fetuses are endangered not only by alcohol and drugs, but also by poor nutrition and smoking. The development of the fetus's internal structures, organogenesis, is sensitive to sublethal teratogens, agents that can induce structural and functional defects in a surviving infant. These include alcohol and other drugs and workplace toxins. Damage to embryos is often localized, producing localized defects such as anencephaly. Anencephaly occurs at the beginning of organogenesis, when there is improper formation and closure of the neural tube. Most of the brain may be missing, while the brain stem is relatively intact. The degree and kind of defect vary with the nature and intensity of the damaging agent and the stage at which the damage occurs. Each organ has its own sensitive development schedule. There are critical periods for various parts of the embryo, most frequently the second to eighth weeks (Grobstein, 1988). This increases the problem because many women may not be aware that they are pregnant and may be exposed to alcohol, drugs, cigarette smoke, radiation, or toxins.

For example, for years scientists and health officials have warned women in the Great Lakes area not to eat the fish from the lakes because of potential damage to fetuses. The state of Michigan issued advisories to women about lake fish in the early 1970s, when mercury was found in Lake St. Clair, and later extended the advisory basinwide due to discoveries of dichloro-diphenyl-trichloro-ethane (DDT) and polychlorinated biphenyls (PCBs) in fish.

Cindi John, a member of the Ottawa tribe, fishes Lake Michigan with her tribe. She gave birth to a daughter in 1990 whose blood was contaminated with industrial toxins from the lake, including PCBs and DDT. Cindi John stopped eating lake fish when she learned that she was pregnant, but this was already too late (St. John, 1992). Although PCBs were banned in the 1970s, they are still present in the lake's food chain. PCBs can deform babies and cause cancer.

Researchers have been tracking children who have been exposed to these toxins to determine their effect. Sandy and Joseph Jacobson, child psychologists from Wayne State University, surveyed 8,482 new mothers in lower Michigan in 1981 and from those selected 236 women who ate an average of two to three fish meals a month. They tested the blood of those women and found PCBs, and they tested the children and found that at birth these babies were 160 to 250 grams lighter than other infants in the study (about the same weight as infants whose mothers smoked during pregnancy). Four years after birth, they were still an average of four pounds lighter than their peers and had slightly diminished memory. Although the researchers had no conclusive findings, they were concerned that there was enough cause and effect to warn of diminished potential in children, and they continued their research (St. John, 1992). Tim Eder of the National Wildlife Federation in Michigan said that, based on the work of the Jacobsons and others, "it's really frightening. Really an entire generation of Great Lakes kids doesn't have the intelligence potential they should have" (St. John, 1992:6A).

There are a growing number of studies on how a mother affects the fetus. In 1982 a new understanding of how a mother affects her unborn child emerged from a landmark series of studies based on nearly 60,000 births in the United States. The studies of pregnancies occurring from 1959 to 1966 in the Collaborative Parental Project of the National Institute of Neurological and Communicative Disorders and Strokes were directed by Dr. Richard L. Naeye, professor of pathology at the Milton S. Hershey Medical Center in Pennsylvania. Underlying most adverse effects, he noted, was reduced blood supply to the fetus. Although chromosomal defects are commonly thought to be the most serious risk in pregnancies among older mothers, blood flow disorders were a much greater risk. Reduced blood flow could result in placental defects and intrauterine infections, jeopardizing fetal growth and survival. Increased risk of prematurity increased the risk of mental disabilities. The study pointed out the risks of poor nutrition, inadequate weight gain, cigarette smoking, advanced maternal age, and employment involving lengthy standing past the eighth month of pregnancy (Brody, 1982).

It is now well known that there is a high mortality rate and a high rate of physical and mental health problems associated with infants born too small.

Major birth defects are diagnosed in 3 to 4 percent of infants during their first year of life (Centers for Disease Control, 1988). Many infants with birth defects have intrauterine growth retardation (IUGR), are born prematurely, or both; so the rate of birth defects varies by birth weight. Analysis of the Metropolitan Atlanta Congenital Defects Program (MACDJP) data shows that 22.3 percent of 13,074 infants born with major birth defects in Atlanta between 1970 and 1984 had intrauterine growth retardation; and of 48 defect categories, 46 were associated with intrauterine growth retardation, with the findings most striking in infants with chromosomal anomalies (73.3 percent for anencephaly and 83.7 percent for trisomy 18 syndrome) (Khoury, Erickson, Cordero, and McCarthy, 1988). Of the infants born with birth defects, 21.3 percent were born prematurely (less than 37 weeks of gestation) compared with 5.6 percent of controls (Khoury and McClearn, 1990). Anencephaly associated with polyhydramnios was one of the fetal congenital malformations that seemed to be associated with premature birth (Creasy, 1984). Research has shown a strong inverse relationship between the birth defect rate and the birth weight. One study found that the birth defect rate was 16.2 percent for newborns weighing less than 1,500 grams, 13.2 percent for newborns weighing from 1,500 to 1,999 grams, 6.2 percent for newborns weighing from 2,000 grams to 3,999 grams, and 2.8 percent for newborns weighing 4,000 grams or more. That research also showed, by analysis of the type of defect, that most birth defects were significantly associated with low birth weight. Down's syndrome was only one of five birth defects significantly associated with the highest birth-weight class (Mili, Edmonds, Khoury, and McClearn, 1991).

Attempts to prevent low birth weight do not yet seem to have had much impact. The low birth-weight rate (the proportion of live births weighing less than 2,500 grams) has changed very little. From 1970 to 1988, the low birth-weight rate in the United States declined very little, only 13 percent, and the very low birth-weight rate (involving births weighing less than 1,500 grams) actually increased from 1.17 percent to 1.24 percent (National Center for Health Statistics, 1991). Research to impact this condition has been carried out concerning prenatal care, maternal nutrition, cigarette smoking, infections, maternal anemia, drug and alcohol consumption, psychosocial stress, occupational stress, work and physical activity during pregnancy, and other possible correlates. Kramer (1987) concluded that the prevalence of intrauterine growth retardation could be reduced by up to two thirds by elimination of maternal cigarette smoking, low caloric intake or low weight gain, and low prepregnancy weight. But for the three fourths of preterm births which are unexplained, there is no preventive direction indicated (Kiely and Susser, 1992).

Research is also addressing neural tube defects. A review of research studies involving nonrandomized and randomized intervention trials and case control and cohort studies (Willet, 1992) indicates that women using folic acid supplements or multivitamins in the first six weeks of pregnancy experienced a three- to fourfold decrease in neural tube defects in their infants. This work indicates that there is a subset of women in the United States who are not receiving sufficient folic acid to minimize the risk of such defects. Willet (1992) recommends identification of high-risk populations, including those with prior neural tube defects, family histories of neural tube defects, prior use of some anticonvulsants and other medications, and poor diet; encouragement of the use of multivitamins at the time a pregnancy is planned or as soon as it is detected; improvement of the U.S. diet through increased intake of fresh vegetables; and consideration of fortification of flour or other basic foods.

Recent actions in the state of California show the current direction of state prevention policy. The 1990-91 California Governor's Budget included $17 million for development and implementation of the largest birth defects monitoring program in the world. The budget also included $4.6 million for the Perinatal Substance Abuse Program, which was begun as a pilot program in 1990 in four counties. The program was scheduled to be expanded to two additional counties in 1990-91, with up to 10 other counties receiving planning and development grants (State of California, 1990:65, 73).

These varied studies and actions are but a sample of the kind of research and legislation which is developing and establishing a growing knowledge base about maternal behavior, which can be used for prevention of mental disabilities. One of the greatest concerns is the effects of alcohol and drugs.

ALCOHOL ABUSE AND FETAL ALCOHOL SYNDROME

Nolan (1990) estimated that 6,000 to 8,000 infants per annum are born with fetal alcohol syndrome (FAS). Abel and Sokol (1987:51) estimated that as much as 11 percent of annual costs of all mentally retarded institutionalized persons are attributable to FAS. Growth retardation and other FAS disorders may cost $321 million annually. Several studies on fetal alcohol syndrome state that alcohol abuse may be accompanied by other effects, such as fetotoxicity and placenta abruptio (Abel and Dintcheff, 1986; Marbury et al., 1983).

Studies have difficulty defining "moderate drinking." In addition, most studies are based on client response, which is sometimes an inaccurate measure because women may underreport their actual intakes. Another consideration in the studies performed is binge drinking. Marbury and her associates (1983) found that women who consumed more than three glasses of wine per week had an increased number of stillbirths compared to those women who drank less. In their study, women were asked how many drinks of alcohol they consumed per week during each trimester of their pregnancy. Additionally, they were asked if the alcohol was from wine, beer, liquor, or all three. Smoking was an issue as well, with each participant stating how many cigarettes were smoked per day. Findings concluded that women in the highest consumption category were older, single, smoked more, and had higher gravidity. Also, with the increase of alcohol intake there was an increase in stillbirth and placenta abruptio. It was concluded that alcohol causes placenta abruptio, which then leads to stillbirth.

In another study performed by Lenzer, Hourihan, and Ryan (1982), the behavioral and physical abnormalities associated with prenatal exposure to alcohol were researched. Findings concluded that the developmental malformations present at birth from mothers who consumed alcohol can be broken down into four categories: (1) growth deficiencies, (2) facial abnormalities, (3) somatic and brain malformations, and (4) cognitive and behavioral deficits. Those children with facial deformities, growth abnormalities, and who were diagnosed as mentally retarded were grouped as having FAS. Those who possessed cognitive and behavioral abnormalities were believed to be suffering from some type of alcohol exposure. The behavioral deficits associated with "social drinking" were similar to, but not as overpowering as, the behavioral deficits found in damaged offspring of chronic alcoholic mothers. Additionally, risk and severity of symptoms were directly proportional to the average daily consumption of alcohol during pregnancy. These researchers also found that low levels of alcohol resulted in long-lasting changes in behavior of the offspring. One father's odyssey in discovering his adoptive son's FAS and the personal tragedy involved in raising such a child is told beautifully in the award-winning *The Broken Cord* by Michael Dorris (1989). His book not only chronicles his search for the cause of his son's disabilities, but it provides much information on the research involving FAS, the extent of the problem among North American Indians, and the difficulties for a family dealing with FAS.

Mr. Dorris's experience with FAS changed his whole viewpoint as a father.

A person's genetic history is a long chain, and the latest link begins with conception, not birth. Adam [his adopted son] carried aspects of his ancestors in every chromosome, in every bead of his DNA string, in every gene. They were his raw material, literally the stuff he was made of. The parents who raised him, biological or adopted, could tease out the inherent strengths or unleash the weaknesses, but they couldn't change the outer limits of potential (p. 79).

Dorris found he could no longer ignore his son's ancestry or past. He knew that Adam's mother was a Sioux woman who drank and died before she was 35. He knew the biological father had frequently been arrested for drunk and disorderly conduct and had also died young. The search for his son's past led him to the discovery of his son's FAS, the staggering statistics on alcohol problems among many Indians, and the growing FAS problem on some Indian reservations.

Drinking may have more serious consequences for women than men. Scientists in Italy and the United States, directed by Dr. Charles S. Lieber of Mt. Sinai School of Medicine in New York City, have found that, in general, about 30 percent more alcohol appears in the bloodstreams of women than of men of similar weight after up to two drinks have been consumed. A stomach enzyme which helps break down alcohol is half as active in women as in men, so more of what women drink enters the bloodstream in the form of pure alcohol. Enzyme activity was lower in alcoholics, particularly women. Alcoholic women had no discernible protection which may partially explain their greater susceptibility to liver damage. Less alcohol is also broken down by the enzyme when people drink on an empty stomach or use antiulcer drugs, such as Tagamet (Cimetidine) ("Alcoholism," 1990). This research demonstrates why relatively low alcohol intake in women may have serious consequences for a fetus.

Researchers have not found any specific group of people associated with FAS or drug-dependent babies. However, as already noted, some Indian tribes are affected severely by the problem, and some studies have focused on disadvantaged black and Hispanic women (Moss and Hensleigh, 1988; Staples, 1990).

In 1986 the National Coalition of Hispanic Health and Human Services Organizations established the Hispanic Health Research Consortium (HHRC) to analyze the landmark Hispanic Health and Nutrition Examination Survey (HHANES) conducted by the National Center for Health Statistics (NCHS) to provide health and nutritional status information on Puerto Ricans, Mexican Americans, and Cuban Americans. The data were to focus on the health status and health care needs of the 23 million Hispanics in the United States. HHANES is the largest and most comprehensive Hispanic health survey ever carried out in the United States. Data were collected for 1982-84 in three regions of the United States. The HHANES survey represented approximately 76 percent of the total 1980 U.S. Hispanic civilian, noninstitutionalized population aged six months through 74 years.

The HHANES data indicated that there was a significant positive correlation between acculturation (the process of change that occurs as a result of continuous contact between cultural groups) and alcohol consumption, especially for the women in each sample. The dominant norms of alcohol consumption among non-Hispanic women are more liberal than the cultural norms for Hispanic women. Generally, non-Hispanic women drink more frequently and drink greater quantities of alcohol than Hispanic women. As Hispanic women are more influenced by the norms and practices of the dominant group, their drinking increases (Marks, Garcia, and Solis, 1990). Acculturation was found to be related positively to alcohol consumption by younger Mexican American women. Although acculturation was not important among middle-aged women, there was evidence that women of that age group might be turning to alcoholism in response to poverty and marital disruption. Unemployed middle-aged women were less frequent drinkers but were heavier drinkers than employed women (Markides, Ray, Stroup-Benham, and Trevino, 1990).

Research has also found that rates of low birth weight babies were higher for second-generation Hispanics of Mexican descent compared with first-generation women. No significant difference was found for miscarriages. A Mexican cultural orientation appeared to protect first-generation, Mexico-born women from the risk of low birth weight. Second-generation Mexican American women showed a higher educational and income status and used more health care, but certain behavioral characteristics such as drinking and smoking increased in the second generation (Guendelman, Gould, Hudes, and Esenaji, 1990).

This research indicates that mental health and lifestyle issues may override the benefits of factors which typically promote better physical health. This is a major study which shows the drinking patterns of Hispanic women and the effect of acculturation on drinking. It would appear that if increasing acculturation leads to increased drinking, this also places minority populations at risk for increased FAS children. Prevention policies need to address differences in subpopulations and the effects of acculturation.

The Surgeon General of the United States issued an advisory on alcohol and pregnancy in 1981, which was reinforced in 1988 in the Surgeon General's report. This has resulted in many doctors warning their patients that there is no safe level of alcohol while pregnant or nursing.

DRUG ABUSE AND DRUG-EXPOSED INFANTS

Other drugs are also a threat to fetuses. In June 1990 New York Senator Daniel Moynihan presided over Senate Finance Committee hearings on the scope of the drug-exposed baby crisis. Two reports released at the hearing indicated that estimates of between 100,000 and 375,000 drug-exposed infants born a year may be far too low because many hospitals do not screen and test pregnant women for drug use. A 1988 survey by the National Association for Perinatal Addiction Research and Education found that approximately 11 percent of pregnant women in the United States used heroin, cocaine, methadone, amphetamines, PCP, and marijuana. The most commonly used drug was cocaine (National Institute on Drug Abuse, 1989). A 1989 survey in Florida showed that 15 percent of pregnant women tested positive for alcohol, opiates, cocaine, and marijuana. Although rates were similar for blacks and whites, blacks used cocaine more often and whites used marijuana more often (Chasnoff, Landress, and Barrett, 1990).

The National Institute on Drug Abuse (NIDA) (1989) estimates that 375,000 infants per annum are affected by their mothers' drug use. A review of birth and death certificates in New York City revealed that infant mortality rates of children born to substance abusers was almost 2.5 times higher. Only 42 percent of those women were reported to have had prenatal care. The reporting of maternal substance abuse rose from 6.7 per 1,000 live births in 1981, to 20.3 in 1987 (Chavkin, Driver, and Forman, 1989). Nolan (1990) reports that one third to one half of children born to substance-abusing parents are placed in foster homes or reared by non-parental guardians.

Drug use may occur legally and while under a physician's care. A Swedish study released in 1987 indicated that women who took certain painkilling drugs during labor increased the risk of their offspring becoming drug addicts later in life (Wilstein, 1987). Dr. Bertil Jacobson released the findings at the Third International Congress on Prenatal and Perinatal Psychology. Although only a tiny percentage of mothers given barbiturates or opiates at birth produced babies who later became drug addicts, the association was conclusive. The study also looked at 99 addicts with 144 siblings, comparing their birth records. Among addicts to opiates such as morphine or heroin, 24.5 percent were born to mothers who were given opiates and/or barbiturates, while only 9.6 percent of the controls' mothers were given drugs.

At one hospital studied, there was an extreme use of barbiturates for a short time in the 1950s in an experiment to prevent a blood ailment. Nearly four times the usual percentage of women giving birth were given barbiturates, and about four times the usual percentage of babies later became addicts. The Swedish study partially supported the findings of a 1985 American study by Dr. Lee Salk. A University of California, San Francisco, obstetrician and co-chairman of the conference, Dr. Mary Davenport, said that Jacobson's research could have a profound effect and caution should be used in giving drugs to women in labor (Wilstein, 1987).

Illegal drugs which are considered by many not to be dangerous may be dangerous to a fetus. A National Institute on Drug Abuse (1989) study based on research involving 1,226 patients at a pregnancy clinic at Boston City Hospital found that women who smoked marijuana produced babies who averaged three ounces lighter and two tenths of an inch shorter than nonusers' newborns. The research indicated that pregnant women should be warned that smoking marijuana may stunt the growth of unborn babies. The report also said that even a single joint results in prolonged fetal exposure to the drug. Difficulties may be due to malnutrition rather than the marijuana directly, but the results may nonetheless be mental disabilities which are associated with lower birth weights.

Together marijuana and alcohol produce some devastating effects. For instance, Abel and Dintcheff (1986) found that since alcohol and marijuana are synergistic in their actions, combining them has a much greater negative effect than either alone. These researchers found that the combination of alcohol and marijuana had a 100 percent fetotoxic effect in mice, and a 73 percent fetotoxic effect in rats; whereas when these substances were administered independently, their results were no more fetotoxic than placebos. In addition to the fetotoxicity produced, the combination of alcohol and marijuana reduced fetal weight significantly. The effects of marijuana are believed to include a decrease in food and water consumption leading to malnutrition of mother and fetus. The study also confirmed earlier reports showing that cocaine users also produce unusually small babies. The study suggested that a woman who gained only 10 pounds during pregnancy, smoked a pack of cigarettes a day, and used marijuana and cocaine would produce a baby who is 15 ounces smaller than normal.

The effects of drug use may be seen in newborn infants. Severe cases of drug-addicted babies may result in critical withdrawal symptoms requiring intravenous feeding. Long-term studies on the effects of drug abuse and pregnancy are ongoing.

Antedoctal cases paint a disturbing picture. A young woman writing about her experience as a child born to a mother addicted to heroin said that as a child she was very bright, but only in selected areas.

> I learned to write before I started kindergarten, but to this day I cannot print. No one remembers when I began to read. I astounded everyone when I was 3 by reading labels on cans and cereal boxes. . . . My sense of balance was never good enough for me to ride a bike. I never learned to dance because I couldn't understand the patterning. . . . I cannot tell you if a piece of music is classical, country, or jazz because it all sounds the same to me. I find it very difficult to dial a telephone. I cannot balance a checkbook. I cannot count to a hundred. I cannot make change and don't know when someone has cheated me. . . . I can't tell time. I have a ''talking'' clock. . . . I can't follow directions. . . . I am unable to assemble anything or follow a recipe. . . . I avoid social relationships because I'm afraid people will realize how many things I can't do and will think I'm stupid. I enrolled in . . . college and . . . I now have enough credit to complete degrees . . . but I can't. . . because I am unable to pass the exams in math or logic. . . the university may make an exception in my case. . . . I've shed an ocean of tears over my handicap. . . .

The emotional damage has been enormous, but I'm going to make it.
(Landers, 1990:2B).

This young woman was adopted as an infant, and her adopted parents were
not told of her mother's addiction. She only learned of the situation when her
birth mother contacted her years later, attempting to establish a relationship
(Landers, 1990). This situation raises the question of how many adoptee parents
and adopted children are struggling with problems about which they do not know
the true etiology. This underscores the need for full disclosure about birth
parents' history.

Acculturation plays a part in drug use, as it does in alcohol use. Research
has shown that even after sociodemographic variables were considered,
acculturation into U.S. society, as reflected by English language use, was
associated with higher rates of illicit drug use by Hispanic groups. Predominant
use of English was more closely associated with cocaine and marijuana use
among Puerto Ricans and Mexican Americans of lower educational attainment.
The rate of cocaine and marijuana use is higher among Hispanics, especially
among Puerto Ricans, than non-Hispanic whites (National Institute on Drug
Abuse, 1987). Twenty-one percent of Puerto Rican women and 40.6 percent
of Puerto Rican men had used cocaine at some point in their lives, compared to
8 percent of women and 18 percent of men in the general northeast population
(Amaro, Whitaker, Coffman, and Heeren, 1990).   Acculturation, when
accompanied by poor education and poverty, may involve marginalization. The
individual loses essential parts of the previous culture while not successfully
entering the new, larger society. Feelings of alienation and loss of identity lead
to high stress and risk for poor mental health outcomes (Kaplan and Marks,
1990).

These types of studies indicate that there is a great need for prenatal
education on the use of drugs and alcohol by pregnant women and sensitivity to
the effects of culture and acculturation. Regier et al. (1984) suggest that if
epidemiologists, health service workers, and so on wish to participate in setting
a policy which will allocate resources for alcohol, drug abuse, and mental
disorders, then they must join together to heighten the awareness of these
problems.

In June 1990 the Secretary of Health and Human Services, Louis Sullivan,
asked the Public Health Service to educate the public about the risks of drug use
during pregnancy, including the greater risk that the baby will have
developmental and medical problems. He also urged people who knew drug-
or alcohol-using pregnant women (especially babies' fathers) to warn women
away from drugs and alcohol.

Psychologically speaking, pregnancy offers drug-addicted women an
opportunity to feel almost normal. Some try to change their lifestyle for the

sake of their child. Others are welcomed back into their family. Dr. Janet Mitchell of Harlem Hospital says, "It is the most rewarding part of my job to hear [IV drug users] talk about their lives and their babies in such glowing terms. Their pregnancy is the first time in their lives that they feel important. Do we want to take that away from them?" (Mitchell, 1988:22). Of course, this does not address the quality of the children's lives or the issue of sex discrimination in the United States, which makes these women only feel important if giving birth.

The same can be said of poor women who are not IV drug users themselves but are sexually involved with someone who is. In general, women who are poor measure their worth by their ability to have children. Also, they may not have a strong social support system that would allow them to work through all the options available to them. Blacks may be particularly sensitive to this issue because of the fear of genocide (Abraham, 1988). Many of these women do not go to the medical community for help because they are often intimidated by the bureaucracy of the health care system. Some fear their babies will be taken from them, or they will be pressured to abort. In reality, many of these children will wind up under children's protective services and will be placed in foster homes. If the babies are HIV positive, it may be very difficult to find placements for them.

The Centers for Disease Control (CDC) now encourages counseling be offered to high-risk pregnant women on a routine basis because of the risk of the passage of HIV infection to infants (Abraham, 1988). According to the CDC, high-risk pregnant women include IV drug users, prostitutes, partners of high-risk men, residents of communities with a high rate of infection among women, and those who have received blood transfusions between 1978 and 1985.

There is an increasing tendency to frame policy relating to addictions while pregnant in criminal terms. Prosecutors and legislators are seeking criminal penalties for prenatal abuse by using statutes which range from violating child support, to transmitting a controlled substance to a minor, to involuntary manslaughter, to child abuse. Since the late 1980s, the American Civil Liberties Union (ACLU) estimates that 30 women have been prosecuted on these grounds in the United States, with more than half of the cases in South Carolina (ACLU Reproductive Freedom Project, 1990).

MATERNAL-CHILD CONFLICTS AND MENTAL HEALTH

Discussion of potential conflicts between a woman and the fetus is relatively recent and is primarily the result of the new technologies, including amniocentesis, ultrasound, and fetal surgery, which have allowed diagnosis and treatment of the fetus in utero.   Another factor raising this interest is the increased recognition of the extent of substance abuse among pregnant women and its serious and long-term potential effects on fetuses (Merrick, 1990). At a conference of the American Society of Law and Medicine in the mid-1980s, the subject of fetal abuse led to doctors and lawyers discussing the possibility of national standards of behavior during pregnancy.

Physicians must obtain informed consent prior to administering treatment, and a competent adult can refuse treatment. A number of scholars have supported the right of a woman to be free from government interference in decision making regarding her pregnancy.   These arguments are based on greater societal gain (Nelson and Milliken, 1988); women's fundamental rights (Field, 1989; Johnson, 1986); the lawlessness of such an act (Annas, 1990); the undermining of informed consent and the usurping of women's choice during obstetrical care (Rhoden, 1987); the risk of life and limb (Rhoden, 1986); and autonomy and the destructive affect on the physician-patient relationship (American College of Obstetricians and Gynecologists, 1987).

Issues involving loss of choice, risk of harm, loss of autonomy, and destruction of the physician-patient relationship raise mental health issues for the woman. Risk of harm certainly includes the risk of mental illnesses and nerve or brain damage. Loss of choice and autonomy raises the concern of increased powerlessness leading to depression, suicide, or other mental health problems. Destruction of the physician-patient relationship raises concerns involving loss of trust, which could lead to avoidance of health care providers or increase the difficulty for other physical or mental health care providers to be able to establish a relationship with the woman.

On the other hand, actions of the pregnant woman can result in damage to the fetus, which may leave a child with life long brain or neurological damage leading to long term mental disabilities. The view that parents have moral and legal responsibilities to their child leads scholars to argue that inherent in entering into a relationship is some loss of autonomy, and at times there may be legal restraints (Blank, 1986; Robertson, 1983).   It has been argued that responsibility extends to the pregnant woman regardless of the issue of viability, and responsibility also extends to her partner in respect to any behavior which might also affect the fetus, such as transmitting the AIDS virus (Blank, 1986; Losco, 1989).

The Supreme Court has ruled that the state has a legitimate interest in potential life and that interest begins with viability (*Roe v. Wade*, 410 U.S. 113 1973:163; *Webster v. Reproductive Health Services*, 1989 57 U.S. L.W.:3057, July 3). The court has not determined when life begins and human rights start. Robertson (1983) argues that a fetus has no right to be conceived or to be carried to viability, but if the woman decides not to terminate the pregnancy, a viable fetus has rights concerning the way the woman conducts her life.

Parental discretion becomes limited if the woman's conduct would injure the viable fetus. Blank (1990) argues that a reasonable standard of care must be developed for pregnant women which balances the mother's right to control her body and her responsibility to the fetus. This would mean a greater standard of care for behaviors with more severe effect. Simon (1978) has argued for a variable standard of care based on the parent being held to a minimum standard of knowledge, which would be commonly known in the community, while at the same time holding a parent with superior knowledge to a higher standard of care.

It seems a problematic stance to hold women to different standards of care based on trying to prove their level of knowledge, and it poses the possible recognition by women that their safest legal stance is to have as little knowledge as possible. This seems counterproductive to prevention approaches based on prenatal care and education of expectant women. It also raises the specter of different standards for people with mental disabilities.

Balisy's (1987) approach suggests negligent conduct of a high degree before a woman should be held liable for prenatal injury. Defining what is negligent conduct to a high degree might be difficult. Such an approach, however, probably would be less of a threat to preventive approaches involving increasing parental knowledge.

Although Robertson (1983) may be right that a state could prohibit pregnant women from obtaining or using tobacco, alcohol, or drugs based only on a "rational basis" test, such an approach would not resolve the issue of the first one to three months of pregnancy, when many women are unaware of their pregnancies. The first trimester in many cases is the time when the most damage could occur. If this approach were taken, how far would the state have to go to enforce it? Would women of child bearing years have to show a current pregnancy test to show they were not pregnant before they could buy or use cigarettes, alcohol, or drugs? What do social control approaches like this do to women's self-esteem and sense of empowerment? How does this affect their mental attitude about becoming pregnant or carrying a child? How does this affect the societal view of women as just for reproduction? Do we know enough about the psychological impacts of these kinds of approaches to adopt this kind of policy?

As Robertson (1983) points out, criminal law could also be changed to allow the state to prosecute women who refuse medication or knowingly expose themselves to harmful substances. Blank (1990) calls attention to the fact that this view could encourage abortion. In addition, women could avoid prenatal care to avoid detection and prosecution. Since the population most likely to be affected by this approach (addicts and alcoholics) is often difficult to get into prenatal services, this social control approach would probably worsen the situation by driving them across jurisdictional boundaries and into hiding.

California is one state where action is being taken against drug using pregnant women. In 1977 in *Reyes v. Superior Court* (75 CA App. 3d 214, 141 Cal. Rptr. 912), a California appellate court ruled that a pregnant woman who had been warned by a public health nurse not to use heroin could not be prosecuted under the state child abuse law for using heroin because that statute did not refer to an unborn child. In 1987 in the case *The People of the State of California v. Pamela Rae Stewart* (No. M508197 San Diego Mun. Ct., Feb. 26), the court dismissed the case against a woman who was charged under a child support law for failure to provide appropriate medical care for her fetus. She had been warned by her doctor not to use drugs or engage in sexual intercourse and to seek prompt medical attention if she began to bleed. Her son was born brain damaged with traces of amphetamines in his blood, and he later died. The prosecution claimed she took amphetamines and marijuana, engaged in sexual intercourse during her pregnancy, and did not seek prompt medical attention when she began to bleed. The court's dismissal was based on their view that the legislature had not intended the child support statute to be used to prosecute pregnant women for not following a doctor's advice.

In November 1988 California's Butte County began a new program, the first of its kind in California, to prosecute mothers of drug-addicted babies. The county district attorney said that local hospitals had agreed to inform authorities whenever newborns were found to be suffering drug withdrawal symptoms and had traces of cocaine, methamphetamine, or heroin in their urine or blood. Unless the mother agreed to undergo a voluntary drug treatment program, she would be subjected to prosecution under a penal code which carried a mandatory 90-day minimum jail term upon conviction. Investigators would go to the hospital as soon after the birth as possible to insure proper collection of evidence and to question the mother. The risk to the child would also be assessed and a determination made of whether the parent was incapable of adequately and safely caring for the child. It was estimated that there would be 50 to 75 cases per year, with maybe five cases tried. A 20-member panel of representatives from community agencies had worked for a year on a protocol to deal with drug-addicted mothers and their infants. The protocol was to weave together the services of county agencies to aid drug-addicted mothers. Some members of the panel were concerned about the announcement of the county attorney's program (Austin, 1988).

Although drug-addicted babies are less of a problem in Butte County than some places in California, the three hospitals in the county that deliver babies began in 1987 to refer mothers with a history of suspected alcohol abuse or who had delivered babies with traces of controlled substances in their urine to child protective services. Methamphetamine and cocaine appeared to be substances of choice (Austin, 1988). In-service training to recognize the problem had occurred throughout the county. Many people involved were concerned that the new policy would be more a hindrance than a help.   As of 1993, no prosecutions had been carried out.

In a Florida case in 1989, a woman who gave birth to a baby advised hospital personnel that she was cocaine addicted.   The woman and the baby were tested and found to have a form of cocaine in their systems.   The woman was charged with delivering a controlled substance during the delivery of the baby and was also charged regarding a son who was born in 1987.   The children were not born addicted.   She was acquitted on a child abuse charge and convicted on a controlled substance charge.   The judge found she had introduced the cocaine into her body and then passed it to the children during the time between delivery and severing of the umbilical cords.   He found her addiction not to be a defense.   He viewed the situation in terms of choosing to use drugs and choosing to be pregnant (*State of Florida v. Jennifer Clarise Johnson*, Case No. E89-890-CFA, Cir. Ct. 18th Judical Cir., Seminole Co., July 13, 1989).

The trend appears to be to look at maternal-fetal substance abuse in terms of criminal prosecution.   "The imposition of criminal punishment presupposes the capacity of the defendant to voluntarily conform her conduct to the requirements of law.   If psychoactive substance dependence is acknowledged to be a compulsive medical disorder, then it would appear logical that criminal sanctions alone cannot deter this behavior" (Chavkin, 1990:485).

Imprisonment of pregnant women and prosecution of women who give birth to addicted babies does not address the fundamental problem, which is a mental health problem.   Viewing the problem from that point puts the emphasis on educating the public on the effects of alcohol and other drugs on the fetus. Primary prevention involving educating people prior to pregnancy is of major significance because many disabilities may be caused by substance abuse before a woman is aware of her pregnancy.   Secondary prevention involves educating all pregnant women on the effects of substance abuse.   Tertiary prevention calls for identifying pregnant substance abusers and making available to them immediate alcohol or drug treatment.

As research indicates, drug abuse and dependence is not an easy problem to address.   Simplistic responses such as believing that the woman can just stop drinking or taking drugs are in reality not so easy to carry out.   While the hereditary relationship of alcoholism has been well established for years, the hereditary relationship of drug dependence is just beginning to be studied. Increasingly more studies are being done involving neurochemical research, with the most recent studies involving opiates and cocaine (Kaufman and McNaul, 1992).   For example, research shows that some drug use may change the way in which brain chemistry functions in the brain of the user.   Chronic use of stimulants may cause catecholamine receptor supersensitivity.   Chronic cocaine abuse may cause dopaminergic autoreceptor supersensitivity, which may decrease dopaminergic transmission (Gawin, 1988).   Newer psychodynamic theories relate the experiences and consequences of substance abuse to the underlying organization of the personality of the user (Treece and Khantzian, 1986). Thus, we know we are dealing with a situation involving genetic predispositions, brain chemistry changes, and the underlying organization of personality. This is not a problem with an easy solution. Extensive psychotherapy and pharmacologic treatments have been developed, and such treatment may require months or years.

One of the major barriers to treatment for pregnant substance abusers is the lack of immediately available treatment services. Many programs do not serve pregnant women at all. In New York City, 54 percent of treatment programs exclude all pregnant women and 67 percent reject pregnant women on Medicaid (Chavkin, 1990). In Florida in 1989 few programs accepted pregnant women, and there were only 135 residential beds available for 3,500 reported pregnant addicts and 10,425 estimated unreported pregnant addicts (American Public Health Association, 1989). In Butte County, California, there is no methadone maintenance program for heroin addicts; they must drive 85 miles to Sacramento. One pregnant woman returned to heroin use when her car broke down in the belief that the drug would be less harmful to her fetus than withdrawal.

Treating the addicted pregnant woman through the criminal justice system increases problems of mother-fetal/infant conflict, increases the chance that women will avoid prenatal care to reduce the likelihood of detection, may increase trust problems with mental health and medical personnel, and may negatively influence fetal/infant bonding. The U.S. Supreme Court recognized addiction as a medical matter over 60 years ago. Women who are addicts are unlikely to be deterred by the threat of criminal prosecution. These women do not intentionally harm their children, but they require treatment. Currently, even motivated women have difficulty finding programs to treat them. It is difficult to see how a criminal justice policy focus can be pursued when there has been a failure to provide access to treatment through our mental health policy. How can dollars be put into the criminal justice system for this problem when insufficient dollars are put into the mental health system? Will this problem be defined by casting the women in the role of criminals?

The American Public Health Association (APHA) Council in 1990 reaffirmed its position that illicit drug use by pregnant women is a public health issue and should not be the focus of punitive measures. The Council also said that drug treatment facilities should provide half-way houses for at-risk women, their newborns, and other dependent children and should provide programs for newborns exposed in utero. APHA's 1990 policy statements included support for educational efforts, laboratory quality assurance, and adequate reimbursement for maternal serum alpha-fetoprotein screening and follow-up (APHA, 1990). The National Association for Perinatal Addiction Research and

Education (NAPARE) (1990), a nonprofit organization, in its policy statement also viewed prenatal drug use as a health care issue and not a legal issue. NAPARE believed that criminalization would be counterproductive and would deter women from seeking prenatal care. Criminalization also placed health care practitioners in conflict with their requirements to provide patient confidentiality. NAPARE had also seen evidence of selective reporting, meaning that low-income, minority women were most subject to reporting.

What will be the end result for the mental health of parents and children placed in these conflict situations? We do not know. Another area of conflict is the right of women to work in environments potentially hazardous to fetuses.

JOB-BASED HAZARDS

Many employers banned all fertile women from high-risk jobs based on the risk of reproductive hazards. A 1987 survey in Massachusetts found that employers used fetal protection policies in 20 percent of the chemical and electronics industries, while the Congressional Office of Technology Assessment reported that 15 major multinational corporations had some type of restrictive policy (Murphy, 1990). Many reproductive hazards issues involved the risk of mental disabilities.

In May 1990 the California Supreme Court unanimously denied review of an appellate decision that ruled that women cannot be banned from jobs that expose them to lead because fetal protection policies amount to sex discrimination. Johnson Controls Inc., Fullerton, had attempted to ban fertile women from jobs that would expose them to lead. The Fourth District Court of Appeals by a 3:0 margin on February 28, 1990 ruled (*Johnson Controls v. California Fair Employment and Housing Commission*, 267 Cal. Rptr. 158, Cal. App. 4 Dist., 1990) that the policy was "blatant, overt gender-based discrimination" based on "unfounded, unscientific stereotypic notions about women," and that "we are in an era of choice. A woman is not required to become a Victorian brood mare." The opinion said that the company apparently assumed that all fertile women would become pregnant and that women could not be trusted to make decisions about maternal and fetal health. The decision was based on California's Fair Employment and Housing Act. Johnson Controls had argued that the employer had a "legitimate interest in protecting the health of unborn children when their work places endangered such health." The California appeals court agreed with research that has shown that high concentrations of lead are linked to birth defects in both male and female parents. The company disputed those research findings.

Johnson Controls, Inc. had a national policy. That policy was upheld in a Wisconsin case in 1990 by a federal appeals court. That case, *International*

Union, United Automobile, Aerospace, and Agricultural Implement Workers of America, A.U.W. et al. v. Johnson Controls, Inc. (111 S. Ct. 1196, 1991) was accepted to be heard before the U.S. Supreme Court. It challenged Johnson Controls' national fetal protection policy as violating Title VII of the 1964 Civil Rights Act, the federal antidiscrimination statute. The union and eight employees, who underwent sterilization to keep their jobs, were the plaintiffs against the lead battery manufacturer.

Johnson Controls developed its 1982 policy based on evidence that a fetus's direct exposure to maternal blood lead levels can cause irreversible injuries to the brain and central nervous system. The company required mandatory sterilization for women to stay in their jobs "for the future well being of the race" (a statement with a familiar eugenics ring) (Murphy, 1990:1). The firm also feared suits by children of women employees claiming punitive and compensatory damages for exposure to high lead levels. The policy was based on grounds of a moral duty to protect the fetus and fears of toxic tort liability. The employees claimed that the company did not protect prior wages of any women who chose transfer over sterilization and did not guarantee transfer. A brief filed by the American Public Health Association and other health groups and officials argued that data from federal health regulators indicated that men, women, and fetuses all required protection. The Occupational Safety and Health Administration had shown male workers may be rendered infertile, and research by the company's medical experts did not measure paternal exposure and did not rule out that paternal exposure could be a contributing factor in their detection of a number of correlations between the umbilical cord blood lead levels and physical and neuropsychological development in children.

The federal appeals court applied Title VII's only statutory defense to discrimination, "a bona fide occupational qualification reasonably necessary to the normal operation of that particular business or enterprise" (BFOQ), and upheld the company policy. Federal attorneys urged the Supreme Court to reverse the judgment based on the evidence of possible harm to male workers, while the unions argued that only requirements relating to effective performance could constitute a BFOQ defense. Issues involved in the case included the use of fetal protection policies as a massive discrimination tool against women; the need for regulatory agencies to control policy in this area rather than case-by-case court decisions; the need for safe work environments for all workers; and, in cases where technology does not exist to provide a safe work environment, the need to determine whether a product is essential or should be banned.

In the spring of 1991 the Supreme Court handed down a decision finding the Johnson Controls policy discriminatory. The decision banned fetal protection policies in which employees do not allow women of childbearing age to work in certain hazardous jobs. The court felt such policies were excuses to deny women equal employment opportunity. The court also held that decisions about the welfare of future children were up to the parents (111 S. Ct. 1196, 1991). This means protection must be at the preventive level through education of employers and employees to change workplaces and behaviors which place children at risk for mental disabilities.

GENETIC COUNSELING FOR MENTAL DISABILITIES

One approach to preventing mental disabilities is to prevent disability before birth. Prenatal diagnoses are important for identifying potential mental and physical disabilities. About 18,000 infants (.5 percent) in the United States are born with a chromosomal abnormality, 36,000 (1 percent) have a dominant genetic disease, 9,000 (.25 percent) have a recessive disease, and 324,000 (9 percent) have an irregularly inherited disorder (Scriver, 1985). If mental diseases or disorders can be identified specifically as genetic, then genetic counseling can be used to educate and make decisions regarding marriage and procreation. Since the early 1970s, carrier screening programs have been in place in some states and localities for Tay-Sachs disease. Recessive diseases occur in 25 percent of the offspring of two people carrying the gene. Tay-Sachs screening has been voluntary, and Jews of Azkenezi descent, among whom Tay-Sachs disease is prevalent, usually go for screening and may avoid marriage to someone when there is genetic risk.

Genetic counseling is a new, developing profession (Rollnick, 1984). The first training program began at Sarah Lawrence College in 1971. The first wave of counselors were largely well-educated, predominantly white, middle-class suburban women returning to careers after raising children. A second wave of younger, more ethnically diverse counselors were largely women postponing childbirth for careers. Therefore, most counselors have not experienced the technology about which they counsel. Rapp (1988) sees these counselors as gatekeepers between social experiences and science, regulating the quantity and quality of genetic information used in decisions while identifying with their women clients and representing the claims of their profession.

About 50 percent of clinic patients and 10 percent of private patients break their appointments for genetic counseling. Of 1,000 women counseled by genetic counselors in a year, about 750 have amniocentesis. Middle-class professional families who have delayed childbirth may be more convinced by statistics to have amniocentesis. For some minority, low-income people the possibility of mental retardation is not a significantly greater problem than others they face. One Haitian father rejected testing of his baby because "the counselor says the baby could be born retarded. What is this retarded? They always say Haitian children are retarded in the public schools. If we send them to the Haitian Academy [a community-based private school], they learn just fine'' (Rapp, 1988:113).

The development of DNA probes to identify polymorphisms (genetic variations) marking a particular trait means that in the near future, there will be more carrier screening tests available for recessive genetic diseases and for genetic trait makeup. A molecular probe for Huntington's Disease was found in 1983. Research to find genetic markers is ongoing in several areas affecting mental health, including Alzheimers, bipolar disorder (manic depression), schizophrenia, alcoholism, and drug addiction.

The use of diagnostic tests in mental health areas has been voluntary. However, states could require diagnostic procedures with statutes based on public health grounds. Privacy rights might be overridden by public health being used as the compelling state interest, which could override the constitutionally protected privacy right (Robertson, 1983). Sickle-cell screening has been mandatory in some states and has raised controversy because of the trait's concentration among blacks.

In some cases diagnosis may lead to treatment, but in most cases the only choice is abortion. The situation is complicated by court cases allowing children to sue their mothers for failure to obtain diagnostic tests. *Grodin v. Grodin* (102 Mich. App. 396, 301 N.W. 2d 869, 1980) recognized the right of a Michigan child to sue his mother for failure to obtain a pregnancy test. Blank (1990) has raised concerns over prenatal diagnosis becoming mandated legally through such tort liability actions. Increasingly physicians may be required to inform pregnant women of the availability of different types of tests. They may also be increasingly encouraging or requiring such tests in order to protect themselves from malpractice suits. As more women are informed of such procedures and tests, if they refuse them, liability may shift to them. Blank (1990) also has raised the issue of whether there is a duty of carriers of genetic diseases or traits that increase susceptibility to conditions not to have children or to use reproductive technologies such as artificial insemination.

As identification techniques become more sophisticated, how many people are going to be free of negative traits? If people want a biological child, are they going to have to make genetic screening part of their criteria for who they marry? Some Azkenezi Jews already do this. Do people decide not to have a biological child based on the risk of one negative trait occurring? How many of their positive traits might have been passed on? How serious does the negative trait have to be to override the positive, and who decides and how? Are negative mental health traits viewed as more detrimental because of long-term stereotyping of mental disabilities? What does this do to our perception of ourselves? Does one negative trait give us a negative view of ourselves? How do we regard people with traits that are viewed as negative? Does this increase our stereotyping and stigmatizing of people? What mental health effects occur when people give up becoming a biological parent? These are many of the unanswered mental health questions.

The genetic aspect of mental health conditions will probably be only one component of many affecting the likelihood of any individual having the condition. This means there will be no black and white decision making. Will such genetic indications be used only for educational purposes, or will they influence abortion decisions? If used educationally, will the knowledge assist preventive actions, or will it result in self-fulfilling prophecies? Will the information lead to restrictions on the persons carrying the traits? Will they be refused certain jobs because they might be susceptible to a mental disorder? How will the confidentiality of this information be maintained? The 1972 Vice-presidential candidate Thomas Eagleton had to withdraw from candidacy when his mental health record was revealed (Altheide, 1977). What happens to politicians if it is revealed that they have genetic markers for mental disorders?

4

Identification and Early Intervention of Mental Disabilities

Prenatal intervention has been manifested primarily in the form of prenatal diagnostic tests. Technological developments such as amniocentesis and Chorionic Villus Sampling (CVS) have made it possible to identify certain chromosomal abnormalities for identification and treatment of mentally handicapped fetuses. This technology can also be used to recognize Rh incompatibility between the fetus and the mother. Early diagnosis of this condition combined with treatment has successfully reduced the frequency of blood diseases and brain damage caused by incompatible Rh-factor pregnancies. Furthermore, these technologies can help doctors select the optimal time for intervention by providing valuable information about the relative risk of delayed or premature delivery of the infant, which might result in brain damage.

Neural tube defects, which are frequently associated with mental retardation and occur in approximately 6,000 infants born each year, in many cases can also be detected. The largest numbers of neural tube defects are anencephaly and spina bifida (Main and Mennuti, 1986). Anencephaly results in much of the brain being absent, while spina bifida is a congenital defect characterized by imperfect closure of the spinal column, which leaves exposed some of the nervous system and often results in hydrocephalus, mental retardation, and paralysis.

DIAGNOSTIC TECHNOLOGY AND MENTAL HEALTH ISSUES

In 1973 an association was found between elevated levels of maternal serum alpha-fetoprotein (AFP) and open neural tube defect. The level of AFP can be determined from maternal serum or amniotic fluid taken between the fourteenth and twentieth weeks. In over 90 percent of neural tube defects, there are no prior indications of the problem. After one affected pregnancy, there is only a 2 to 3 percent risk of a recurrence (Macri and Weiss, 1982). AFP measurement is recommended for the small number of women known to be at risk. Mass serum AFP screening is not recommended because of the high rate of false positives (approximately one in 10,000). This occurs because of the normal changes in AFP levels during pregnancies and the overlap in the distribution of AFP levels in normal pregnancies and neural tube defect pregnancies. Discriminating techniques are not yet well enough defined. Also, there appear to be heightened levels of maternal serum AFP in black women with normal pregnancies (Johnson, Palomaki, and Haddow, 1990). So different screening protocols may be necessary for different racial groups. This type of policy making is difficult because of the need for being sensitive to discrimination concerns. The Federal Drug Administration has approved a diagnostic kit for testing for neural defects. Concerns were raised by medical, scientific, and consumer representatives that the test might not be used as a preliminary screening device leading to further testing but might lead directly to abortion decisions. The high rate of false positives might result in aborting normal fetuses.

Both amniocentesis and CVS were developed to diagnose fetal chromosome abnormalities and other genetic diseases. Amniocentesis, the older process, can be used in the second and third trimesters of pregnancy. The newer CVS procedure can be used during the first trimester. Both procedures are usually safe and effective; however, they can cause spontaneous abortions. Amniocentesis has been conducted as early as 14 weeks but is usually performed at 16 to 18 weeks for optimal safety.

In 1980, 29 percent of women aged 35 and over and 4 percent of those under 35 had amniocentesis (Fuchs and Perrault, 1986). Parents with previous children with Down's syndrome or other chromosomal abnormalities, older mothers, and those with possible Rh incompatibility may be appropriate candidates. The age at which amniocentesis is suggested, around 35, is drawn from the intersection of the incidence of live birth with Down's Syndrome at that age (about 1 in 360) with the added risk of miscarriage (1 in 330). If the technology resulted in less risk, the recommended age to use the procedure would drop. This has been demonstrated in that as amniocentesis has become safer, the recommended age has fallen from 40 to 35.

Amniocentesis involves removing approximately 20 cubic centimeters of amniotic fluid by inserting a needle attached to a syringe through the abdomen. The live body cells found in the fluid are cultured for approximately two weeks. Karyotyping of the chromosomes identifies chromosomal abnormalities and the sex of the fetus. Biochemical assays can identify up to 120 metabolic disorders and about 90 percent of neural tube defects. The waiting period for amniocentesis and its results is long and stressful. The procedure usually occurs after the sixteenth week of pregnancy, and lab work requires an additional three to four weeks for results.

Barbara Katz Rothman (1986) has studied the effect of amniocentesis on the woman/fetus relationship, which is the initial phase of the mother/child relationship. This relationship may be impacted when a woman waits for a diagnostic technology to pronounce judgment several months into the pregnancy that the fetus is free of detectable abnormalities. For the woman who may consider termination of the pregnancy, waiting for the technology causes separation and distancing. The woman avoids moving toward attachment, a process which normally would begin much earlier in the pregnancy. We don't know what, if any, long term consequences occur as a result of late attachment.

The personalities of women using amniocentesis have been assessed for anxiety, information retention, and rational response to risk factors. Rapp (1988), in studying 45 African American, Hispanic, and white families (stratified by occupation and payment method) who underwent amniocentesis, found that most people could describe Down's syndrome, but few knew about neural tube defects (spina bifida), and almost none knew about other chromosome problems.

For most women the test's results are negative, but a few women must face the stress of a positive finding. Two percent of amniocentesis results will indicate a disability. Most women choose abortion, but this varies by diagnosis, with close to 100 percent abortion rates for Down's syndrome and 50 to 75 percent for sex chromosome abnormalities (Rapp, 1988). Because of the low rate of positive amniocentesis results, women who have this experience feel very isolated. Rapp (1988) found that no women in her study had met another woman with the same experience.

The highly medicalized and confidential aspects of genetic testing have reinforced this isolation. Consideration should be given to lifting this veil. Women in large urban areas might have a support group made available, but because of low numbers in nonurban areas, support groups would not be an option in much of the country. Another solution might involve women volunteering to allow their names to be made available to other women who would like to discuss the experience, just as people get referrals from cosmetic surgeons of others who had the surgery and who would be willing to talk to them.

CVS involves a biopsy of the placenta. The placenta has the same DNA as the fetus. CVS can be done transabdominally by extracting the tissue by a needle put through the abdomen or transcervically by using a pump-type sampler to aspirate a specimen of placental tissue while visualizing through a laprascope. CVS can accurately diagnose more than 80 serious disorders, including Down's syndrome, Tay-Sachs disease, and some malformations of the head and spine. CVS has a substantial advantage over amniocentesis because it can be performed between 8 and 12 weeks of gestation. The earlier diagnosis reduces the stress of waiting and allows for early intervention for corrective procedures. Emotional attachment to the fetus does not have to be suppressed so long. If a decision is made to terminate the pregnancy, an abortion can be done at an earlier stage of the pregnancy. An earlier abortion is not only easier and physically safer, but also may reduce the emotional stress. A disadvantage of CVS is that it has a higher false-positive diagnosis (2 percent) than amniocentesis (.3 percent). False positives are defined by Cole (1990) as cases in which abnormality was detected on prenatal diagnosis that was not found in follow up amniocentesis, abortion, or neonates.

Amniocentesis has been believed to have a lower risk of spontaneous abortion, and the procedure has been performed for over 20 years (Nadler, 1986). However, recent studies indicate that CVS is just as safe as amniocentesis (Clark, Bissonnette, Olsen, and Maginis, 1989; Ledbetter et al., 1990). However, some controversy remains. CVS may have a significantly higher spontaneous abortion rate in women over 35 years of age. Cohen-Overbeek, Hop, Ouden, Pypers, Johoda, and Wladimiroff (1990) believe late first trimester CVS in older women is still justified because the spontaneous abortion rate and the procedure related abortion risk do not exceed the risk of fetal chromosomal abnormality.

McCormick, Rylance, Mackenzie, and Newton (1990) researched patient attitudes toward CVS. The majority of the patients interviewed were at high risk because of previous genetic problems requiring diagnosis, and the rest were of increased maternal age. Most of the patients thought the procedure was satisfactory. A small yet significant percentage found the procedure to be embarrassing because the transcervical position meant entrance through the vagina (as opposed to entrance through the abdominal wall, as in amniocentesis). The patients felt that the main benefits were avoiding a late termination and an early reduction of stress during the pregnancy.

Prior to making a decision to have either procedure, a woman should be informed fully of the possibility of spontaneous abortion. In cases where a spontaneous abortion does occur during or following a procedure, referrals to mental health services should be available. Loss of a fetus as the result of a procedure may result not only in grief, but may also result in feelings of guilt or blame for having the procedure. Counseling services should be available to both the mother and father.

The options of amniocentesis and CVS provide parents who are having children later in life or who have concerns about genetic abnormalities with assurances concerning the outcome of the pregnancy. Both procedures, however, have a false-positive rate. Although that rate is relatively low in CVS and even lower in amniocentesis, there are still some fetuses aborted because of error. It is essential that women receive adequate, well-informed informational counseling about identified conditions so they can make an informed choice. They should be informed of the risk of false positives, and additional testing should be discussed with them. In cases where abortion is chosen and an apparently normal fetus is aborted, the parents should be informed and counseling services provided.

DECISION MAKING AFTER DIAGNOSIS

Children with Down's syndrome and spina bifida now have much better survival rates and better life outlooks due to changes in early and community-based treatment. For some families of children with disabilities, the experience is life enriching and leads to emotional growth and development. But some families with this type of life crisis are unable to cope and the family may dissolve, resulting in parental divorce and emotional problems for some family members. Clearly different individuals and families react in different ways, but all should receive extensive and up-to-date information and counseling support.

If tests to identify disability are available and women do not use them, or if they continue with the pregnancy of a fetus with a disability, responsibility and blame may be placed on the woman. Considerable pressure may be placed on these women. On the other hand, women who choose abortion may also be blamed and pressured. The ultimate decision should rest with the woman, and she should be provided with supportive responses and counseling service regardless of the decision.

The choice of whether to have or keep a disabled child must remain with the individual family. They are best able to judge the emotional impacts, positive and negative, that aborting, having, keeping, or making available for adoption a disabled child would have upon the family.

Abortion

Many of the identified defects, such as Down's or Lesch-Nyhan syndromes, cannot be treated successfully in vitro. If the woman chooses abortion, the earlier the decision the less risk physically, and probably also psychologically. Grobstein (1988), for example, believes that termination of a pregnancy of a fetus with anencephaly may be more beneficial for the parents by eliminating the psychological trauma of continuing the pregnancy.

Attitudes toward selecting abortion vary and are influenced by culture. A middle-class, professional couple chose abortion after a diagnosis of Klinefelter's syndrome (XXY), a sex chromosome anomaly, based on the view that children have to face a lot of problems anyway and this would be an unfair burden. A couple who were poor and recent immigrants made their decision based on the belief that if the child was "slow" he wouldn't get "a shot at being President" (Rapp, 1988:110-111). Rothman (1986) found that it was the husbands who, after a prenatal diagnosis of genetic or developmental defect, decided to end the pregnancy and persuaded their wives to go along. Decisions to continue or end pregnancy are based on psychological and cultural world views. In another study it was found that black men were especially resentful if their partners decided to abort if they wanted the pregnancy to continue and if they ascribed to the wider cultural view of male dominance. They were disturbed by both not becoming fathers and also not deciding the matter (Shostak and Mclouth, 1984). Culturally sensitive counseling services should be available to all couples to try to ease long-term impacts of the decisions.

Some studies report that the majority of parents of children with genetic disorders do not consider abortion acceptable for such disorders as Down's syndrome (Elkins, Stoval, Wilroy, and Dacus, 1986), X-linked disorders (Lubs and Falk, 1977), and Huntington's disease (Markel, Young, and Penney, 1987). However, other studies involving fragile-X (Meryask and Abuelo, 1988) and X-linked conditions (Beeson and Golbus, 1985) indicate that parents of children with genetic disorders may be more willing to abort than the general population. Attitudes toward abortion are based on the perception of the severity of the condition. Severe mental retardation is seen as the condition most likely to result in choosing abortion (94 to 97 percent of women with prenatally diagnosed fetal abnormalities involving severe mental retardation choose abortion) (Golbus, Loughman, Epstein, Halbasch, Stephens, and Hall, 1979). Only 62 percent of women choose abortion for sex chromosome abnormalities such as X Turner syndrome or XXY Klinefelter syndrome, which have a low association with mental retardation (Benn, Hsu, Carlson, and Tannenbaum, 1985).

In 1989 a study was conducted which surveyed 395 parents of children with cystic fibrosis (CF) at 12 New England CF centers (Wertz, Rosenfield, Janes, and Erbe, 1991). CF does not involve mental retardation or significant physical handicaps, but it reduces life expectancy and increases morbidity. Since 1985 prenatal diagnosis has been available through DNA probes linked to the CF gene (Farral, Law, and Rodeck, 1986). The research study was conducted to determine how parents of affected children viewed abortion for CF and where they placed it in a wider spectrum of other disorders/conditions that might justify abortion (Wertz, Rosenfield, Janes, and Erbe, 1991). Questions were asked about attitudes toward abortion in 23 situations, including 11 conditions affecting the child and 12 affecting maternal or family situations.

The researchers found that only 20 percent of CF parents would abort a CF fetus. This was reflected in their optimism that their child would reach age 40, hold a full-time job, and marry (currently 75 percent survive to their late teens, half reach the age of 26, and about 40 percent reach 30, but few survive into their forties) (Boat, Welsh, and Beaudet, 1989). The majority believed that legal abortions should be available for all 23 conditions in the first trimester and for 20 of the conditions in the second trimester. Severe mental retardation was the only fetal characteristic for which the majority (58 percent) would themselves choose abortion. For other conditions the percent choosing abortion were as follows: bedridden for life but with no mental retardation (41 percent), death before age five (Tay-Sachs) (40 percent), moderate mental retardation (35 percent), mild mental retardation (16 percent), severe untreatable obesity (12 percent), severe disorder at 60 (Alzheimer's) (7 percent), treatable physical defect (3 percent), susceptible to alcoholism (2 percent), and sex selection (.4 percent). The researchers felt generally that the respondents would not abort frivolously, but they were concerned at the response to the obesity question as they felt that it indicated a willingness to abort for cosmetic reasons.

The trimester did not have much affect on willingness to abort; only about 5 percent fewer women would abort in the second trimester than in the first. "This result suggests that newer methods of prenatal diagnosis, such as CVS, which make first-trimester abortions possible, may have little effect on deeply held attitudes" (Wertz, Rosenfield, Janes, and Erbe, 1991:995). Men were more likely to say either that abortion should be prohibited by law or that they would abort. They avoided the middle ground, which women were willing to choose, of saying they would not abort but they would permit others to have abortions. With the exception of sex selection, all attitudes toward abortion were associated with the respondent's perception of the attitudes of their spouse, mother, father, and siblings toward abortion. The majority thought their relatives (51 percent siblings to 65 percent spouses) would disapprove. The researchers felt that genetic counselors should acknowledge the effects of extended family on patients' views and encourage the patients to discuss the relationship between personal and family values. They also found that the attitude of the physician who cared for the child could influence the parents' decisions. The researchers, in addition, felt counselors should discuss these parental perceptions regarding "the clinically necessary optimism conveyed by pediatricians, rather than the doctors' actual views" (p. 995). Perhaps such physicians should be educated to give a more balanced view of future outcomes for children.

Blank (1990) found that the response to a pregnancy termination was more intense in terminations that occurred after the first trimester. Grief reactions could last a year or longer. The research did not suggest that early terminations did not cause grief processes but suggested that many factors are involved, including support of spouse, extended family, and understanding friends.

Although patients who experienced voluntary terminations or spontaneous miscarriages entered into a grief process, earlier diagnosis seemed to lessen the anguish. Research has also shown that abortions of wanted pregnancies because the fetus has been diagnosed with a disability are distressing even to women who philosophically do not oppose abortion (Rothman, 1986). Counseling services should be available to all women undergoing abortion.

Another important issue for parents when there is a spontaneous or induced abortion is what is to happen to the fetal tissue. In some cultures, such as the American Indian and New Zealand Maori, there are important cultural norms regarding handling and burial of fetuses and even birth matter. For other parents, choosing to have fetal tissue released for research or choosing to have a burial may be important to grief processes. Policies should give the mother or (in the event of her death or incapacity) the father or nearest relative the opportunity to decide what should be done with fetal tissue. Even for normal births, if family custom calls for a prescribed method of handling the afterbirth, policy should accommodate the cultural preference. This raises issues regarding the use of fetal tissue in experimentation, which will be discussed later.

People are moved emotionally by fetuses. The right to life movement has played upon this fact. Recognizability of the fetus as a human in appearance or behavior may impact people emotionally, whether other criteria of humanness are present or not. This may be an important factor in the "burnout" reported in health professionals who assist in many second-trimester abortions. The argument has been made that if desensitization occurs to these empathic responses, moral consciousness may be dulled and this may lead to reduced sensitivity to helplessness in general, including the mentally disabled (Grobstein, 1988). Because of these and other emotional issues, Employee Assistance Programs (EAPs) or other counseling services should be available for personnel engaged in abortion services.

ULTRASOUND AND MENTAL HEALTH ISSUES

Another major prenatal diagnostic technology is ultrasound (sonography). A noninvasive technology, ultrasound involves high-frequency, nonionizing, nonelectromagnetic sound waves which provide a visual image of the inner structures of the abdomen. Ultrasound examination of all pregnancies has been suggested by some individuals (Rosendahl and Kivine, 1989), but others believe it should be used only under carefully defined protocols. The technique allows observation of fetal development, fetal movement, and detection of some skeletal-muscular malformations. In conjunction with magnetic resonance imaging (MRI), it may provide diagnosis of nervous system abnormalities (Williamson, Weiner, Yuh, and Abu-Yousef, 1989).

Although fetuses in appearance and development are no different now than in the past, technology has allowed them to be visualized. This visualization has led to an increasing mental and emotional identification of the fetus as a person (Fletcher, 1983). Ultrasound allows fetal movements to be seen as early as nine weeks and by the second trimester human features can be perceived. Observing the fetus on ultrasound, which often includes a videotape to take home, helps women to perceive a fetus as their baby. This may have a positive influence in enhancing the closeness the woman feels for the fetus and for encouraging maternal bonding (Fletcher, 1983). This could have a positive impact, because research indicates that negative effects may appear later in children who were unwanted during pregnancies. A wanted child enriches the lives of the genetic parents during its development. An unwanted child is felt as a growing burden. Sometimes an ambivalent or negative mother experiences emotional bonding on experiencing the fetus through ultrasound (Grobstein, 1988).

Ultrasound has sometimes been used to foster bonding in cases of anxiety or ambivalence, but it has also been used routinely and multiply. Sarah (1988) believes this may interfere with natural responses to pregnancy and preparation for children. The natural process involves feelings which include anxiety, ambivalence, fear, and self-discovery. Practitioners uncomfortable with feelings may try to short circuit these feelings. Cutting this process short by using a machine to show a woman a baby and that she is a mother may not help the woman to deal with her feelings and growth. She is being given a model for dealing with feelings by turning to authority figures, not developing inner resources.

Thus, we have conflicting views of the effects of this technology on mental health and bonding, but we do not have definitive research regarding its negative or positive effects. However, we do know that the technology makes available the ability to make choices based on sex.

Sex Selection

In October 1983 the *New England Journal of Medicine* published two studies showing that ultrasound as early as the fourth month of pregnancy can accurately reveal fetal sex. Improved ultrasound equipment provides clear images of sex organs. Dr. Jason C. Bernholz's research was conducted at Rush-Presbyterian-St. Luke's Medical Center in Chicago. He said that ultrasound will "provide information for parents that will help them appreciate that little person that's inside and plan their families" ("Ultrasound Tells . . .," 1983:A12). In Bernholz's study doctors judged the sex of 69 percent of 855 fetuses, and they were right 99 percent of the time. The fetuses were 15 weeks gestation or older. Drs. John D. Stephens and Sanford Shiven at the University of California Medical Center in San Francisco correctly identified the sex of all 100 fetuses examined when they were between 16 and 18 weeks gestation. In an accompanying editorial, Dr. John C. Hobbins of Yale Medical School suggested that an advantage of knowing the sex was that "theoretically it may be better for some parents who are disappointed in the sex of their fetus to work through their disappointment before the baby is born" ("Ultrasound Tells. . . .," 1983:A12). Where genetic diseases run in a family, identification of the sex of the fetus also could lead to other tests to confirm the sex ("Ultrasound Tells. . . .," 1983).

Roberta Steinbacher, a sociologist at Cleveland State University, estimated in 1983 that if sex selection became available, as many as 140 boys would be born in the United States for every 100 girls (Faith and Steinbacher, 1983). By 1986, 75 percent of the 450 couples who had selected the sex of their child had opted for boys (Robinson-Haynes, 1986). This disproportionate favoritism for male infants can be seen to an astonishing degree in particularly provincial areas of the People's Republic of China, where government policy to allow only one child per family has resulted in many efforts, even including infanticide of girl babies, to ensure a male child. In Barcelona, Spain, a court allowed a woman to choose a female embryo for implantation in an in vitro process because of the woman's depression. This raises the issue of using preconceived ideal children to resolve mental health problems with nothing known about the later mental health consequences for the child.

There has also been biomedical research on enhancing the chances of conceiving a particular sex. The Ericsson Method or the Albumen Separation Method for male sex selection was developed by Ronald Ericsson, a reproductive physiologist and president of Gametrics, Ltd. of Sausalito, California. It was used in 17 sperm centers worldwide between 1979 and 1984 with a success rate of 75 to 85 percent. The procedure required the woman to be artificially inseminated with her partner's male-separated sperm. About one third of women became pregnant in the first two cycles, but the average was four to six cycles. The cost and level of education required to monitor ovulation limited who could use the procedure. The technique was not foolproof, and some obstetricians who offered the service had patients request abortions if they did not get the requested sex. The technique has been supported as a way to benefit families with genetically carried disease affecting only one sex. Supporters have also said it filters out all the weak sperm, so there are fewer congenital abnormalities and spontaneous abortions (Robinson-Haynes, 1986). But obviously the procedure can be used for other reasons than prevention.

Sex selection could result in the sex ratio being changed with unforeseen results, including the possibility of increased older brother/younger sister families. This has implications for increased male dominance. There are many possible mental health consequences related to artificially changing birth order

(Toman, 1988). One can only speculate about the mental health consequences of reinforcing sexual stereotypes, or of having large imbalances of the male to female ratio in countries such as China.

FETAL SURGERY AND OTHER INTERVENTIONS

Fetal surgery was first performed in 1981 when Dr. Michael Harrison of the University of California, San Francisco, began using open fetal surgery to correct obstructed urinary tracts, fetal tumors, and diaphragmatic hernias. Dr. Harrison and his colleagues noticed that the operations left no scars, and that opened up possibilities for reconstructing congenital deformities before birth. Such surgery might be used for cleft palate, which afflicts 1,200 babies, and other facial abnormalities associated with such conditions as Apert's syndrome or even Down's syndrome. Fetal wound healing is also being studied to learn if a way can be found to prevent scarring in adults (Harrison et al., 1981). Prevention of scarring also could have major mental health affects in preventing self-esteem problems associated with major scarring.

Shortly after these early surgeries, surgeries affecting mental health began with the implantation of shunts in the brains of fetuses diagnosed with hydrocephalus (Rosefeld, 1982). Hydrocephalus is a condition characterized by an abnormal increase in the amount of fluid in the cranium, which causes enlargement of the head. If this cannot be controlled by means of shunts implanted by surgery which drain the fluid away, wasting of the brain and severe mental retardation occur. Left untreated, hydrocephalus results in a dangerous buildup of fluid in the brain, which can result in mental retardation and eventual death. A shunt can allow drainage from the brain to the amniotic sac. Fetal surgery has also allowed doctors to abort one twin fetus with Down's syndrome while saving the other twin ("Fetus Operated on. . .," 1981).

Fetal surgery presents high risks of spontaneous abortion or early delivery. The surgery may also result in the birth of a physically or mentally disabled child who otherwise would have not survived pregnancy. The surgery may put the mother at physical risk, with all the potential risks of surgery including disability and death. In addition, it may place the mother at risk for her mental health.

Courts have invaded both women's bodies and their psyches to provide medical care for fetuses. Haverkamp and Orlean's (1982) evaluation of the negative impacts of the use of fetal monitors included some factors which impact mental health: the restriction of patient movement, which tends to force patients to remain flat on their backs during labor (taking control from the woman); the monitor becoming the focus for partners, physicians, and nurses rather than the woman; and the monitor medicalizing the labor and interfering with motion, freedom, and relaxation, which may result in negative biofeedback and cause anxiety that can interrupt labor. Active labor may be slowed by a woman lying on her back to allow a fetal monitor to get the best tracing. That position may also impair blood flow, causing fetal distress. A fetoscope or Doptone can be used for monitoring without these constraints. Sarah (1988), a midwife, describes how she has often seen women in labor rooms frightened, alone, and confined to their beds while husbands and medical personnel cluster around a fetal monitor.

The President's Commission for the Study of Ethical Problems in Medicine and Biomedical and Behavioral Research (1982) has recognized that gene surgery or therapy with fetuses may further erode the principle that a competent adult may refuse medical procedures in nonemergency situations as pressure builds to treat fetuses in utero. The mental health field has yet to resolve consent issues for incompetent adults, but it increasingly has been seeking a solution based on a surrogate decision maker who decides based on what he/she believes the person would want if competent. Clearly, we are seeing decision making by competent adults being breached before we can even resolve the issue for the incompetent.

A questionnaire of directors of training programs in maternal-fetal medicine found 21 cases of court orders being sought on behalf of fetuses for obstetrical intervention against the wishes of the pregnant woman. Procedures sought were Caesareans, intrauterine transfusions, and forced hospital detention. Court orders were obtained for 80 percent of the cases within six hours. Nearly half of the training directors favored detaining mothers whose actions threatened fetal health. Minority women were most likely to be involved in these cases (Kolder, Gallagher, and Parsons 1987). Court orders involving women, both prenatal and at birth, include cases ordering women to have a Caesarean section performed (*In re Madyun*, 114 Daily Wash. L. Rptr. 2233 D.C. Super. Ct., July 26, 1986) and to be held in detention to receive prenatal care (Kolder, Gallagher, and Parsons, 1987).

In the case *In re Madyun* (1986), the pregnant woman was in labor at the time she had to attend a court hearing, which ordered her to submit to a Caesarean section. Sarah (1988) believes Caesarean section is probably the most resented and feared intervention in birth. The emotional experience can be devastating. The necessary Caesarean is not usually a negative emotional experience, but women who undergo what they find out to be unnecessary surgery may experience sorrow and anger. Large numbers of unnecessary Caesareans are done in the United States, exposing many women to unnecessary emotional as well as physical risks.

In 1981 in *Jefferson v. Griffin Spaulding County Hospital* (247 Ga. 86, 274 S.E. 2d 459), the Georgia Supreme Court declared a fetus in the third trimester as having a legal right to the preservation of its life which overrode the mother's religious freedom. The Human Resources Department was given authority to give consent for surgical procedures for the mother. The order was never used, as the woman successfully completed a normal delivery. Finnamore (1981) views the *Jefferson* case as having gone beyond *Roe v. Wade* by weighing fetal rights against the mother's rights and creating a legal duty for the mother to safeguard the life of the fetus at the expense of her constitutional rights (and probably her mental health as well). In a 1983 case, *Taft v. Taft* (388 Mass. 331, 146 N.E. 2d 395) in Massachusetts, a husband sought a court order to require his four months pregnant wife to submit to a cerclage operation to suture closed her cervix to prevent a miscarriage. The woman refused the procedure on religious grounds. The trial court gave consent to the husband, but it was reversed by the Supreme Judicial Court. The court, however, indicated that under other circumstances the decision might have been different. The mental health effects of forcing a woman to have her cervix sutured closed are unknown. But there is certainly potential for later sexual problems, marital problems, and perhaps resentment leading to problems in bonding with the child.

A survey of obstetricians in 45 states (Kolder, Gallagher, and Parsons, 1987) reported that in 21 court orders over a five-year period in 70 percent of the cases the hospital was aware of the situation for one day or less before pursuing a court order. In 88 percent of 16 cases, it took six hours or less to obtain a court order, 19 percent of orders were issued in an hour or less, and at least one order was issued over the phone. As 81 percent of the women were black, Asian, or Hispanic, and 24 percent did not speak English as their first language, the study also showed that minority women were much more likely to have orders sought against them.

This raises the concern of whether the impact of the action on the mental health of the woman was considered. Considering the short time frames of many of the decisions, time is not allowed for psychological assessment by a mental health professional or for counseling to ameliorate the effects of the decision. Questions must also be raised by the high minority status and language difficulties of the women involved. This replicates the long-term problems in the mental health system, where minorities are overrepresented in psychiatric institutions (Kemp, 1992) and where at the turn of the century immigrants with language difficulties were diagnosed as mentally ill and were both placed in psychiatric institutions and deported for mental disorders (Fox, 1978). If these legal processes are used largely on those who are at a power disadvantage in the society—women, racial and religious minorities, and the foreign born—what are the mental health implications for these women and their children by their being made even more powerless during childbirth?

Prenatal diagnosis may be inaccurate, and women who have fled and gone into hiding to escape court-ordered Caesareans have sometimes given successful vaginal birth (*Jefferson v. Griffin Spaulding County Hospital*, 1981:458). In these cases, the women and their fetuses are put at risk by being forced to escape medical care and are placed under great mental stress, with unknown short- and long-term results.

The court's intervention may also result in death. A 27-year-old Washington, D.C., woman, Angela Cardner, who had a previous history of cancer from the age of 13, was diagnosed with terminal cancer at 26½ weeks gestation. She agreed to treatment to extend her life to 28 weeks in case a Caesarean section became necessary. The following day, while Cardner was heavily sedated, a trial court convened at the hospital and appointed the District of Columbia to serve as *parens patriae*, and ordered a Caesarean section be performed. When Cardner was informed of the court order, she agreed briefly to the surgery but then opposed it. The court again ordered the Caesarean. A court of appeals denied a stay. The surgery was performed and the baby girl died within two hours, and Angela Cardner died two days later (*In re: A.C. Appellant*, D.C. Ct. App., April 26, 1990). There appears to have been no consideration of the additional mental anguish and stress caused to Angela Cardner and her family. The family was left to deal not only with the death of Angela Cardner and her child, but also with the knowledge of the way in which the system contributed to those deaths by reducing the quality of Angela Cardner's last days and the dignity of her death, and perhaps by reducing the length of her life and causing the death of her daughter.

The appeals court, as a result of a requested review by the American Civil Liberties Union, issued a written decision vacating the trial court's order. The District of Columbia Court of Appeals held that the rights of all patients to make informed decisions about their treatment should, in virtually all cases, be decided by the pregnant woman for herself and the fetus. It refused the argument of maternal obligation to rescue the fetus by stating that the courts cannot compel one person to permit a significant intrusion upon her body for the benefit of another person's health. It also excluded consideration of the quality of the patient's life. The court spoke to the issue of competency by stating that where a patient cannot offer informed consent, the court should appoint a surrogate who would advocate the choice the woman would have made if she were competent. The court also recognized the interest of the woman in avoiding physical or mental impairment for her child by allowing consideration of her prognosis, the viability of the fetus, and the probable results of treatment or nontreatment for both. The court emphasized that it would be an extraordinary case in which a court would override the woman's wishes and authorize a surgical procedure (*In re A.C. Appellant*, 1990).

This case is significant not only for its protection of the patient's right to decide, but also for its decision to protect incompetent patients with a surrogate who must present the view of the patient as if she were competent. This decision supports the direction in which policy has been developing for incompetent mentally disabled and for the dying.

Annas (1990) emphasizes the importance of the case by stressing that it would be almost impossible to think of any case where the woman's decision would be overruled by a judge. He stresses the significance of the decision in preventing force from being used to physically restrain a competent woman. "Not only surgery, but blood transfusions, injections, and even forcing a pill down a woman's throat, are to be prohibited" (p. 29).

When other scholars such as Merrick (1990:10) advocate the position that "the court should only intervene when risk to the child is great, while risk to the mother is low," emphasis should also be placed on the issue of mental health risk as well as physical risk. Psychological pain can be just as long term and damaging as physical injury, and it may have more effect on the quality of the parent-child relationship and the long-term emotional development of the child. Humans suffer psychic trauma as well as physical trauma.

Women who receive a message about their lack of worth by being forced into a procedure they have refused may have long-term mental health problems. Also, there is a growing body of knowledge regarding the link between physical illness and mental states including stress, lack of control, and feelings of worthlessness. Mental states may lead to physical illness, which may result in death (Glasser, 1981; Padus, 1986).

Advocates have developed to protect the rights of the mentally disabled; they also have been proposed to represent the interests of the fetus (Clewell et al., 1982). The advocate would seek the best treatment for the fetus and protect it from unnecessary assaults. This clearly is best interest advocacy. And who would protect the fetus from the advocate? This could place two advocates in conflict, one for the mother and one for the fetus. It would seem that there would be little to gain from fetal advocacy but maternal-child conflict with potential negative mental health impacts for both.

NEWBORN CARE AND MENTAL HEALTH

Undeniably, technological advancements have resulted in developments in many areas of health care. Care for the newborn is such an area. Newborn intensive care developed in the early 1960s because certain important technological advances made possible the miniaturization of ways to evaluate and treat very small subjects (Stahlman, 1989). Technological advancements in this particular area of health care include the development of infant respirators, micro blood gas analyzers, small-bore endotracheal tubes, and plastic umbilical catheters.

Technology has changed infant health care. With the increasing complexity of the technology surrounding underweight sick infants, more personnel with special areas of expertise are needed. Care is fragmented, from one physician and one nurse who knew everything about an infant, to many individuals, each knowing a great deal about fragments of the infant's problems and needs. Decision making is fragmented, and it is less apparent who is primarily responsible.   The impersonalization of care, made possible because of technological advances such as the computer, has brought about potentially deleterious affects on the mental health of an infant. Due to technology, the time spent at the bedside has been shortened and the number of beds increased. The needs of newborns for touch has been recognized only recently and the human element returned to the technological setting.   Changes have been introduced in nurseries to encourage touching, holding, and talking to the infant.

Sonograms which allow doctors to examine the baby's brain have also led to treatment changes. Sonograms revealed that the blood vessels of up to 40 percent of premature infants burst and hemorrhaged into the brain because the pressure in ventilators was too high (Ubell, 1983). Sonograms allowed for countermeasures to be taken. New technological devices measure oxygen in the blood, so doctors can adjust the ventilator to deliver the most oxygen at the least pressure (Ubell, 1983).

Technological advancements in the health industry were accompanied by an increase in expenses. The monetary cost can be measured in billions of dollars per year for newborn intensive care. This raises policy issues of overuse of technology and inappropriate use of technology in order to pay for all of the new equipment and procedures.

Low birth weight is the most common life-threatening condition. In the first few hours of life, it is very difficult for medical staff to determine a correct prognosis. Infants may die, develop normally, or survive with severe physical and/or mental disabilities (Rhoden, 1986). Although we do not know the long-term emotional effects of intensive treatment of newborns, by 1983 infant intensive care units were achieving a 60 percent survival rate in infants under two pounds.   Ten years earlier, only 1 percent of those infants survived. Advances have been in three areas: diagnosis, artificial feeding, and mechanical breathing (Ubell, 1983).

Policy issues are also raised because newborns are unable to make their own treatment decisions. The President's Commission for the Study of Ethical Problems in Medicine and Biomedical and Behavioral Research (1982) stated that since newborns will never be able to make decisions, they will need surrogates who in most cases will be parents with the advice of physicians. The commission put faith in parents being able to make decisions in the best interest of the infant.

Although most treated premature infants survive and become normal children, a significant number do not. This raises the issue of when and whether preventive or treatment measures should be taken. Richard McCormic

(1981:383), a Catholic theologian, believes the value of life requires some potentiality for human relationships. If that potentiality is absent or totally subordinated to the effort to survive, then "life can be said to have achieved its potential." According to Grobstein, "personal individuality is very closely linked to the sense of self—and the security of self is a persistent and fundamental individual concern" (1988:20). Furthermore, "a fundamental characteristic of human beings is their inner sense of being that is variously designated as sentience, self-awareness, consciousness, or more generally psychic individuality. This term underlies the uniqueness and particularity of inner awareness as it is experienced by individuals designated as persons. The critical question then is when, in the course of development, a person first exists to experience such individuality in at least minimal forms" (Grobstein, 1988:33). Lacking any firm definition, the door is open to conflict over when to treat.

Rostain (1986) describes how medical personnel, hospital personnel, and parents reach a consensus on forgoing treatment and prepare for an infant's death. This includes a sad ritual and the sentiment that what is being done is for the best. However, without clear institutional guidelines participants are placed in an increasingly difficult decision-making atmosphere of uncertainty, fear, and mistrust.

Infants who survive serious illnesses or disabilities may be left with chronic health conditions. These children may also experience the burden of childhood illness. Chronic childhood illnesses also have a substantial public policy cost and impact. In 1988 chronically ill children accounted for 41 million school absences, 37 million bed days, 92 million physician contacts, and over seven million hospital days. At an average daily hospital cost of $581 plus $36 for intermediate-level pediatric visits, the cost of hospital and physician care is estimated to be $7.5 billion annually (Newacheck and Taylor, 1992).

Mentally Handicapped Newborns

The 1982 Baby Doe case in Indiana involved an infant with a mental disability, Down's syndrome, associated with mental retardation and a deformed esophagus that prevented normal eating or drinking. The baby's parents decided against surgery to repair the esophagus or intravenous feeding, a decision which would result in starvation. The hospital went to court. The court ordered the hospital to comply with nontreatment (*Doe v. Bloomington Hospital, 104 S. Ct. 394*, 1982). The Indiana Supreme Court refused to hear the case, and the week-old baby died before an appeal to the U.S. Supreme Court could be made. This death focused attention on withholding treatment from infants with disabilities and allowing them to die.

Advocates for persons with mental retardation lobbied President Reagan. The administration drafted regulations published March 7, 1983 requiring hospitals receiving federal money to post notices that failing to provide food or treatment to a handicapped infant may violate the law and could lead to prosecution. A 24-hour, toll-free hotline was established for anonymous reporting of violations to the U.S. Department of Health and Human Service's Office for Civil Rights.

The American Academy of Pediatrics, Children's Hospital National Medical Center of Washington, D.C., the National Association of Children's Hospitals, and related institutions sued, arguing that the regulatory procedures were "arbitrary and capricious" and intruded into the family-physician relationship (Merrick, 1988:3). The physicians were concerned about being second guessed in life-or-death situations and were concerned that government intervention would prolong the pain and suffering of patients who would not live. The Association for Retarded Citizens (ARC) filed a brief in support of the administration.

Between March 1983 and January 1984, the Department of Health and Human Services issued a series of rules which were struck down by the federal courts. A U.S. District Judge, Gerhard A. Gesell, overturned the Reagan administration regulation in April 1983. He found the hotline informer procedure ill considered. He did conclude that in some circumstances section 504 of the Rehabilitation Act of 1973 authorizes the government to protect handicapped newborns from discriminatory denial of medical care.

In 1983 Baby Jane Doe was born with spina bifida and related complications in Long Island, New York. Her parents refused surgery and agreed to the physician's advice of conservative treatment, including antibiotics and dressings. An unrelated person filed suit, and a trial court authorized surgery. The appellate division of the court reversed. The New York Court of Appeals subsequently found the trial court in error for allowing nonrelated persons to bring suit. (This is becoming an increasing problem. When nonrelated persons, often those who never have even met the family, enter the situation, this adds enormous stress by threatening the family identity and control. We know nothing of the long-term mental health effects of this.) New York's Child Protective Services Agency also investigated and found no cause to intervene (Annas, 1986). Health and Human Services (HHS) sought the baby's medical records, and when the hospital refused it filed suit for their release. The Federal District Court found for the hospital (*United States v. University Hospital of the State University of New York at Stony Brook, 575 F. Supp. 607, 1983*). Health and Human Services appealed to the Second Circuit Court, which found that section 504 did not apply to such investigations, and it was not correct to assume that Congress intended for the federal government to enter the child care field, which had traditionally been under state jurisdiction.

In *American Hospital Association v. Heckler* (585 F. Supp. 541, S.D. N.Y., 1984), the court issued a summary judgment that the final regulations were not authorized by the Rehabilitation Act. On the appeal to the U.S. Supreme Court, the court ruled in *Bowen v. American Hospital Association* (106 S. Ct. 2101, 1986), in a plurality decision written by Justice Stevens, that the requirements for notices, reporting, and access to records were not founded on evidence of discrimination and were not within the authority of the Secretary. The Rehabilitation Act was determined not to permit intervention with state jurisdiction and the decision making of parents and physicians. The court also noted that HHS had not shown any case in which a hospital had denied treatment solely for reason of a handicap.

In the fall of 1984 public policy shifted to the legislative arena when legislation dealing with Baby Doe cases was passed by Congress. The legislation was backed by pediatricians and hospitals. Congress passed amendments to the Child Abuse Prevention and Treatment Act. The amendments brought failure to treat a handicapped infant under the federal definition of child abuse and neglect (Child Abuse Amendments of 1984, Public Law No. 98-457, 121, 98 Stat. 1749, 1752, 1984). States were required to establish separate government offices to handle complaints of withholding of medical treatment from handicapped infants. Complaints could be brought by physicians, nurses, hospital workers, or individual citizens. States would be required to intervene if the care was withheld when treatment was "medically indicated" (Moskopord Saldania, 1986). Quality of life was not addressed by the amendments (Moskop and Saldania, 1986). The affect on the mental health of the family was not considered; nor was the future quality of life of the infant.

HHS was given the power to promulgate rules to implement the act. Only states receiving federal funds for operation of child protective services (CPS) were covered by the amendments, and the only means of enforcing compliance was withdrawal of those federal funds. In the spring of 1985 the Department of Health and Human Services released a final regulation under the 1984 legislation covering the Baby Doe cases, in which infants with severe or multiple handicaps might be denied necessary medical treatment and allowed to die. Three cases were specified in which doctors were justified in withholding medical treatment: when the infant was chronically and irreversibly comatose, when treatment prolonged an inevitable death, and when treatment was so extreme and so likely to be futile that it was inhumane to administer it.

The final rules issued in April 1985 required medical neglect as part of the definition of child abuse and required hospitals receiving federal funds to designate a contact person and allow child protective services access to medical records. Hospitals were encouraged to establish Infant Care Review Committees to review individual cases, recommend institutional policies, and educate families and hospital personnel. The Joseph P. Kennedy Foundation argued that failure to treat handicapped newborns was infrequent. A 1987 survey of state programs upheld this view by showing that all states had systems in place for notification of CPS agencies for reporting potential Baby Doe cases. The systems had been in operation for years, and there was "no significant increase in the volume of reports received . . . cases [were] essentially [handled] the same way even before the Federal law was passed" (Merrick, 1988:5). Between October 1985 and April 1987, the states received a total of 19 reports of suspected medical neglect of handicapped newborns. All were investigated, but in only six cases did CPS intervene in the treatment. None of the children recovered or went home to live with their family. One child died after a change of treatment; one remained in a chronic nonresponsive state; two were sent to children's convalescent hospitals; one was placed in foster care; and one remained in the permanent custody of the state CPS agency (Merrick, 1988). We have no information on the mental health effects on the families who went through these processes.

HHS studied the establishment of Infant Care Review Committees in 10 large hospitals in eight major cities (Office of the Inspector General, HHS, 1987). One established a committee, while the other nine already had ethics committees prior to the regulations. Most handled a range of cases, not just involving infants. Although membership varied, all had hospital administrators, social workers, medical specialists, and nurses, and most had clergy, ethicists, patient representatives, and members of disability groups.

Dr. William Weil (1986:32), chair of the American Academy of Pediatric Bioethics, suggested that avoidance of legal challenges could lead to worsening bed shortages in neonatal intensive care units and cause unnecessary emotional and financial stress on families. Prolonging the life of "the most compromised infants" could result in higher morbidity and mortality for all infants needing intensive care. Further development of decision-making roles for committees and courts moves away from a history of relatives and/or legal guardians making decisions for patients who are not able to make their own decisions (Merrick, 1988).

MENTAL HEALTH ASPECTS OF PAIN AND SUFFERING

One of the most disturbing aspects of treatment of both fetuses and babies is the question of pain. How much pain and suffering is acceptable in carrying out treatment? Fetuses probably do not feel pain during the early weeks of development, but they probably do in later weeks, and babies clearly do.

Adult pain is dependent on a neural substrate with several identified neural requirements. There are two aspects of pain: informational, allowing identification of the source and intensity of a stimulus, and the experience or feeling itself. Pain may also be followed by general feelings such as fright, anger, or anxiety. If inner experience and pain depend on a significant degree of brain function, then it would not exist during the first trimester (13 weeks) and would be unlikely up to 20 weeks. The first synapses among cortical neurons do not appear until 18 to 20 weeks, and the first fibers from the thalamus do not enter the cortex until about 22 weeks. At around 25 weeks, thalamic fibers begin to synapse with cortical neurons and to develop the branching characteristic of the adult cortex. Technology is helping in the understanding of these processes. Electrical patterns shown by electroencephalograms show a change in electrical patterns around this time; they become more regular and resemble adult patterns of sleeping and waking states. This indicates that seven months (30 weeks) of development may be necessary for a sufficient neural substrate to experience pain as we know it (Grobstein, 1988). Development of this kind of information is important to policy decisions where quality of life is considered and where abortion is considered.

Until recently, babies were forced to suffer many procedures without proper anesthesia, and medical personnel often discounted their ability to feel pain. With improved anesthesia, physicians are being educated to no longer ignore infant pain. Many young children of the 1950s and earlier have appeared as adults in counseling with serious mental health issues which can be linked to childhood experiences of pain and fear from inadequate anesthesia and poor psychological preparation for surgeries. We are only beginning to discover the mental health effects of children suffering pain and trauma. What are the long-term mental health effects for infants who are subjected to procedure after procedure involving trauma, pain, and even near-death experiences?

One study (Wilstein, 1987) shows that various types of birth trauma are associated with higher suicide rates among adolescents or young adults. Although very few babies who suffered trauma at birth later committed suicide, the association between birth events and destructive behavior later in life was conclusive. The Karobinska Institute research indicated that people who committed suicide by violent means, such as leaping from heights or using firearms, had more often experienced mechanical birth trauma including forceps delivery, umbilical cord entanglement around the neck, and breech presentation (20.8 percent compared to 9.1 percent of controls). People who committed suicide by asphyxia, including hanging, drowning, and gas poisoning, more often suffered loss of oxygen (asphyxia) during birth (10 percent compared to 2.3 percent of controls). The research examined 412 birth records of young people who killed themselves or died of drug or alcohol abuse between 1978 and 1984, and 2,910 control subjects born at the same five Stockholm hospitals in the same years. This kind of research points out how little we know about long term consequences of our treatment of infants.

As we learn more about pain and suffering of near-term fetuses and infants, will this open up further tort actions? Already malpractice suits involving the birth of children with mental disabilities are widespread, and wrongful life suits are growing.

WRONGFUL LIFE AND MALPRACTICE

Forty states have had lawsuits involving children born with abnormalities or deformities and wrongful life. A tort for wrongful life is a suit brought on behalf of an affected infant against a physician or other health professional for alleged negligence in informing the parents of the possibility of their having a severely defective child, thus preventing parental choice in terminating the pregnancy. Various types of cases have arisen, including alleged negligence in genetic counseling, failure to recognize the presence of genetic disease in the parents, failure to advise the parents of the risk of having an affected child, and failure to advise the use of appropriate prenatal tests which could detect the problem. There are also cases involving physicians and laboratories in regard to negligence in processing or interpreting the prenatal diagnostic tests. In addition, there have been cases involving failure to diagnose or advise of the effects of a maternal medical condition impacting fetal health, such as rubella (Blank, 1988).

The unusual aspect of all of these cases is the assumption that a life has occurred which should not have been, and it is the negligence of the defendant which has led to this birth. The suits are usually brought on behalf of the affected child. The harm claimed for a lawsuit for monetary damages is based on being born, and damages are asked on the basis of that existence. Such suits raise the issue of whether the infant can be a plaintiff when the harm occurred before conception or during the time as a fetus.

Wrongful birth suits are brought on behalf of the affected parents. Increasingly courts are accepting these actions. Physicians have been held liable for damages in cases involving wrongful birth of children born with mental or physical defects. Successful lawsuits have occurred against physicians who did not advise patients over 35 of the availability of amniocentesis. In 1987 Virginia enacted a no-fault liability coverage for birth-related severe neurological injuries. Chapter 540, Laws of 1987, applies to live, full-term births. Infants must have suffered permanent and severe impairments as a result of injury to their brain or spinal cord caused by mechanical injury or oxygen deprivation occurring during labor, delivery, or resuscitation immediately after birth.

A 1988 Florida law became the second in the country to cover a narrow class of severely injured infants with a no-fault reimbursement system. The Florida medical liability law provides for voluntary arbitration, with incentives for defendants to arbitrate. The law caps noneconomic damage awards at $250,000 in arbitrated cases. If a patient goes to court, awards for pain and suffering and punitive damages are limited to $350,000. If a doctor refuses to arbitrate, awards can be unlimited. Awards for economic losses are not limited.

In 1988 the U.S. Supreme Court barred a Missouri couple whose child had Down's syndrome from suing their doctor for failing to tell them a test would have revealed the disorder prior to birth. The court without comment refused to review a wrongful birth claim by parents who said they would have chosen abortion if they knew the child had the disorder. Mrs. Barbara Wilson was 36 at conception and 37 when she gave birth to a son with Down's syndrome. The Wilson's cited medical evidence that the risk of a child having the disorder is about 1 in 1,000 when the mother is in her twenties and about 1 in 30 when she is 36. The Wilsons said Dr. Kuenzi failed to inform them that the disorder could be detected by amniocentesis. The Wilsons sued the doctor for negligence on their own behalf, a wrongful birth claim, and on their son's behalf, a wrongful life claim. The Missouri Supreme Court dismissed the suit, ruling that permitting such suits conflicted with the state's policy on personal injury claims or torts. "A finding . . . that we will not recognize either, a new tort for wrongful birth is in our opinion totally compatible with the policy considerations expressed by our legislature in attempting to limit the statute of limitations for malpractice actions." The Missouri Court noted that wrongful birth suits have been permitted in some states. But the Missouri court said those states have had trouble explaining how a genetic disorder is the result of "any injury negligently inflicted by the doctor" ("Missouri Parents . . .," 1988:8A).

Sixty-seven percent of the money awarded in obstetrical lawsuits is for claims of brain damage resulting from oxygen being cut off from an infant during labor and delivery. Most cases of cerebral palsy, which occurs in 1 in 300 births, are blamed on this lack of oxygen at birth. Cerebral palsy (CP) involves a complete or partial paralysis of the muscles, primarily of the limbs. It is caused by a brain abnormality, and the degree of handicap varies. Limbs may be immobile or the movements may be weak and poorly controlled or jerky. This spasticity may be mild or severe. Many children have some degree of mental retardation, but other children are highly intelligent. Hearing loss, visual defects, and convulsions may also occur. For most children, the cause is not known. CP may result from abnormal development of the brain or from brain damage before, during, or shortly after birth. Later on, brain damage can be caused by head injury, severe convulsions, or meningitis. In many cases, the CP will not be recognized until well into the baby's first year. CP is the most common crippling disorder of childhood, and it is especially common in babies who are premature or under 2½ grams (5½ pounds) at birth (Kunz, 1982). Dr. Richard Naeye, a pathologist at Penn State University College of Medicine, Hershey, and his associates studied more than 56,000 pregnancies and concluded that only 10 percent of severe cases and 2 percent of mild cases of cerebral palsy are caused by birth asphyxia. Dr. John Freeman, director of pediatric neurology, Johns Hopkins University, Baltimore, who studied the same pregnancies and other cases of birth asphyxia in the world in a study co-authored with Dr. Karen Nelson of the National Institutes of Health, agreed with Naeye's study. Their study concluded that mild degrees of asphyxia are very common during labor and delivery (Freeman and Nelson, 1988). In order to cause permanent neurologic damage such as cerebral palsy, oxygen loss must be both severe and prolonged. Infants with severe and prolonged oxygen loss show symptoms at birth of breathing difficulty, sucking difficulty, seizures, or coma. These disturbances of function in the first few days of life are clinically defined as neonatal encephalopathy (NE) (Nelson and Leviton, 1991). Freeman and Nelson (1988) concluded that an infant without those symptoms probably does not have severe asphyxia during labor. Most children with cerebral palsy do not show those signs. Birth asphyxia has led to a major crisis in obstetrical lawsuits. The American College of Obstetricians and Gynecologists concluded that the studies could greatly reduce the cases filed against obstetricians (Friend, 1988).

Treatments aimed at preventing death or long-term neurologic deficits from birth asphyxia will soon be available (Espinoza and Parer, 1991; Vannuci, 1990). As these therapies are powerful and potentially risky, they will require the ability to identify very rapidly infants whose problems are secondary to asphyxia and serious enough to warrant some risk in their treatment. Nelson and Leviton (1991) examined this issue and concluded that although there are signs that infants have suffered cerebral injury due to asphyxia at birth, their evolution has not yet been captured and quantified in a way which permits predictive use. Most of the characteristics that allow for origin are features that cannot be recognized until hours or days after birth. The problem with this time delay is that most proposed interventions would occur very soon after delivery. Thus the signs of NE are nonspecific, and birth asphyxia sufficient to produce NE is not easy to distinguish from other causes within the moments after birth. As most severely asphyxiated children who survive are later clinically normal (Jain, Ferre, Vidyasagar, Nath, and Sheftel, 1991), proposers of clinical trials of new therapies, which have shown risks in animal testing but have effects that are not fully predictable in humans, "will be under a strong obligation to judge that the treatment is not worse than the disease" (Nelson and Leviton, 1991:1329).

Early Diagnosis

There is a growing body of knowledge regarding early diagnosis of mental disorders. For example, in 1991 research was reported ("Schizophrenia Signs . . .," 1991) that an irregular pattern of infant growth, including lags and spurts in muscle development, may indicate a tendency toward schizophrenia. A four-year study of children of schizophrenic adults showed that not all children with the pattern developed schizophrenia, but none of the children without the symptoms developed it. The work was an extension of research begun 40 years ago in the 1950s by Joseph Marcus, who studied Israeli children with at least one schizophrenic parent. He discovered that 50 percent of these children had subtle neurological symptoms, including lack of attention, hyperactivity, and below-normal muscle coordination (a condition now called schizotypal personality disorder). In the 1950s Barbara Fish began studying 12 children of schizophrenics and 12 children of nonschizophrenic parents in New York City. She concluded that there were definite infancy warning signs. In testing her findings, she studied 58 infants who Marcus was researching from birth to elementary school. Without knowing their identities or their parents, she identified which children went on to become schizotypal. The ability to make an earlier identification can lead to ways to prevent or lessen the effect of mental disabilities.

Phenylketonuria (PKU) is an inborn metabolic error. It is an enzyme disorder which leads to a newborn's inability to oxidize phenylalanine, a substance found in most high-protein foods. It is inherited as a recessive trait and can lead to mental retardation, but it can be minimized with effective neonatal care. Currently the only treatment is dietary. A baby can be identified as having PKU through blood tests. The PKU diet is then begun early in life. It is a very restrictive diet which controls for phenylalanine intake. Although there are some dangers associated with the diet, the risk is small compared to the damage which can be caused by PKU (Evans, 1983). To supply the recommended daily allowance of carbohydrates, fats, and proteins, special casein hydrolysate formulas are used. Various low-protein solid foods are added gradually to the diet as the child grows older. Fat and cholesterol levels consumed tend to be lower than in the general population. But research has indicated that families with a child with PKU have lower serum total cholesterol values than the general population, and the levels of serum cholesterol in their PKU children are influenced more by genetic factors than diet (DeClue, Davis, Schocken, Kangas, and Benford, 1991). With careful monitoring, most children with PKU develop "near normal" intelligence (Sells and Bennett, 1977).

Since the 1960s a number of states have mandated PKU testing of newborns. Mental retardation caused by the disorder has declined (Gearhart and Litton, 1977). PKU is only one of several disorders causing mental retardation which can now be detected through blood testing. Neonatal tests also exist for galactosemia, histidinemia, homocrystinuria, hypothyroidism (cretinism, which is still a major problem in some countries such as Nepal), and maple syrup urine disease. These are treatable disorders when treated early. However, not all states require testing for these disorders even though the testing cost per child is very low (Evans, 1983).

Perhaps the greatest hopes for prevention in the future lie with genetics. Genetics hold out the hope of eventual prevention of many diseases and conditions. Genetics may also be used in understanding and eventually treating many disorders.

As genetic counseling, diagnostic technologies, fetal surgery and intervention, and newborn care become more sophisticated, they hold out the hope for better identification, decision making, and treatment. But at the same time they raise new ethical and legal concerns regarding sex selection, control of decision making, quality of life, effects of pain and suffering, and increased lawsuits.

5
Drug Treatments and Mental Disabilities

Psychiatry has been influenced from the beginning by concerns regarding mind and body, the problem of trying to define and differentiate the psychological and environmental factors and the physiological and biological factors. The psychological and behavioral effects of drugs were noted even in primitive medicine. Psychopharmacology is tied to a search for physiologically or chemically defined states in psychiatry (Tourney, 1978). Psychopharmacology has developed as a scientific discipline. There has been a lengthy conflict between environmental or psychosocial versus biological approaches. In recent years there has been a strong resurgence of the biological orientation.

Psychopharmacology is related closely to the field of biological psychiatry. The belief that there is an organic deficit in mental disorder is not a new one. This belief has led to many somatic therapies, including experimentation with many drugs. Psychopharmacology focuses on the ability of drugs to alter behavior and mentation, and thus to treat mental disorders. It has attempted to define mental disorders as physiological and chemical and has focused on reducing psychopathology to chemical or metabolic disturbances in function (Tourney, 1978).

DISORDERS TREATED WITH DRUGS

Disorders of the brain and nervous system are frequently treated successfully with drugs. These disorders may range from epilepsy to schizophrenia. Typically drug treatment does not eliminate the nervous system disorder, but corrects or modifies it. This brings symptom relief or in some cases results in restoration of normal functioning and behavior. Drugs may encourage the action of the inhibitory neurotransmitters and lower activity, as in drugs used to treat insomnia and anxiety, or stimulate the excitatory neurotransmitters to increase the level of activity as in drugs used to treat depression. The major drug groups include antidepressant drugs, antipsychotic drugs, antianxiety drugs, sleeping drugs, analgesics, nervous system stimulants, anticonvulsant drugs, antiparkinsonism drugs, antiemetic drugs, and drugs used for migraine.

Many mental disorders are commonly treated with drugs. Among these disorders are affective disorders and schizophrenia. Their etiology remains obscure. Increasingly it is believed that there is a genetic component, but most researchers do not believe that genetics are the total cause for these conditions. Studies of brain chemistry and function are becoming primary.

Affective Disorders

Affective disorders are mood disorders. They consist of a mood or affect that involves subjective feelings, thoughts, wishes, or fantasies. They usually have both physical components and behavioral consequences. Among the affective disorders is depression. There are two types of depression: exogenous depression, which appears to be precipitated by external stress such as loss of a loved one or work stress, and endogenous depression, which appears to arise from within the individual as the result of biochemical or hormonal imbalance and is not related to external factors. Bipolar disorders, involutional depression, and postpartum depressive psychosis are believed to be endogenous (Atwood and Chester, 1987).

The affective disorders have been a focus of modern neurochemical research. By 1960 a number of biogenic amines were discovered in the brain, and a number of drugs were discovered to have important effects upon mood. These were found to have significant action on the biogenic amines of the brain. Reserpine, which had been used to treat hypertension, was found to have a side-effect of depression in about 10 percent of cases and was found to deplete the brain of norepinephrine and serotonin. Several drugs which were used to elevate or treat depression, including tricyclic antidepressants, amphetamines, and monoamine oxidase inhibitors (MAOs), were found to enhance the activity of norepinephrine at its central synapses (Kety, 1978). Meanwhile, Coppen (1971) and others connected the involvement of serotonin to manic depression and other affective disorders. This evidence included the finding of a significant reduction of a major metabolite of serotonin, hydroxyindoleacetic acid, in the cerebrospinal fluid of patients in depression, mania, or remission.

Depression is now thought to be caused by a reduction in the level of various chemicals in the brain, neurotransmitters, that affect mood by stimulating brain cells. Antidepressants increase the level of excitatory neurotransmitters. The tricyclics are the most widely used group of antidepressants and are usually the first given to a patient. Some, such as amitriptyline, are mostly sedative and are used for people who are also having trouble sleeping. Others, such as imipramine, have a stimulant effect and are used for people who are lethargic. Excitatory neurotransmitters released by brain cells are usually taken up rapidly again into the cells. Tricyclics block the re-uptake of neurotransmitters, thus prolonging the stimulatory effect on the brain. The second most common group of drugs used, the MAOs, are usually given to people who have not responded well on tricyclics or who for some reason have counterindications for tricyclics. They are particularly useful for people who are anxious or have phobias as well as depression. They block the action of a brain enzyme that normally breaks down the excitatory neurotransmitters and allow the neurotransmitters to build to a high level and stimulate the brain.

Schizophrenia

Schizophrenia is now believed to be a group of diseases with similar symptoms but different causes. However, because these diseases are not yet differentiated clearly, schizophrenia is still largely treated crudely as one disease, but this is beginning to change. Schizophrenia is now accepted as an illness presenting two major syndromes regarding symptoms, negative symptoms (social withdrawal, loss of emotional expression, lack of drive, and loss of interest) and positive symptoms (psychosis). Scales have now been developed to assist therapists in the assessment of schizophrenia. The Positive and Negative Syndrome Scale (PANSS), for instance, provides a standardized evaluation of psychopathology dimensions to help characterize a clinical profile and to monitor changes with treatment. The scale involves a rating of 30 symptoms along a seven-point scale and yields separate scores along nine clinical dimensions, including scales for Positive syndrome, Negative syndrome, Depression, Composite Index, and General psychopathology (Kay, Opler, and Fiszbein, 1990). The development of increasingly refined means of assessing and monitoring mental disabilities enhances the opportunity for more individualized treatment.

Schizophrenia may have a gradual onset (prodromal phase), or its onset may be sudden. The acute or active phase of schizophrenia may involve delusions, hallucinations, distortions in thinking, and disturbances in feelings and behavior. After an acute episode the person may enter a chronic or residual phase involving listlessness, trouble concentrating, and withdrawal. Acute phases of the disease may reactivate over time. There are several different types of schizophrenia: disorganized, catatonic, paranoid, undifferentiated, and residual. Symptoms of schizophrenia include thought disorder, thought broadcasting, delusions, hallucinations, disturbance of feeling or affect, ambivalence, sensitivity, physical symptoms such as slowing of physical activity or excitation and overactivity, lessening of drive, social withdrawal, and changes in habits and ability to function (Kerr, Thompson, and Jeffries, 1988).

Even though the underlying brain pathology was not clearly understood, drug treatment went forward to treat the symptoms. Some results began to be seen as follow-up studies showed that about one third of patients with schizophrenia remitted, another third stayed the same, and one third deteriorated. The use of drugs such as haloperidol, an antipsychotic drug, changed short-term study results. Within one year, approximately 70 to 80 percent of treated schizophrenics improved (Cole, 1964). However in longer follow-up studies of five years or more, the results remained in the approximately one third divisions (Gottlieb and Frohman, 1978).

There have been many theories over the years regarding the cause of schizophrenia. The latest research indicates that schizophrenia may be caused by irregularities in brain chemistry and that there may also be a genetic factor. Chemical hypotheses about mental illness were developed by Hippocratic physicians, but the modern biochemical approach to schizophrenia probably started with Thudichum in 1884. He believed that many forms of mental illness were probably the result of toxic substances in the body. He spent a 10-year research grant from the British parliament studying the brains of cattle, which he obtained from a slaughterhouse. In this work he laid the foundations of modern neurochemistry (Kety, 1978). After World War II, Kety and other researchers (Kety et al., 1948) concluded that in schizophrenics there was no difference in the circulation of the brain or in its oxygen consumption compared to other persons, and they believed that if there was a biochemical disturbance it was probably "in much more subtle and complex processes than in the overall circulation and energy metabolism of the brain" (p. 41). In the 1950s it was postulated that a defect in the metabolism of epinephrine might lead to the accumulation of adrenochrome, which might cause hallucinations (Hoffer, 1957). But when this could be examined in the early 1960s, no evidence was found (LaBrosse, Mann, and Kety, 1961).

With the discovery in 1974 of receptors for the protein dopamine in the brain, questions about the role of dopamine in schizophrenia were raised. Was there too much dopamine, too little dopamine, an excess of receptors for dopamine, or an oversensitivity to dopamine? Was the brain's dopamine system the problem, or was the dopamine problem only a symptom of some other problem in brain chemistry? It is now recognized that there are at least two subtypes of dopamine. Research on dopamine and other brain chemistry research is of growing importance. Anti-psychotic drugs are known to bind to D2 (dopamine) receptors and also to sigma receptors. Sigma sites have been identified, and researchers are trying to find drugs which bind to sigma receptors but not to D2 receptors. Serotonin is also being researched, and it is believed to have 8 or 10 neurotransmitter sites. The effect of glutamate on the brain is also under examination (Stahl, 1990).

One of the major problems in the use of psychoactive drugs is that they are not localized to a specific area of the brain. They go to every part of the brain and affect many brain pathways. This causes unwanted drug side-effects, which are discussed later in this chapter.

In 1988 researchers reported that they had isolated the gene that acts as a blueprint for the D2 dopamine receptor. The receptor gene was first identified in rats and then humans. The receptor, which is made by brain cells, rests on the surface of the cells and is where antipsychosis drugs exert their effects on the brain. Normally the receptor responds when adjacent brain cells secrete dopamine, allowing brain cells to communicate. If a family of dopamine receptors can be found, then drugs may be able to be designed that affect only the receptors linked to disease. That would allow the avoidance of side-effects of current medications. Research could lead to knowledge about how the receptor gene is turned on and off and that could provide information on how schizophrenia occurs. Research might also help scientists study the inheritance of a tendency toward schizophrenia and possibly other diseases, which could lead to better matching of patients and medications ("Discovery of Schizophrenia . . .," 1988).

With the recognition that there are both negative and positive symptoms in schizophrenia, a new sophisticated pharmacotherapy is under development which allows the two syndromes to be approached separately. It has been suggested that drugs with D2 receptor antagonistic activity (antipositive or psychotic drugs) are more effective for the control of positive (psychotic) symptoms. Drugs which have action on other neurotransmitter systems and are less selective on D2 (antinegative or deficit symptom drugs) have been suggested to be therapeutic for the negative symptoms. "In the future, psychosis may be controlled by one agent whereas the negative or deficit symptoms may be treated by other means" (Jones, 1990:4). The stage of illness may come to determine the type of treatment, with acutely ill patients being treated with drugs which are able to antagonize dopaminergic activity quickly and potently while other drugs are given for maintenance treatment as the psychosis resolves and the brain's ability to adapt takes over. That stage may call for drugs which are modulators or regulators of neurotransmitter action. Drug treatment will become much more complex. "Antipsychotic drugs will simply be one weapon in a more vast armamentarium ultimately resulting in true antischizophrenic drug treatments" (Jones, 1990:5). Learning more about how antipsychotic drugs work may also lead to a better understanding of the biological mechanisms underlying psychotic disorders.

The hope of people with schizophrenia and many other mental disorders is that research will lead to the identification, in a highly specific way, of the parts of the brain and the brain pathways involved in the disorder and that very specific drugs can be developed to affect only an identified area without affecting other parts of the brain and causing many side-effects (in other words, that research will enable the successful move from a shotgun approach to specific targeting).

Other Disorders Treated with Drugs

Among other disorders treated with drugs are many disorders in children. Children dual diagnosed with conduct disorder and attention deficit hyperactivity disorder (ADHD) often receive drug therapy involving stimulant medications which have been used for over 50 years. Attention deficit hyperactivity disorder is characterized by inattention and hyperactive or impulsive behavior. If these symptoms are severe enough, they may interfere with a child's adjustment at home and in school. ADHD is one of the most common behavioral disorders of children in the United States.

Behavioral disorder was recognized in the early nineteenth century, and behavioral symptoms were associated with insults to the brain such as injuries or infections of the central nervous system. Originally labeled ''brain damage syndrome,'' the terminology was later changed to ''minimal brain dysfunction'' (Shaywitz and Shaywitz, 1990:2270).

Drugs used to treat adult mental illnesses have also been used for childhood disorders. Lithium and carbamazepine (an anticonvulsant) are used for children who are explosively aggressive. Lithium is also used along with beta blockers and maltrexone for children with mental retardation who are extremely self-injurious and aggressive. Haloperidol is among the drugs used to treat children with autism (NIMH, 1990).

Another common disorder treated with drugs is anxiety. Anxiety involves fear or apprehension which is not caused by real danger. If certain brain chemicals become disturbed, the increased brain activity can result in fearful feelings and stimulation of the sympathetic nervous system, resulting in physical symptoms such as shaking, palpitations, breathlessness, headaches, and digestive disorders. Antianxiety drugs are referred to as anxiolytics or minor tranquilizers. They are used to alleviate symptoms but do not address underlying causes, which may be dealt with by psychotherapy. The two main classes of drugs used are benzodizepines and beta blockers. Benzodizepines are the most common and are usually given for short periods to create relaxation. They are also, as noted later in this chapter, subject to much abuse. Many of them also have a sedative effect to address insomnia, which often accompanies anxiety. They depress activity in parts of the brain dealing with emotion and promote the action of the chemical gamma-animobutyric (GABA), which attaches itself to brain cells and blocks the transmission of electrical impulses. This blocking reduces communication between brain cells. The beta blockers are used mostly to reduce the physical symptoms of anxiety. They act on the release of norepinephrine, a chemical released by the sympathetic nervous system. By blocking the action of norepinephrine, they reduce the physical symptoms of anxiety (Clayman, 1988).

With increasing knowledge about brain chemistry, new treatment possibilities become available. For example, researchers at Stanford University have used research regarding dopamine to explore the cause of debilitating shyness. They found that many shy people have lower amounts of dopamine in their brains. Dopamine makes a person more talkative, active, and excitable—more outgoing. Columbia University researchers have used MAO inhibitors, which increase levels of dopamine in the brain and have been used for depression, to treat shyness ("Antishyness Drug," 1988). Previously only psychotherapy had been available as a treatment for shyness.

Physical diseases with mental health components can also be treated by drugs. For example, AIDS dementia can be treated with azidothymidine (AZT), which can return people to approximately 90 percent of their previous mental functioning (NIMH, 1990). Parkinsonism can be treated by a number of drugs, including anticholinergics and dopamine-boosting drugs such as Levodopa. Parkinsonism has a variety of causes, including degeneration of the dopamine-producing cells in the brain (Parkinson's disease), brain damage, and narrowing of the blood vessels to the brain; and it can be a side-effect of certain drugs, particularly antipsychotics, which will be discussed later in this chapter (Clayman, 1988).

Drug Treatment and Mental Retardation

There has been a problem with persons with developmental disabilities being overmedicated with antipsychotic drugs. These negative experiences have led to psychotropic drug regulations in many states. These regulations have had a detrimental effect on providing mental health services to dual diagnosed persons (Gadow and Poling, 1988). There is also a problem in diagnosing mental illness in persons with mental retardation. Mental illness may go unrecognized due to the effects of mental retardation (Sovner, 1986). Sovner (1988) believes that in cases where a drug-responsive disorder is present, drug therapy is the treatment of first choice. The use of psychotropic drug therapy to treat behavioral and emotional problems in persons with developmental disabilities is a distinct clinical discipline which requires knowledge of how mental retardation influences the diagnostic process, an understanding of the normal behavioral and emotional responses of the developmentally disabled, an understanding of the impact of drug therapy upon rehabilitation, and an empirical database for diagnosing drug-responsive disorders and selecting the most appropriate drug (Sovner, 1987).

DRUG USE AND ABUSE

People have self-medicated themselves for centuries, seeking relief of psychological pain. Alcohol, opiates, and hashish have been used widely for self-tranquilization. Abuse of some of these substances has led to their control. At times these drugs have been used to treat mental illness.

In the mid-eighteenth century Young reported the effects of opiates in the treatment of mania and melancholia. By the mid-nineteenth century, however, they had reached their height of use and began to gain disfavor with psychiatrists, who had begun to recognize their addictive qualities (Tourney, 1978).

The first drugs to be abused were probably narcotics, including the naturally occurring opiates (opium, heroin, morphine, and codeine) and the later synthetics such as Darvon, Demerol, and Percodan. Narcotics are central nervous system depressants that slow down physical and psychological responses. Hypnotics and antianxiety drugs can also be abused. They can create temporary psychosis involving auditory hallucinations and paranoid delusions. They may also interfere with short-term memory and recall and impair judgment and motor performance. In contrast, stimulants stimulate the central nervous system. They range from caffeine to amphetamines, methamphetamine, dextroamphetamine, and cocaine. Abusers of stimulants may have sleep disturbances, and they are more likely to experience drug-induced psychiatric disturbances than any other abusers. Such disturbances can mimic the manic phase of bipolar disorder, resemble schizophrenia, or appear as panic attacks (BACCUPP, 1990). By reducing inhibitions, stimulants can result in increased risk of violence. Some drugs which have been made illegal are seen as relatively harmless, such as marijuana, while others such as LSD are seen as very dangerous.

Hashish and Marijuana

In 1845 J. J. Moreau de Rours made the first scientific study of hashish. He postulated that hashish produced a state similar to insanity. He presented the first model psychosis in psychiatric literature. He also postulated a relationship between dreams, insanity, and states produced by hashish. Tourney (1978) considers this work the beginning of psychopharmacology. Ever since, hashish and marijuana have been studied. It is now recognized that marijuana usually results in changing levels of consciousness rather than hallucinations. It has the unusual ability to create physical symptoms similar to depression, such as relaxation and drowsiness, and to mimic effects of stimulants, such as increased heart rate and respiration. Chronic long-term use can result in a number of physical effects, including respiratory problems, decreased strength of heart contractions, reproductive problems, increased rate of chromosomal breakage, and possible negative effects on growth-hormone production and on the immune system. Mental health effects include behavioral and learning difficulties in children of maternal users of the drug as a result of reduced oxygen during pregnancy, worsening of prior psychotic states, and memory impairment. Episodic users of marijuana may experience panic attacks, flashbacks, and suffer from impaired judgement (BACCUPP, 1990). In 1990 Dr. Richard H. Schwartz reported a pilot study at the Georgetown University School of Medicine, which concluded that teenagers who often use marijuana may suffer short-term memory problems for at least six weeks after they stop smoking. Heavy users scored much lower in terms of their ability to remember than nonusers (Schwartz, 1991).

Most researchers who study drug use and addiction believe that it is a combination of factors—psychological, biological, social—which turn a user into an addict (Franklin, 1991). Genetic and biological research are adding increasingly to information in this area. Scientists from the National Institute of Mental Health in 1990 said that they had cloned a "button" that marijuana presses in the brain. Their work revealed the chemical makeup of a protein structure on the surface of brain cells to which marijuana's main ingredient, cannabinoid, binds. The study originally described the brain-cell structure of rats, but further study showed a virtually identical human structure.

Marijuana use has been allowed on a limited basis by prescription for some medical conditions, such as glaucoma or nausea during cancer treatment. Through research, medications might be developed which could mimic the drug's therapeutic effects without affecting mood or thinking. Pain, epileptic convulsions, high blood pressure, nausea, asthma, and glaucoma might be treated (Bonner, 1990). Consciousness-altering street drugs such as marijuana may be particularly harmful to someone with a mental disability, as they can counteract the effects of antipsychotic medication and return schizophrenic symptoms such as hallucinations and paranoid feelings (Thornton, Seeman, Plummer, and Jeffries, 1985). For many years the debate has continued over whether to legalize marijuana. Large sectors of the public view it as relatively harmless. Yet it has not sustained enough public support for legalization. The growing body of research about marijuana shows that legalization may not be as easily justified as was once thought.

Lysergic Acid Diethylamide

Lysergic acid diethylamide (LSD) was synthesized in 1938 in Switzerland by Dr. Albert Hofmann for Sandoz Laboratories. He discovered its hallucinogenic properties in 1943. Psychiatrists saw the drug as having potential because it induced in normal people many of the symptoms of schizophrenia, including hallucinations, paranoia, intense anxiety, feelings of depersonalization, and unusual color perceptions. There was hope that LSD would allow the creation of artificial model psychoses which could be studied under laboratory conditions. Much investigation occurred in the 1950s in the area of model psychoses (a term coined by Emil Kraeplin in 1910). Mescaline, amphetamines, and phencyclidine were also used to create model psychoses. Griffith's studies showed that with high doses of amphetamines, all subjects, eventually developed a paranoid psychosis (Angrist and Gershon, 1971).

LSD revived interest in biological theories of causation at the peak of belief in Freudian theories which blamed the family for schizophrenia. A focus was placed on the possibility of a metabolic dysfunction (Isaac and Armat, 1990). But this work also showed that the individual's personality was a critical variable in how the model psychoses were expressed. The type of behavior change was dependent on the personality of the subject. Although altered behavior was induced in all subjects if there was an adequate dose, some subjects did not produce a model psychosis but showed altered thinking processes without definite psychotic behavior. The individual's personality was thus found to be a critical variable along with mood, setting, psychological expectations prior to the drug response, and cultural factors (Tourney, 1978). The use of LSD first spread under the guidance of these research psychiatrists.

By 1959 at an international conference on the use of LSD in therapy, there was major conflict over its use. Paul Hoch, a psychiatrist who had studied the effects of LSD on patients, felt that LSD disorganized the psychic integration of the individual and made patients worse. He said that he had never had a patient who wanted LSD a second time (Lee and Shlain, 1985). Aldous Huxley (1963), who had used the drug himself (1963) and used the drug to treat alcoholics, was among the minority who supported the drug's use.

Timothy Leary, a faculty researcher at Harvard, began to experiment with LSD and other mind-altering drugs in the 1960s. Dismissed from Harvard University, he became a crusader for altering human consciousness through psychedelic drugs. LSD was legal until 1966, but its rapid spread through the growing counterculture resulted in its change of status to an illegal drug. Thus some drugs which have been experimented with to address mental illness have become major substance abuse problems.

Illegal Use and Abuse

A subsequent problem is that LSD and some of the other mind-altering drugs have become a major problem in the illegal use and abuse of drugs. Some of the possible negative effects of hallucinogens are panic reactions, flashbacks, high anxiety, loss of contact with reality, depersonalization, paranoia, confusion, psychosis, and hallucinations. PCP users are known for their potential for violence and their lack of response to pain combined with the appearance of super strength (BACCUPP, 1990).

Illegal drugs such as LSD, amphetamines, cocaine, and other hallucinogens may be particularly harmful to people with mental disabilities. People with mental disabilities have an increased risk of undesirable reaction when taking street drugs (Thornton, Seeman, Plummer, and Jeffries, 1985). Studies show that mentally ill persons admitted for acute inpatient care are increasingly identified as also having chemical abuse problems. Alcohol, which is a depressant, has long been recognized as a problem among psychiatric patients. However, now it is being replaced or augmented by a variety of other legal and illegal drugs. Other depressants include narcotics, sedative-hypnotics, and antianxiety medications. Some industrial products such as solvents and aerosols, which are inhaled for their mind-altering properties, also create depressant-like effects (Haugland, Siegel, Alexander, and Galanter, 1991).

The severity of their symptoms or impaired impulse control may increase the risk of psychiatric patients abusing drugs (Bukstein, Brent, and Kaminier, 1989; Schneier and Siris, 1987). A New York study found that in 1987 almost one third of psychiatric admissions also had substance abuse problems. In metropolitan areas 75 percent of patients with substance abuse problems had a drug abuse disorder, while in rural areas 88 percent of patients with substance abuse disorders abused alcohol. Both community- and hospital-based aftercare services were less available to these dual diagnosed patients. This was most true in metropolitan areas with dual diagnosed drug abuse (Haugland, Siegel, Alexander, and Galanter, 1991). Dual diagnosed people may have difficulty finding treatment in either psychiatric facilities or substance abuse treatment facilities.

Pharmacological Treatment of Drug Abuse—Methadone

In turn, drugs may be used to address drug abuse problems. The most commonly known use is methadone to treat heroin addiction. Heroin addicts may suffer irreversible metabolic changes. Methadone treatment is based on the model of insulin treatment for diabetes. Methadone is used to relieve the metabolic deficiency and to allow the person to function more normally (Moccia,

1983). Methadone, an opiate like heroin, allows addicts to cope without heroin. Addicts are provided with a daily 20- to 30-milligram dose. Methadone does not provide the euphoria of heroin, but it prevents the symptoms of withdrawal and it provides an effect which lasts 24 hours without the highs and lows of heroin. Monitoring of drug levels is done by urinalysis. To receive treatment addicts usually have to show proof of at least two years of addiction (Robinson-Haynes, 1990). Sometimes counseling is provided at the same time to address the psychological aspects of addiction.

Methadone was developed during World War II in Germany as a synthetic painkiller to replace low supplies of morphine during the war. Drs. Vincent Dole and Marie Nyswander began a program in the 1960s in New York for treating addicts with the drug.

Confidentiality is a necessary part of program services involving methadone maintenance. Many patients have employers and family members who are unaware of their use of the program (Robinson-Haynes, 1990). In the early 1970s a New York prosecutor attempted to use photographs of people attending a methadone clinic in order to identify a murder suspect. The courts in that case eventually upheld the right to confidentiality (Newman, 1977). Other public policy issues that have been raised concerning methadone maintenance have been the use of public funds to supply a drug to addicts and the determination of neighbors to prevent treatment clinics from being established in their neighborhoods.

Pharmacological Treatment of Cocaine Addiction

Pharmacological responses to treating drug addiction are being looked at for other drugs than heroin. Cocaine abuse has been associated with neurological and psychiatric symptoms. Cocaine can have effects on the brain which range from mild agitation to seizures, convulsions, and death. Research has led to increased knowledge about cocaine-induced neurochemical disruptions which may be addressed by other drugs. Cocaine abuse is now recognized as having clear biological components. Researchers are proposing the use of medications to treat the craving and withdrawal states involved in cocaine addiction (Gawin and Ellinwood, 1988; O'Brien, Childness, and Arndt, 1988). Significant alterations are believed to occur in the pleasure centers of the brain, and these disturbances are believed to lead to withdrawal and craving states. Craving plays a major role in recidivism and continuation of the addiction. Recreational use can progress gradually to a compulsive addiction which dominates the addict's life. Alterations in the reward centers and the intense euphoria of intoxication classify the drug as physically addictive. Euphoria and craving alternate repeatedly, resulting in a cycle of entrenched and uncontrollable addiction. Craving may be a signal from the brain for more cocaine to address a temporary dopamine depletion (Gawin and Ellinwood, 1988). Bromocriptine might be used for cocaine craving and withdrawal, and other agents might be used to restore the balances in serotonin, norepinephrine, thyroid, and other systems. Drugs might also be used to reverse cocaine overdose, progression of addiction, cocaine-induced depression, and cocaine euphoria (Dackis and Gold, 1990).

PSYCHOPHARMACOLOGY

Since 1850 a number of drugs have been experimented with and used in treatment for anxiety, depression, and overactive behavior, including hypnotics, sedatives, and stimulants. In the 1850s bromides were introduced, including hyoscyamus, belladonna, and conium, which were tried and eventually abandoned. In 1869 chloral hydrate was introduced and in 1882 paraldehyde. The barbiturates appeared in 1903, amythal and the amphetamines in the 1930s, and penicillin was used for general paresis (syphilis), which could lead to brain damage, in 1945.

In 1951 the modern era of psychopharmacology began with Laborit's synthesis of chlorpromazine (Tourney, 1978). Like many other drugs, it was first developed for another purpose (a hypothermic agent for use in surgery). Its tranquilizing effect was noticed, and it was first used to treat psychiatric disorders in 1952. This was soon followed by reserpine and other pheonothiazines to treat schizophrenia.

In May 1954 Thorazine appeared on the market. Within eight months it was administered to over two million patients. Initially it was unknown how these drugs worked. Psychoanalytic psychiatrists regarded the antipsychotic drugs as powerful tranquilizers that had the ability to calm patients and make them amenable to psychoanalysis (Tourney, 1978).

New York was the first state to introduce chlorpromazine on a large scale in the mid-1950s in its state hospitals. After its apparent success on an experimental group, Paul Hoch, Commissioner of Mental Hygiene, requested $1.5 million for "tranquilizers" to be used on all patients (Isaac and Armant, 1990). However, his deputy mental health commissioner and statistician warned of the dangers of overoptimism. They feared this could lead to premature deinstitutionalization. They also called for critical evaluation of any innovation (Brill and Patton, 1962). But, in spite of this cautionary note, New York became the first state to adopt a complete program of treatment with neuroleptic drugs in all its state hospitals. There has been debate about the role of the widespread use of neuroleptic drugs in deinstitutionalization. There are those who believe their large-scale use in 1956 was a major impetus to deinstitutionalization (Brill and Patton, 1962). Goffman, in his famous book *Asylums* (1961), however, ignored the neuroleptic drugs because he refused to accept mental illness as a medical disease and to accept the medical model. This has remained a minority view.

Dr. Nathan Kline of New York's Rockland State Hospital pioneered the use of drugs to treat depression (Tourney, 1978): After marsilid was observed to elevate mood, antidepressants of the monoamine oxidase inhibitor type began to be used in 1954 to treat depression. In 1959 tricyclic antidepressants were introduced, and many minor tranquilizers came into use around this time (Tourney, 1978).

Arvid Carlsson, a Swedish scientist, published papers in the early 1960s which advanced the hypothesis that neuroleptic drugs blocked dopamine receptors in the brain. In 1973 Solomon Snyder and Candace Pert in the United States proved that receptors did exist in the brain, and in 1974 Snyder found receptors for dopamine in rats' brains (Kuhar, Pert, and Snyder, 1973). Over a period of 20 years, three classes of drugs were developed: phenothiazines, butyrophenones, and thioxanthenes. All of these drugs blocked dopamine receptor sites, and they all also had sedative qualities which were not always in the best interests of the patients (Luby and Bielski, 1978).

Supporters of Drug Treatment

There are many supporters of the benefits of psychopharmacology. Dr. Leo Hollister has said that the extensive literature of evaluation trials "constitute[s] the most massive scientific overkill in all clinical pharmacology" and has "demonstrated the value of anti-psychotic drugs in all forms of schizophrenia, at all ages, at all stages of illness, and in all parts of the world" (Hollister, 1978:154). However, there remain some patients who are not helped by medication. It is estimated that 10 to 20 percent of patients are treatment-resistant (Issac and Armat, 1990). For those that can be helped, the financial savings may be significant. During the past 20 years, lithium treatment of bipolar (manic-depressive) illness has saved the United States an estimated $39 billion in lost productivity (NIMH, 1990).

SIDE-EFFECTS AND MISUSE OF DRUGS

The side-effects of psychoactive drugs are worse than the drug treatment used for many chronic diseases because the frequency of permanent side-effects is higher with psychoactive drugs. Many of the side-effects are reversible if the drug is no longer taken, and many side-effects can be controlled by taking additional medication (Bouricius, 1989). These unwanted effects may occur if a dose is given too high or too fast or if a drug is stopped too suddenly.

For neuroleptic drugs used for schizophrenia, a serious effect which sometimes occurs is akathisia, a motor restlessness which makes it almost impossible to sit still. Another serious side-effect is pseudo-parkinsonism, which produces rigidity and tremor, a shuffling gait, and sometimes a mask-like face.

Tardive Dyskinesia and Tardive Dystonia

Tardive dyskinesia is a serious neurological disorder which can affect people using neuroleptics for schizophrenia or affective disorders. It is characterized by involuntary irregular movements. These are often of the mouth and face, chewing and smacking movements of the lips or a darting tongue, but sometimes the involuntary movements are of the limbs. In many cases it is irreversible, and the prevalence is quite high among patients who take high doses for long periods. It is estimated that the rate among psychiatric outpatients is between 20 and 30 percent. However, less than 5 percent have serious symptoms of the disorder (Bouricius, 1989).

A British study of facial dyskinesia of 109 female survivors of a mental hospital population originally surveyed in 1965 showed in 1981 that the prevalence of dyskinesia had risen from 18.4 percent to 46.5 percent. That study found a significant association between its development and neuroleptic dosage. The study also found a significant association between development of dyskinesia and enlarged ventricals of the brain. Cognitive impairment was also significantly associated with a longer duration of schizophrenia. The study raised the question of whether neuroleptic drugs had wider neurodegenerative manifestation. Dyskinesia was also associated with reduced life expectancy, and all patients who had severe dyskinesia in 1965 died by the follow-up 16 years later (McClelland, Metcalfe, Kerr, Dutta, and Watson, 1991).

An even more serious side-effect is tardive dystonia, a disorder in which muscles contract without any synergy. The body may be twisted or the head bent backward, and there may be severe pain. Monitoring examinations can be used for tardive dyskinesia and tardive dystonia. Medical personnel and physicians in some inpatient and outpatient facilities can complete monitoring exams in 5 to 10 minutes. Of the many monitoring systems and standardized assessment scales available, the most commonly known are the Abnormal Involuntary Movement Scale (AIMS) and the Simpson Tardive Dyskinesia Rating Scale (TDRS) (Tardive Dyskinesia and Tardive Dystonia, 1990). Monitoring can lead to changes in the individual's medication and treatment plan.

It is not surprising that with all these problems in terms of side-effects, consumer movements have focused upon the issue of drug therapy, consent, and the right to refuse treatment. However, the research and medical communities have sought to find ways to control the side-effects.

Control of Side-Effects

Antiparkinsonian agents are probably the second most frequently prescribed medication for schizophrenia (Thornton, Seeman, Plummer, and Jeffries, 1985). They are used to address the muscle side-effects of the neuroleptics, particularly muscle stiffness and tremor and sometimes restlessness. However, they also cause their own side-effects, including blurred vision, dry mouth, and a toxic confusional state which can be mistaken for a mental disorder relapse. Some psychiatrists use these drugs for their prophylactic effect of reducing the reluctance of the patient to take antipsychotic medication because of the muscle side-effects.   Other psychiatrists only use antiparkinsonian drugs if muscle symptoms develop because of the potential side-effects of those drugs (Thornton, Seeman, Plummer, and Jeffries, 1985). Traditionally levodopa (L-dopa) was used to treat Parkinson's, but in 1989 a newer drug, Deprenyl, came into use. Parkinson's is an incurable disease whose cause is not known. It results in the death of brain cells, and its symptoms include palsy, shuffling gait, speech difficulties, a fixed expression, and sometimes emotional instability.

A common approach to controlling side-effects is to use as low a dose as possible. However, the drug still must be given in a high enough dose to get into the bloodstream, get past enzymes trying to destroy it, get through the blood vessel wall into the brain, dissolve into the fatty membrane encircling the nerve cell, and attach to a specific site on the cell to facilitate or inhibit the cell's electrical impulses. Patients vary individually regarding the amount of dosage needed, because some individuals are poor absorbers or fast metabolizers while others experience drug interaction with other drugs, foods, or hormones (Thornton, Seeman, Plummer, and Jeffries, 1985). Injections can be given intramuscularly and used to bypass the absorption phase of pills, thus providing a more direct approach to the bloodstream. This avoids the long "halflife" (long absorption time) of most neuroleptics and can provide a quicker effect in an emergency situation. Some drugs given intramuscularly, however, can be given in a slow-release or depot form, which allows the drug to be released slowly from the muscle. However, the drug's rate of release can be affected by exercise. Another approach which has been used is to take the patient off drugs periodically (a drug holiday), but increasingly this is seen as not beneficial (Bouricius, 1989).

Reactions of drugs with other substances also must be considered. The growing study of pharmacokinetics, what happens to drugs after they enter the body, has led to greater awareness of how drugs get absorbed and used by the body. Food has been found to play a significant role in the use of many medications. Sometimes food enhances the absorption of drugs, but more often it delays the entry of drugs into the bloodstream or prevents it completely. Mixing certain drugs and foods can be dangerous. Foods high in tyramine (an amino acid), such as pickled herring, certain cheeses, salted dried fish, meat extract, stored beef liver, avocado, and red wines, if combined with antidepressants such as isocarboxazid (Marplan), phenelzine (Nardil), or tranylcypromine (Parmate), can result in a dangerous reaction of rising blood pressure (Graedon and Graedon, 1988). Unfortunately, this is an area of knowledge to which professionals may not pay sufficient attention, and consumers are often uninformed or not sufficiently warned.

Alcohol can add another dangerous element for people with mental disabilities. Mixing alcohol and the drugs used to treat mental illnesses can be lethal. Alcohol can also make certain drugs, such as benzodiazepenes, function more potently. Alcohol and street drugs are of particular concern because of the growing recognition of dual diagnosis (mentally ill substance abusers).

Adding to the problem are drugs which were developed to treat other disorders but which may have mental health effects. People with mental disabilities might also be more susceptible to the mental health effects of such drugs. For example, in 1991 the Upjohn Company came under increased attack for its sleeping drug Halcion. The British government decided to ban permanently the use of the drug, and in the United States the television program "60 Minutes" was very critical of the drug. The drug has been linked to depression and short-term memory loss in some patients. Worldwide, Halcion has been the most widely prescribed sleeping medication, and in the first nine months of 1991 it brought in 8 percent of Upjohn's sales, about $2.5 billion ("Health: Upjohn Defends ...," 1991). The Upjohn Company defended its drug Halcion from both the critical "60 Minutes" report and the British government's ban on the medication.

Numbers and Complexity

Another problem with drugs are their numbers, complexity, and the constant addition of new drugs. Even back in the 1970s the problem was acute, as noted by Domino (1978): "The field of psychopharmacology has expanded enormously since the majority of us went to medical school. Most of the drugs now used in treating psychiatric patients were not available then. It is now a full-time effort for me just to keep abreast of current knowledge of psychoactive drugs. As new ones become available it becomes progressively more difficult to choose the right drug, in the right dosage for a specific patient" (p. 2ll).

This situation is compounded by the fact that approximately 80 percent of all prescriptions written for neuroleptics are written by physicians other than neurologists or psychiatrists (Tardive Dyskinesia/Tardive Dystonia National Association, 1990).

There are some 5,000 substances loosely referred to as drugs. Virtually all drugs in current use have been developed in laboratories and are manufactured through chemical processes. Many drugs are synthetic forms of naturally occurring substances, and a few come from botanical or animal sources. All drugs have three names. The generic name is the official medical term for the basic active substance. It is chosen by the U.S. Adopted Name Council (USAN). The brand name is chosen by the manufacturer. There may be several brands by different manufacturers which contain the same generic substance and which in reality have only slight changes relating to absorption rates, digestibility, and convenience. A drug may be available by brand name, generic form, or both. Some brand names have several generic substances. The third name is a chemical name, which is the technical description. Drugs may be grouped by chemical similarity, such as the benzodiazepines, but usually they are classified by use or biological effect. Most drugs are in one group, but some have multiple uses and are listed in several categories (Clayman, 1988).

All new drugs are required to undergo testing before they are approved for marketing by the U.S. Food and Drug Administration (FDA). Testing often takes several years. Recent federal regulatory changes have been attempting to shorten the testing and review period. Federal law requires drugs to be safe and medically effective. The drug's risks also have to be weighed against benefits. In reality, the FDA does not do its own testing but relies on the research and documentation of the drug companies, which in many cases is overwhelming in terms of sheer size of documentation. Federal and state law regulate which drugs can be sold over the counter and which require a physician's prescription. Controlled substances laws regulate drugs by five schedules. Schedule I drugs are almost all illegal, have a high potential for abuse, and cannot be prescribed. These include heroin, LSD, and peyote.

Nine states have multiple-copy prescription programs (seven are triplicate programs) for preventing the diversion of controlled substances. Usually the physician is required to prescribe Schedule II controlled substances which have a high potential for abuse, on a triplicate form provided by the state. One copy stays with the physician, one goes to the pharmacist, and one goes to the state regulating agency. In 1989 New York became the first state to place benzodiazepines on the list of controlled substances requiring a triplicate prescription (Applebaum, 1992).

Research shows that there has been a significant reduction in inappropriate prescribing and illicit diversion. However, there are some research reports that indicate a significant increase in the prescribing of benzodiazepine substitutes that are less effective and safe, and there are some increases in overdoses of some substitute drugs. Schwartz (1992) concludes that changes in legitimate prescribing may reflect fears of breach of confidentiality, cumbersomeness of the procedure, and fear of regulatory agency investigations which could damage a career. Applebaum (1992) believes that unless educational efforts promoted by professional associations and non-prescription-based tracking systems show effectiveness equal to New York's reduction in prescribing under the triplicate program, other states will adopt the New York approach.

Misuse of Prescription Drugs

Misuse of drugs has also occurred. In 1989 the American Psychological Association declared that elderly people in the United States were being inhumanely and needlessly drugged by doctors who relied on drugs to control behavior and who were inexperienced in treating older patients. Spokespeople for the association urged that antipsychotic drugs be used only for specifically documented, appropriate reasons and not to just control behavior. While the elderly make up about 12 percent of the population, 35 to 40 percent of prescribed sedatives and hypnotics were used for the elderly. The Association urged the use of nondrug therapies, such as psychological counseling, and a reduction in dosages of drugs that were given (Clifton, 1989). The American Psychiatric Association started a program in 1987 to better train physicians in prescribing psychotropic drugs, and the 1989 Medicare regulation revisions put even stronger controls on the use of antipsychotic drugs in nursing homes.

Minor tranquilizers are abused widely. They are overused and perhaps in many cases, have been prescribed by physicians who would prefer not to confront the cause of the problem, which might be handled more appropriately by referral to a psychologist or counselor. Many cases of anxiety, compulsive disorders, and so on are thus inappropriately handled. By 1977 Valium topped the federal government's Drug Alert Warning Network (DAWN) List as the drug most often mentioned in prompting emergency room visits. The use of tranquilizers and other drugs, legal and illegal, contributes to car and other accidents; thus alcohol and other substance abuse contributes to one of the major causes of death in the United States, especially among the younger population. Research shows that 7 to 13.4 percent of drivers in fatal car crashes test positive for marijuana (Simpson, 1986).

Tranquilizers may impair psychomotor skills and cognitive performance. Benzodiazepine tranquilizers were introduced in the United States in 1962, and they are now prescribed widely. One study of benzodiazephine tranquilizers and the risk of accidental injury examined the pharmacy claims submitted to a third-party payer, involving 4,554 persons' prescriptions for benzodiazepine and

13,662 persons' prescriptions for drugs other than benzodiazepine. During 1986-87 all accident-related care received by those persons was reviewed during a three-month period before their first observed prescription and six months later. Accident-related care was found to be more likely among persons who had been prescribed benzodiazepine. The probability of an accident-related medical encounter was higher during months in which a prescription for benzodiazepine had been filled recently. Also, persons who had filled three or more prescriptions for those tranquilizers in the six months following the beginning of therapy had a significantly higher risk of accident than those who had filled only one prescription. After controlling for sex, age, and prior utilization, there was an approximately twofold risk of accident-related care (Oster, Huse, Adams, Imbimbo, and Russell, 1990).

There has been concern that stimulant drugs have been abused in treating children. These concerns include that they have been used inappropriately to treat inattentiveness rather than hyperactivity and they that have been used without addressing the underlying causes and individual management of hyperactivity (Stephenson, 1975). One of the drugs used to control attention deficit hyperactivity disorder in children which has caused concern is Ritalin.

Ritalin is also one of the drugs which has raised concern about some drugs and a potential connection to violence. Methylphenidate (Ritalin) is a mild central nervous system stimulant. It was first sold in 1955 to improve mental performance in the elderly and to reduce fatigue. But it has become a very popular treatment for attention deficit disorder (ADD) in children, along with pemoline (Cylert) and dextroamphetamine (Dexedrine). The ability of stimulants to calm hyperactive children has been known since the 1930s, and now it is believed that as many as 80 percent of attention deficit disorder children may be helped by drug treatment. Approximately 30 percent of children seem to have major improvement on drug therapy while others improve to varying degrees. Although Ritalin has been available for over 50 years and has been marketed for over 30 years, how it works biochemically or physiologically is still not understood completely. It is known that the drug stimulates the brain to produce chemical messengers that the brain cells use to alert and stimulate other cells. It is believed that this increase in brain chemicals has something to do with the drug's beneficial effects. The positive effects are decreased distractibility, improved concentration, and less fatigue. Usually the side-effects of the drug are mild and pass quickly (Haney, 1988). In addition, the drug may affect performance negatively on tasks which call for cognitive flexibility or "divergent thinking" (Solanto and Wender, 1989:900).

Ritalin has also been accused of causing violent behavior. The defense in a highly publicized 1986 Massachusetts murder case, involving a 15-year-old male charged with killing another young man with a bat, claimed that his violent behavior was caused by Ritalin. The perpetrator and the victim both took

Ritalin. The trial became a debate over the drug in terms of how it could, in combination with other treatment, help children and how its casual use could allow deeper problems to go undetected. Guidelines of the American Academy of Pediatrics state that Ritalin should only be used in combination with counseling and careful monitoring after a detailed diagnosis. The defendant in the Massachusetts case, Rod Matthews, received the drug without other therapy. He took the drug for over five years, but he went off the drug a few months before the killing. A few weeks later he asked for the drug and received it, and it was found in his school locker after the killing. But no one knows if he was taking the drug at the time of the killing (Bayles, 1988).

Another drug under questioning is Prozac. Prozac was introduced in 1988 to treat depression. It was highly promoted and by 1990 its sales for Eli Lily were over $700 million. However, reports soon appeared that the drug could make some users feel suicidal. A New York woman sued Eli Lilly for $150 million, and Prozac survivor groups were established in several states. Prozac was tested originally on more than 5,600 patients. Since its introduction, over two million people have used it (Toufexis, 1990b). Most reports of Prozac and suicidal behavior have been anecdotal. However, one study (Teicher, 1990) documented six cases of depressed patients who became obsessed with violent suicidal thoughts (four tried to kill or harm themselves) two to seven weeks after beginning treatment with Prozac. Although some of the patients were on other medications as well as Prozac and some had previously contemplated suicide, the suicidal compulsion subsided when they were taken off Prozac. The researcher also found that the nature of their suicidal thoughts while using Prozac were different than prior suicidal thoughts. In addition, while on the medication, the urge to commit suicide was described as an irresistible impulse.

Prozac is not the first drug to have its effects on depression questioned. Benzodiazepines, which are the most commonly used class of sleeping drugs, have generally been considered to have comparatively few adverse effects and to be relatively safe in overdose (Clayman, 1988). They have also been used frequently to treat anxiety, but their relationship to depression and suicide has been questioned.

An early report in 1968 presented seven cases of worsening depression and development of suicidal ideation in patients diagnosed as having depressive disorders and taking diazepam (Valium). There were two actual suicides and two serious attempts. The survivors all improved within three to four days after discontinuing the drug (Ryan, Merrill, and Scott, 1968). There are a number of reports in the literature that note an association between benzodiazepine use and the emergence of depressive symptoms (Hall and Joffe, 1972; Lydiard, Hosell, and Laraia, 1989).

Smith and Salzman (1991) concluded after a review of the literature that although there are no data to support the belief that depression is a regular or frequent side-effect of benzodizepine use, it should be recognized that such treatment can lead occasionally to significant depression and suicide. Although how the drug may cause such symptoms is unknown, there is no evidence that any particular benzodiazepine is more likely to cause the problem. However, higher doses may increase the risk, and patients with low trait anxiety may be more susceptible. If the problem arises, it can be resolved by switching drugs or treating with an antidepressant. As previously noted, benzodiazepines such as diazepam (Valium) have been abused widely.

Balancing the Benefits and Risks

The risks of the use of psychotropic drugs and any drugs which can have a mental health effect have to be weighed against the benefits in each individual case. More care needs to be taken to see that individual patients are treated individually and monitored carefully. There is a tendency when a drug is found to be successful to want to apply it to most patients without assessing carefully each individual and considering the full range of options. Too often drug monitoring is perfunctory and routine, especially when resources and personnel are short (Torrey et al., 1990). This may mean that unsatisfactory side-effects or results are not caught and addressed early and that complaints of clients about medications may be ignored improperly.

OPPOSITION TO DRUG TREATMENT

In 1978 the North American Conference on Human Rights and Psychiatric Oppression demonstrated at the offices of Smith, Kline, and French, makers of Thorazine, demanding an end to the production of Thorazine and other psychoactive drugs. A Thorazine protest was also held in 1982 in Toronto at a meeting of the American Psychiatric Association.

With success in curtailing psychosurgery and eletro convulsive therapy (ECT), ex-patients opposed to any somatic treatment focused on the antipsychotic drugs. Drugs were referred to as a chemical lobotomy (Breggin, 1983). The National Alliance of Mental Patients (NAMP) took a stand against drugs, and this was later followed by the National Alliance of Mental Palients (previously the National Mental Health Consumers' Association). The National Alliance of Mental Patients opposed any involuntary treatment under any conditions. The National Association of Psychiatric Survivors, as the National Mental Health Consumers' Association under Joseph Rogers, originally supported involuntary treatment in very extreme and rare cases. But in 1990, when Paul Dorfner took over the organization, the same stance was taken as the

National Association of Psychiatric Survivors (Isaac and Armat, 1990).

The American Psychological Association has also spoken out against the dangers of antipsychotic drugs. It has called them "high risk treatment" and has referred to them as having a "mind altering effect," which has First Amendment implications because of their ability to intrude on the formation and communication of ideas (American Psychological Association, 1988).

Not all advocacy has been opposed to necessary treatment. Wald and Friedman (1979) distinguish between two main types of advocacy, which they believe have caused tension in the entire advocacy system. Civil liberty advocates are concerned with the deprivation of liberty by commitment and intrusive procedures, while the services-oriented advocates want the right to treatment expanded and feel that commitment is all right if treatment is provided.

Treatment issues have also been fueled by conflict between psychiatrists and other mental health professionals. Psychologists and psychiatric social workers appropriated the status of psychotherapist in the community mental health centers of the 1970s, and psychiatrists complained that they were only needed to write prescriptions. This resulted in many psychiatrists returning to private practice (Clark and Vaccaro, 1987). Psychiatrists are still often seen only in relationship to their ability to prescribe drugs. Concerns are also raised that with a shortage of psychiatrists, other mental health personnel, such as psychiatric nurses, are left to monitor ongoing drug use without psychiatrists having sufficient contact with patients (Tourney et al., 1990).

The Right to Refuse Treatment

Isaac and Armat (1990) argue that from the beginning it was the agenda of the mental health bar to obtain a right to refuse treatment rather than to obtain a right to treatment. Brown (1984) has called the right to refuse treatment the most controversial of the rights of mental patients. He sees this issue as polarizing the movement for mental health reform between external activist reformers and care providers. He sees several reasons for the strong opposition to a right to refuse treatment, including professionals' and institutions' defense of their autonomy against challenges to their professional clinical judgment, an opposition to legal interference, and a belief that the community as well as the patient must be protected.

Mental health providers may be sued over treatment issues. In 1969 a New York court granted an ex-patient $300,000 in damages based on the view that if he had been treated adequately he could have been released in two years rather than the 12 for which he was confined. The court dismissed the hospital's argument that the patient had refused all medication (*Nason v.*

Superintendent of Bridgewater State Hospital, 233 N.E. 2d 908, Mass., 1968).

In 1973 the City Council in Long Beach, New York, passed an ordinance refusing further registration in a hotel if a resident without medication could be a danger to himself/herself or others or not be able to realize the effects of his/her actions. The New York Civil Liberties Union challenged and defeated the ordinance on the basis that it was unconstitutional to, in effect, require discharged mental patients to take medication in order to continue to live in the community (Torrey, 1990).

In 1977 two major cases established a right to refuse treatment: *Rennie v. Klein* (481 F. Supp. 552 D. N.J.) in New Jersey and *Rogers v. Okin* (478 F. Supp. 1342 D. Mass., 1979) in Massachusetts. In the New Jersey case the Third Circuit Court of Appeals upheld the use of a second medical opinion when an incompetent person refused medication. The attorney opposing treatment in the Massachusetts case argued that mental illness was hopeless, so there was no point in treating it (Cole, 1979). The courts in several states have now reaffirmed the right to refuse medication, but in *Youngberg v. Romeo* (457 U.S. 307, 1982) the U.S. Supreme Court supported the right of professionals to make treatment judgments in the case of a severely mentally retarded young man.

By the mid-1970s, nearly all states' statutes provided that hospitalized mental patients remained legally competent unless specifically judged incompetent by a court. This led to the argument that competent patients in mental hospitals should have the same right to refuse treatment as competent patients in general, acute hospitals. A competent patient who was forced to have an unwanted medical procedure could charge assault and battery. In 1979 a federal judge in Massachusetts ruled that state mental hospital patients could refuse medication unless there was a substantial likelihood of suicide, personal injury, or extreme violence (Applebaum and Gutheil, 1980). There have been similar rulings in other states. This places an emphasis on specific court orders for each case.

Also in the 1970s the concept of substituted judgment was developed. This allowed the court to make determinations for an incompetent person based on what the person would have wanted under the current circumstances if he/she were competent. In 1980 in the Richard Roe III case (*In the Matter of Guardianship of Richard Roe III*, Supreme Judicial Court of Massachusetts, 421 N.E. Rep. 2d 40, Mass., 1980), the judges ruled that Richard Roe's guardian, his father, lacked the necessary detachment to decide whether his son should receive medication. The court determined that only it could make the detached investigation necessary and that it would decide not on what was medically in the "best interests" of the person, but it would decide what the incompetent person would want if he were competent. This would be done through deciding the values and preferences of the patient. The attitude of the family was only a relevant factor if the patient wanted to minimize his burden on them. The court viewed itself as conflicted over what was more restrictive—the psychoactive drugs or institutionalization.

Issac and Armat (1990) argue that substituted judgment really means the use of the preferences of the decisionmaker, and they see this as open to abuse by the anti-psychiatric movement through the ability to convince judges of the extraordinariness and dangerousness of antipsychotic drugs. Perry (1987) asserts that substituted consent adheres to fundamental American ideas of personal autonomy within rules that must govern a federal nation while retaining sufficient flexibility to encompass all types of intrusive healthcare decisions.

However, many state courts, including California and New York, have followed Massachusetts in requiring court hearings before incompetent patients who refused medication could be treated. In California the Lanterman-Petris-Short (LPS) Act (1967) had a provision which permitted conservatorship for those "gravely disabled" by mental illness. Its purpose was to provide assistance in managing the affairs of the patient beyond the two-week treatment period. The act allowed court-appointed conservators to make treatment decisions for their conservatees (Morris, 1978). Most patients who remained in hospitals more than 17 days under LPS were gravely disabled conservatees. However, if the patient refused the treatment, this did not prevent the decision from being taken before the courts.

In 1988 a Minnesota court ruled that psychotropic drugs were as intrusive as psychosurgery and ECT and warranted the same rigorous due process before administration (*Jarvis v. Levine*, 418 N.W. 2d 139, Minn., 1988). Also in 1988 the state of Washington established the most stringent criteria in a case involving a prisoner, which was heard before the state Supreme Court (*Harper v. The State of Washington*, Washington State Supreme Court, 1988). The decision established that before a court could rule that antipsychotic drug treatment could be used, the state had to prove that there was "clear, cogent, and convincing" evidence and "a compelling state interest to administer" the drugs and that the administration was "both necessary and effective for furthering that interest." In 1990 the U.S. Supreme Court overturned that decision, ruling that the Constitution did not require a state to prove its "compelling interest" in medicating a prisoner or that the drugs were "necessary and effective for furthering that interest." The court's opinion suggested that the person's interests were perhaps better served by allowing the medical profession to make the decision rather than a judge (*State of Washington et al. v. Walter Harper*, 1990). Although the decision was unlikely to affect states already requiring judicial review, the psychiatrist Paul Applebaum believed that it might have the effect of discouraging other states from moving in that direction (Issac and Armant, 1990).

Implementation of the Right to Refuse Treatment

Patients have not widely applied the right to refuse treatment (Brown, 1984). But even in situations where there has been substantial refusal, appeal processes have overwhelmingly upheld the use of medication. A study by the Massachusetts Department of Mental Health over an 18-month period in 1986 and 1987 of approximately 1,500 cases of patients who refused treatment found that in 98.6 percent of the cases the court ruled the person should be medicated (Hoge et al., 1990). The *Rivers v. Katz* (67 N.Y. 2d 485, 1986) case in New York required judicial review rather than administrative review for involuntary medication. A study of the outcome of that ruling suggested that judicial review produced a better understanding by clinicians of the legal basis for involuntary medication and provided for greater participation in the review procedure. However, the disadvantages were a lack of an independent clinical review and increased costs (Cournos, McKinnan, and Adams, 1988). An Oregon study of 33 state hospital forensic psychiatric patients who refused treatment found that treatment refusal rates were slightly lower among forensic inpatients than nonforensic civilly committed inpatients at another state hospital. Treatment refusers had previous psychiatric admissions prior to arrest. Pretrial patients tended to refuse treatment earlier than those referred by the state psychiatric security review board (Young, Bloom, Faulkner, Rogers, and Pati, 1987).

In Canada 7 of the 10 Canadian provinces have legislation that explicitly or implicitly authorizes the routine imposition of treatment upon involuntarily, civilly committed mental health patients without their consent (Verdun-Jones, 1988).

Treatment may also be required in the community. An example of this is Dane County, Wisconsin. Although Wisconsin has one of the most stringent civil commitment laws based on dangerousness in the United States, Dane County has used a protective services law to provide treatment. Although that law was written primarily for persons with mental retardation and disabled older people, the county has used the law for a minority of revolving-door mental patients. Under the law the county seeks a limited guardianship for treatment and medications. If a judge finds the client incompetent regarding the need to take medication, then a guardian can be assigned that function. In 1989 almost 25 percent of Dane County's chronically mentally ill were under some kind of community compulsory medication court order. Enforcement was through use of contempt of court provisions. If a patient refused medication, a guardian could obtain a court order requiring the police to bring the patient to a mental health center for medication (Isaac and Armat, 1990).

However, there is the danger of legal challenge to such an approach. In Milwaukee there was a successful attempt to prevent patients from being placed indefinitely under protective services or placement. Under that court decision, mandatory annual reviews must be held (*State ex rel. Watts v. Combined Community services Board,* 362 K.U. 2d 104 Wisc., 1985).

An argument has been made to return *parens patriae* concerns to mental health law, so the state would act in behalf of citizens unable to act in their own best interests. Psychiatrist Harold Treffert (1989) has called for a fourth need for treatment standard to be added to the standards of dangerousness to self, dangerousness to others, and gravely disabled. Such a standard would permit involuntary treatment for patients with severe mental disorders who lacked the capacity because of the disorder to make an informed treatment decision.

COSTS OF TREATMENT

The more drug treatment that is provided, the more expensive treatment may become. One of the major problems with drugs is cost. On average it costs $200 million and 12 years to develop a new drug (Stahl, 1990). This then results in a high price tag on the drug. Clozaril, for example, costs almost $9,000 a year. In 1990 only 15 Medicaid programs were paying for it, and if all those who could benefit from it received it, the costs of treating patients in some states would exceed the total mental health budget. As the drug does not cure, patients would require it indefinitely. In addition, for patients who improved sufficiently to earn a living, their Medicaid would probably be terminated, even though they probably would not earn enough to pay for their medication (Isaac and Armat, 1990).

Maier, Miller, and Roach (1992) describe the case of a forensic inpatient in Wisconsin for whom a county mental health board refused to fund his continued treatment with clozapine. After a history of mental health problems, the patient was in a state forensic facility, and when clozapine became available, he agreed to enroll in a Clozaril Patient Management System instituted by Sandoz Pharmaceuticals. The facility held the position that it was ethically bound to identify patients who could benefit from clozapine, was responsible for providing them treatments to improve their quality of life and to help them become eligible for release, and that the cost could be offset by ultimately releasing the patient earlier. Positive changes were seen in the patient within two weeks of treatment. He suffered no side-effects. He transferred to a minimum-security unit and petitioned the court for release. In a release hearing, all three experts testified about the improvement of the patient on clozapine and their belief that the changes would be sustained in the community.

The county mental health board was concerned that it would have to pay the $9,000 annual cost for the drug when the patient would be released to a halfway house. It was also concerned that the patient's improvement would not continue in the community. It recommended another six months of hospitalization while on clozapine. Eventually the mental health board refused to provide the money for the drug. The patient received Social Security Disability Insurance and a small pension, for an income of about $1,000 a month. He offered to pay for the drug if the county would pay for his stay at a halfway house. This was eventually done. The patient paid $688 a month directly to Sandoz Pharmaceuticals. After one year, he stopped taking the drug because he felt he did not need it. He was returned to the institute to be reestablished on clozapine. Although he had no symptoms, the terms of his conditional release required his remaining on the drug.

The institute began its own monitoring program, with a savings of approximately $4,000 per year per patient. Maier, Miller, and Roach (1992) concluded that "as the cost comes down, it will be clear to all that for a significant number of treatment-resistant schizophrenic patients, clozapine removes symptoms, modulates mood, improves self-esteem, and returns them home for a meaningful life. These therapeutic effects cannot be given a price" (p. 178).

Unfortunately, therapeutic effects are given a price every day as public policy decisions are made about how much to budget for mental health and how to expend those limited resources. The Wisconsin case is interesting because it highlights the problems in providing high-cost drugs, illustrates the way in which one institute set up its own monitoring program to reduce patient costs, and points out how mental patients are subject to the continuance of treatment under conditional releases regardless of symptomology.

EFFECTS OF LACK OF TREATMENT

There are also costs to not treating. Most people with mental illness are not dangerous. However, some people with untreated mental illness can be dangerous. As Taylor (1986) concluded, most psychotics who commit serious violence have been psychiatric patients, but only a few of them have received treatment in the six months before the offense. That English study found that 43 percent of those with psychosis who committed a violent act were driven by a delusion. Hafner (1986) found, in a study in Germany, that 71 percent of the offenses committed by schizophrenic patients were motivated by hallucinations or delusions.

In addition to the risks of violence with some untreated or inadequately treated patients, one of the greatest effects of lack of treatment is the effect on families. When there is no or inadequate treatment and support systems, the families usually carry the burden as the care givers. Many families provide mentally ill relatives with a residence and other support. Minkoff (1978) estimated that nearly 65 percent of psychiatric patients were discharged from hospitals to their families. In a survey of mental health professionals, Castaneda and Sommer (1989) found that 92 percent of respondents thought it was important for families to oversee the medication regimen of patients living at home. Although professionals are increasingly acknowledging the importance of a supportive family, families continue to feel that they receive too little information from professionals about the patient (Francell, Conn, and Gray, 1988). Petrila and Sadoff (1992) urge professionals to rethink their concerns about confidentiality and share certain information with families who are care givers. Of course, for some professionals changes in state laws might be necessary to allow them to do this.

Another consequence of lack of treatment may be lifelong problems. Research indicates that untreated childhood and early adolescent depression may lead to chronic problems through the teen years and, particularly in girls, may lead to adult depression. If not treated adequately, anxiety disorders often persist through adolescence and into adulthood. Almost half of children and adolescents diagnosed with conduct disorder become antisocial adults (NIMH, 1990). All of these untreated problems may mean long-term societal costs, which may appear in other policy arenas such as criminal justice, education, and welfare. But treatment does not just mean drug treatment—there are also nondrug approaches available.

6

Nondrug Treatments

When Sigmund Freud opened his practice in Vienna, there were a few physical therapies available. Small shocks of electricity could be given to the affected part, or patients could be sent to a nervous clinic or spa to receive some kind of bath/shower treatment, massage, or rest cure. Treatments of a somatic nature tended to be tried without regard to diagnosis (Valenstein, 1986). Freud was to establish a functional view of mental illness which emphasized life experiences rather than biological determinants (Gay, 1988). This view was to prevail in American psychiatry for many years. But in recent years, there has been a return to organic treatments.

Lee Coleman, a psychiatrist, has argued that the resurgence of organic treatments in psychiatry was a method by which psychiatry could prevent intervention by nonmedical interlopers (Frank, 1973). His was not a new argument. By the 1930s psychiatrists were confronted increasingly by competition from nonmedically trained persons practicing psychotherapy. Psychiatrists frequently felt the need to emphasize the medical and somatic to counter competition (Russell, 1932). Organic/somatic treatments are based on biological and physiological theories. Although drug treatment is a common approach to treatment under these theories, there are nondrug approaches, including psychosurgery. From the late 1900s, psychiatrists engaged in jurisdictional battles with neurologists over who should treat the mentally ill. Neurologists saw themselves as more scientific and focused on somatic therapies. They accused psychiatrists of abandoning medicine and being too focused on psychotherapy. Some psychiatrists, neuropsychiatrists, did adopt many of the somatic therapies (Shorter, 1987). In any case, there were many organic illnesses with psychiatric symptoms, and neurologists focused increasingly on those.

All practitioners must be careful to separate out clearly known organic conditions with psychiatric symptoms from psychiatric illnesses. These conditions may or may not be treated with drugs.

ORGANIC CAUSES OF PSYCHIATRIC SYMPTOMS
AND NONDRUG TREATMENTS

Freud saw many patients who had organic illnesses. In his day the major organic nervous disorder seen was neurosyphilis, a syphilitic infection of the brain and spinal cord which eventually resulted in paralysis, dementia, and death and was most common in middle-aged men. For many years it was not recognized as a late form of syphilis but was viewed as a general paralysis of the insane, general paresis. Its organic basis as a disease which caused physical lesions in the brain went unrecognized.

When there are psychiatric symptoms, it is always important for the clinician to look for underlying organic causes. If an organic cause is diagnosed, treatment may be quite different. For example, from 40 to 100 percent of patients with brain tumors experience psychiatric symptoms, and 1 or 2 percent of patients with a primary psychiatric diagnosis may have undetected cerebral tumors (Lohr and Cadet, 1987). Some of these patients are given a mistaken primary psychiatric diagnosis and are treated inappropriately, with psychiatric drugs or psychotherapy. Israeli researchers, for example, described an unusual case of a man with a lengthy and resistant bipolar affective disorder which was found to be associated with an acoustic neurinoma (Mark, Modai, Aizenber, Heilbronn, and Elizur, 1991). The case involved a man who had been treated periodically for over 10 years with psychotherapy, various tricyclic drugs, and lithium for manic and depressive episodes in the United States and Israel. At the end of a four-year period of no remission, he made a serious suicide attempt, which was not his first. Although the prolonged course of psychiatric manifestations might have led to a wrong diagnosis, a physical exam indicated hearing loss in the right ear, a positive Romberg's sign. This led to a computerized axial tomography scan of the brain, which disclosed "a large space-occupying lesion on the right cerebellopontine angle, with displacement of the brain stem, obstructive hydrocephalus, and enlarged internal auditory meatus" (p. 1258).

This case would probably never have been diagnosed correctly without the technology which now allows the brain to be scanned. The patient underwent two operations to remove the tumor. Although after the surgery he suffered some physical handicap, the affective symptoms were ameliorated completely, and four years later they had not returned. Although there are few reports of mania associated with brain tumors, this type of case points up the importance of a careful physical examination, which now can be enhanced by brain scanning technologies, in order to rule out such physical causes.

Brain Surgery

Brain surgery is one approach that can be taken to resolve organic or psychiatric problems. Before the 1800s brain surgery was attempted only in the case of traumatic injuries. The founder of modern brain surgery was a London surgeon, Victor Horsley. He began doing brain operations in 1886 at the National Hospital for Nervous Diseases. After studying the work of Dr. Horsley, three years later Dr. Elliot of Harvard began operating on brain tumors at Massachusetts General Hospital in Boston. Early brain surgery resulted in many deaths from uncontrolled bleeding or infection. A one-third death rate was not uncommon (Shorter, 1987). As there was no technology to determine the extent of the tumor, physicians guessed at the size by observing it through an area cut in the skull. In Germany in 1896 Wilhelm Röntgen discovered X-rays. In the United States in 1896 Harvey Cushing of Johns Hopkins used X-rays for the first time to diagnose a nervous system disease. Neuroradiology, the imaging of the nervous system, began at that time. However, it was difficult to use X-rays for diagnosis involving the brain because the bony skull blocked details of the brain tissue. Tumors and bleeding vessels could only be seen if there was calcification or a change in the skull around them.

Walter Dandy at Johns Hopkins in 1918 developed a technique, ventriculography, to enhance the visibility of the structures of the brain. He created a procedure to remove some of the cerebrospinal fluid from the ventricles and inject an equal amount of air through a hole drilled in the skull or by a needle inserted between the vertebrae of the spinal cord into the spinal canal (pneumoencephalography). This allowed one to see if the ventricles were normal or in some way enlarged, displaced, or collapsed. Later another process, myelography, involved injecting air into the cerebrospinal fluid of the spine and allowed the air to rise to the ventricles without it being necessary to bore a hole in the skull. However, these procedures were torture for the patient, who was tied to a chair and was then upended, chair and all, by at least three residents (Shorter, 1987:109). This procedure resulted in great pain and vomiting.

Injecting blood vessels with opaque substances, such as lipoidal, had been done successfully but had not been attempted as a diagnostic tool for the brain. However, substances had been injected into the brain through the arteries in the neck to treat patients with general paresis (syphilis). In 1927 in Portugal, Egaz Moniz invented a procedure that involved injecting sodium iodide into the carotid arteries supplying the brain with blood. This was the beginning of angiography, the study of arteries, with a contrast medium. If the artery was pinched off too long, oxygen deprivation of the brain could lead to temporary paralysis of half of the body; a few patients had epileptic convulsions, and some suffered severe pain (Valenstein, 1986). This meant that by the 1930s there were techniques (although often painful and sometimes hazardous) for disclosing the larger defects in the brain, and the main techniques of brain surgery were established.

We now regularly diagnose and treat many organic disorders of the brain involving anatomical or biochemical brain cell damage, including epilepsy, Alzheimer's, and Parkinsonism. Neurologists treat many of these disorders. But surgery is used mostly in relation to brain tumors. Surgery can be quite successful with benign brain tumors because most of them have a capsule of a kind of fibrous tissue that separates them from healthy tissue. They also usually have few blood vessels. Surgery on benign tumors is largely curative, and they seldom come back. But surgery is seldom successful on malignant brain tumors. They have no capsule separating them from the rest of the brain, and they have many blood vessels which allow them to grow quickly, robbing the rest of the brain of nutrients. Surgery on a malignant tumor may just decrease its size and give the patient more time. Even if the tumor is removed fully, there are usually microscopic cells which grow back (Martin, 1986).

MENTAL ILLNESS AND BIOLOGICAL CAUSATION

We do not know how many mental illnesses of today may be of an organic nature. But clearly there is a trend to see more and more mental illnesses as organically based, and research is focusing in that direction. Kraepelin, (1856-1926) a German psychiatrist whose work dominated much of the first half of the twentieth century believed that whereas less severe mental disturbances (neuroses) might be caused by life experiences, major psychiatric illness, (psychoses) were biological in origin. He drew a distinction between schizophrenia (dementia praecox) and manic-depressive psychosis (Zangwill, 1987). But Freud turned away from mental illness as organic and requiring treatment of the brain and nervous system, and toward the view that many mental illnesses had nothing to do with brain disease but were products of anomalies in early childhood socialization which required treating the mind (Gay, 1988). Now we are moving full circle and seeing more and more mental illnesses as actual physical disturbances in the functioning of the brain. Before Freud psychiatrists tended to see mind disease and brain disease as the same thing, and now once again the dominant trend is to see psychiatric symptoms as malfunctioning brain chemistry; thus, mind and brain disease come together. We appear to be returning to the views of Kraeplin that the psychoses are probably of biological origin and the less severe mental disturbances may be caused by life experience. But even less severe mental disturbances may be viewed as biological and treated accordingly. An example of this is Seasonal Affective Disorder.

Seasonal Affective Disorder

Seasonal Affective Disorder (SAD) is a disturbance of mood and behavior which is connected to seasonal change. It is a cyclical illness, with depressions occurring in fall and winter and alternating with normal mood or a mild elation (hypomania) in spring and summer. Diagnosis is now based on the Research Diagnostic Criteria (RDC) for major depression (Spitzer, Endicott, and Robins, 1978) from which the *Diagnostic and Statistical Manual of Mental Disorders* is derived. Research has shown that SAD resembles seasonal behavioral rhythms of lower animals and indicates that approximately 20 percent of normal people complain of moderate to marked changes in mood and energy across the seasons. Symptoms also increase with increasing latitude in the United States SAD usually begins when people are in their twenties or thirties, but some children are affected (Rosenthal, Carpenter, James, Parry, Rogers, and Wehr, 1986). Women are four times more likely than men to experience it, giving it a greater female prevalence than most psychiatric conditions. There may also be a genetic link to other forms of affective illness (Weissman, et al., 1985). Suicide may also be linked to the disorder, as suicides increase in late spring and early summer (Wehr and Rosenthal, 1989). The use of electro-encephalograms has confirmed patients' reports of increased total sleep time during the winter and depressive episodes; slow-wave sleep may also be reduced significantly (Jacobsen, Wehr, Sack, James, and Rosenthal, 1987).

Animal models of light-induced seasonal rhythms led to the conclusion that environmental lighting might be used to treat SAD patients. So phototherapy was developed to treat SAD. The lights used in the home and workplace are of a different spectrum and intensity than natural light. The manipulation of the light was used to try to regulate the hypothalamus of the brain. Most studies on SAD have involved high-intensity, full-spectrum fluorescent light to attempt to get effects similar to sunlight. As a somewhat lengthy exposure may be required, special lights have been developed for patients to use at home and at work. Rosenthal, however, believes that brief, high-intensity treatments are easier to administer and are more effective for most people (Wehr and Rosenthal, 1989).

The cause of the disorder is still under investigation, but there are three major hypotheses. The melatonin hypothesis believes that a change in the length of day causes a decrease in melatonin production, which leads to depression. Under that hypothesis, treatment by phototherapy is only effective if administered before dawn or after dusk. Also, anti-depressant drugs would be as effective because neither treatment would change melatonin secretion. The circadian rhythm hypothesis believes that winter depression occurs because of abnormally delayed circadian rhythms relative to sleep because of the late dawn in winter. Treatment would be given in the morning to prolong the circadian cycle. The final hypothesis, circadian rhythm amplitude, focuses on the shorter range from sunrise to sunset and encourages administration of therapy at mid-day for the greatest effectiveness (Wehr and Rosenthal, 1989). The development of phototherapy treatment for SAD follows a long history of attempts at providing nondrug treatments for mental health problems.

NONDRUG SOMATIC TREATMENTS

In the 1800s several somatic treatments were tried. Hydrotherapy was a popular treatment in the late 1800s and continued in mental institutions into the twentieth century. A medical specialty even developed which dealt with the various therapeutic effects of baths, douches, hoses, spritzers, steam, and wet packs. Fashionable physicians treated the "vapours" with hydrotherapy and electricity (Valenstein, 1986).

In 1883 Julius Wagner-Jauregg, an assistant in a psychiatric clinic in Vienna, observed that the mental state of a psychiatric patient improved after the fever subsided from an attack of a skin disease, which produced a high fever. He had also heard that patients with general paresis (syphilis) had had improvements in mental symptoms after high fever. He concluded that fever was therapeutic. He then attempted to induce fever by inoculating patients with vaccines of tuberculosis, typhoid fever, and recurrent fever. He also believed that malarial fever might be therapeutic for general paresis (syphilis). His malarial fever treatment was adopted widely (continuing in use until the 1940s), and he was awarded the Nobel Prize in Medicine in 1927. Various physical means of inducing fever were also tried, including baths, hot air, infrared-lightbulb cabinets, and radiothermy (Bennett, 1938). This type of treatment was also tried unsuccessfully with schizophrenics.

Until the 1940s some work was done on treating schizophrenia by inducing hypothermia, cooling of the body. Sedated patients were placed in Therm-O-Rite blankets ("mummy bags") which circulated a refrigerant. Body temperature was then reduced drastically. Talbott and Tillotson (1941) reported some success with the procedure.

Surgical Procedures

Several organs were removed through surgery in an attempt to treat mental disorders. In the 1920s tens of thousands of glands and organs, or parts of them, were removed. The endocrine system was seen as involved in mood and influenced by hormonal imbalances. The removal of endocrine glands became very popular, and there also were thyroidectomies. Ovariectomies became popular based on the belief that women became unstable after pregnancy or during the menopause. For many years the belief was retained that hysteria was derived from sexual desires (Ellenberger, 1970). However, males did not escape surgery either, as castrations occurred.

In the 1920s Cotton (1922) developed a focal infection theory. He argued that toxins produced by bacteria at infection sites in various parts of the body were transported by the blood to the brain, where they created mental disorders. He advocated the removal of infected teeth, tonsils, cervix, fallopian tubes, ovaries, uterus, seminal vesicles, and even colon sections. He conducted numerous surgeries. In 1923 a controlled study found that patients who had undergone the surgery did not improve more than did an unoperated comparison group (Kopeloff and Kirby, 1923).

Sleep Therapy

A forerunner of modern dream science was dream incubation, which was used by the ancient Greeks. Ill patients slept in a temple, and during sleep were awakened by priests, who listened to them report their dreams. A diagnostic procedure was used in which certain dream elements represented certain body parts and the action in the dream represented pathological conditions. In the nineteenth century Marquis d'Hervey de Saint-Denis and Alfred Maury in France studied dream access and practiced self-awakening. They were the predecessors of modern sleep lab researchers (Hobson, 1988).

Sleep therapy was popular in the 1920s and 1930s. It was used as early as the 1870s, when drugs were used to produce long periods of unconsciousness. The concept was that deep and lengthy sleep could restore an exhausted, overstressed nervous system. It was believed that actual physiological changes occurred in the brain. Barbiturates or opium derivatives were used to sustain a comatose sleep for one to two weeks. Brief waking periods were allowed during the day for nutrition and bodily functions. The procedure was used with schizophrenics and bipolar disorders (manic depression), with cure rates of 70 to 80 percent reported (Bleckwenn, 1930). The Soviet Union went on to develop electronarcosis therapy, the maintaining of a prolonged sleep state by stimulating the brain electrically.

During the twentieth century much research has been done on sleep, dreams, and their mental health effects. A considerable body of knowledge has accumulated from lab-based research with a new specialty of sleep researchers. In 1953 the rapid eye movements (REM) that occur during sleep and accompany brain activity were discovered. After that, the study of dreaming became more objective and more systematic. The general psychological nature of dreaming was established through collecting thousands of reports from hundreds of people in sleep labs. It became possible to distinguish, through statistics, the strong correlation between dreaming and REM sleep and to distinguish that correlation from other kinds of mental activity in other kinds of sleep. After REM sleep was discovered to occur in all mammals, animals were used to analyze the brain physiology of REM sleep. It is now understood that "human dreaming is tied to a brain process of broad biological significance" (Hobson, 1988:25).

Stimulation of Respiration, Metabolism, and Blood

In the 1920s various attempts were made to stimulate respiration and metabolism to treat mental disabilities. A University of Wisconsin professor in the 1920s experimented with cerebral stimulation by injecting small doses of sodium cyanide in schizophrenics. Later he used a gas mixture with 30 percent carbon dioxide to excite the nervous system (Loevenhart, Lorenz, and Waters, 1929). As the treatment became more popular, patients were given an extended series of inhalation sessions, which might include as many as 150 sessions. Later drugs such as sodium amytal, "truth serum," were used to stimulate talking. Psychoanalysts used it to try to reach the unconscious mind. Attempts were also made to improve metabolism. Catatonic patients were placed in the Navy Laboratory's hyperbolic chamber to increase oxygen. Many studies were conducted on oxygen utilization in the brains of schizophrenics as compared to "normal" brains (Valenstein, 1986).

In the 1930s attempts were made to increase the number of leukocytes, white blood cells, in schizophrenics. This was done by removing some cerebrospinal fluid and replacing it with inactivated horse serum to produce a form of meningitis with some fever. A series of injections were given based on the belief that leukocytes were low during more severe symptoms and high when their condition was improved. The procedure was said to increase lucidity for short periods in some patients and permanently in others (Lundvall, 1915).

Insulin-Coma and Metrazol-Convulsion Therapy

Insulin-coma therapy was first reported in 1933 and metrazol-convulsion therapy in 1935. They were used extensively until the 1950s. Insulin therapy involved introducing an excess of insulin, which deprived the brain of energy and induced coma. Manfred Joshua Sakel, a Viennese physician, discovered insulin-coma therapy accidently when he unintentionally gave an overdose of insulin to a woman who was a diabetic and a drug addict. Because her craving for morphine declined, he proceeded to use insulin therapy with other drug addiction cases. After inducing a deep coma in a dual diagnosed, drug addict/psychotic, he concluded that the patient's mental state improved. He proceeded to use this therapy with schizophrenics, claiming an 88 percent improvement rate (Valenstein, 1986). The procedure required extensive staff time, and patients could die or be brain damaged if left in coma too long. By 1938, 54 percent of U.S. mental institutions were using insulin treatment (Kolb and Vogel, 1942), with 65 percent of patients showing some improvement (Malzberg, 1938).

Metrazol-shock treatment was introduced by Joseph Ladislas von Meduna in Europe. His work indicated that epilepsy and schizophrenia were mutually antagonistic. This was later disproved, but not before some attempts were made to withdraw the blood of epileptics immediately after a convulsion and inject it into a schizophrenic (Valenstein, 1986). This led to inducing convulsions as a treatment for schizophrenia. At first von Meduna injected camphor, but later he switched to metrazol, a synthetic (cardiazol). Eventually the treatment was found to be more effective with depressed patients (Fink, 1984). By 1939, 65 percent of mental institutions in the United States were using metrazol treatment (Kolb and Vogel, 1942). Most of these approaches were abandoned with the introduction of modern psychotropic drugs. However, one somatic treatment which has remained is ECT.

Electroconvulsive Therapy

Electroconvulsive therapy (ECT) involves applying an electrical voltage to the brain through surface electrodes attached to the head. As it produces convulsions which can be dangerous, it is now done under a muscle relaxant or anaesthesia. Wilhelm Erb, a German neurologist, developed the procedure.

ECT is used extensively as a treatment for depression. Approximately 70 percent of psychiatrists believe it is an effective treatment for alleviating intractable depression (American Psychiatric Association, 1978; Millstein and Small, 1985). The best response appears to be related to typical, endogenous, psychotic, or melancholic types of depression (Kiloh, 1982). It has not been studied systematically in the treatment of atypical depression (Pies, 1988). There have been mixed research results, with West and Daily's (1959) patients having a poor response and Van Valkenburg and Winokur's (1979) having an overwhelmingly positive response. Mandel (1975) has suggested that ECT may be effective in cases of chronic pain associated with depression, as some consider chronic pain a form of masked depression (France, Krishnan, Houpt, and Maltbie, 1984).

There is considerable criticism of ECT, and over the years it has become increasingly regulated. It is widely accepted that massive doses of ECT are likely to produce memory and other cognitive deficits (Corkin, 1980).

In California the State Department of Mental Health, Office of Patients' Rights, under Chapter 1252, Statutes of 1977, compiles statistics reported by local mental health directors on the use of ECT and psychosurgery. It submits reports to the legislature and reports any indicated violations of laws or regulations to the Board of Medical Quality Assurance. The number of patients receiving ECT from 1977 to 1986 remained virtually unchanged. In 1986, 2,488 patients received 14,329 treatments (a mean of 6.0). Of the 71 facilities reporting use of ECT, only one was a state hospital (O'Connor, 1986). This reflects the strict regulation of the procedure within state institutions based on the patients' rights movement. This means that state institution patients, who are more often the poor, may be deprived of an effective means of treating some depressions. The majority of patients were treated in other licensed mental health facilities, and some were treated on an outpatient basis by private physicians. The overwhelming majority of voluntary patients, 2,369, received ECT with their consent. While only 23 voluntary patients received ECT without their consent, this does appear to create a paradox in which a voluntary patient receives treatment without consent. Of the 96 involuntary patients receiving ECT, only 31 gave consent. Patients receiving ECT were overwhelmingly older patients (50 percent 65 and over; 26.5 percent 45 to 64). Over two thirds of patients were female, and 92.4 percent were white. Of the 913 complications reported, 907 patients suffered memory loss; three developed apnea; one received a fracture; one had a cardiac arrest; and there was one death reported to a coroner (O'Connor, 1986).

There are concerns that ECT may produce structural brain damage. Such concerns have a negative impact on the willingness to accept ECT as a therapy by both the public and practitioners. The controversy involves the use of electrical stimulation of the brain, seizure production, cognitive side effects, and effects on cerebral physiology and metabolism (Weiner, 1984). Various studies have been conducted on whether ECT causes structural brain damage. These studies have involved experiments with animals and with autopsy and radiologic studies in humans. Neuropathologic studies have been done on animals, including cell counts in regions thought to be of greatest risk. These studies have failed to find evidence of brain damage when seizures replicate conditions of clinical practice (Dam and Dam, 1986; Meldrum, 1986). Studies on humans have been based on the concept that even if animal studies show no damage, the more complex human brain may be more vulnerable. Autopsy studies of people dying during a course of ECT are rare and often difficult to interpret, because most of them die of cardiovascular problems (Coffey et al., 1991).

Brain imaging techniques, including neumoencephalography and computed tomography (CT), have been used to examine people who have received ECT. Most studies have been negative (Coffey et al., 1991). However, a few studies have reported an association between ECT and structural brain abnormalities, either lateral ventricular enlargement (Andreasen et al., 1990) or cortical atrophy (Calloway et al., 1981). These retrospective studies are controversial.

Coffey and colleagues (1991) did a prospective magnetic resonance imaging (MRI) study. They studied 36 inpatients with depression, who received brief-pulse, bilateral ECT. Magnetic resonance imaging was done before and at two to three days and at six-month intervals after the ECT. Analyses were made of measurements of regional brain volumes, and a paired global comparison was done. The researchers found structural brain abnormalities in many patients before ECT. Six months after the course of ECT, there was no acute or delayed change in brain structure as measured by alterations of the total volumes of the lateral ventricles, the third ventricle, the frontal lobes, the temporal lobes, or the amygdala-hippocampal complex. The only change found was in five subjects on the pairwise global comparisons, which showed an apparent increase in subcortical hyperintensity. The researchers believed the increase was due to secondary progression of ongoing cerebrovascular disease. Their work confirmed other studies, which found no relationship between ECT and brain damage.

Thus, the growing sophistication of technologies provides for assessment of the impacts of other technologies, which have been used long before there was any way to assess their impacts. New technologies may help us assess the impacts of treatments before harmful ones become widespread or useful ones are rejected.

Psychosurgery

Psychosurgery refers to operative procedures on the brain designed to relieve severe mental symptoms. The procedures used may remove, destroy, or sever brain tissue. Surgery for mental illness has been conducted since early times. Brain operations were conducted for both paresis (syphilis) and schizophrenia. Burckhardt, a director of an asylum in Switzerland, performed a few brain operations on mental patients in 1890, and an Estonian neurosurgeon attempted some surgery with the prefrontal lobes in the early nineteenth century. However, modern psychosurgery began in 1935 with the Portuguese neurologist Egas Moniz, who would receive the Nobel Prize for his work, and the surgeon Almeida Lima. They performed a series of operations which became known as prefrontal leukotomy. In this surgery they severed the connections between the prefrontal cortex and the rest of the brain (Rodgers, 1992). Of their first 20 cases they reported, seven recovered and seven improved. The best results were reported with patients with affective (emotional) disorders such as anxiety and depression, not thought disorders such as schizophrenia (Valenstein, 1986).

The prefrontal lobotomy procedure was advocated widely in the United

States by Walter Freeman and James Watts and promoted in their book, *Psychosurgery: Intelligence, Emotion and Social Behavior Following Prefrontal Lobotomy for Mental Disorders* (1942). They emphasized the ability of the operation to reduce the intensity of emotions and advocated the cutting of the anterior thalamic peduncle connecting the prefrontal area of the brain and the dorsomedial thalamus. Their theory was that there were brain pathways between the frontal lobes and the thalamus which regulated the intensity of the emotions. They were able to obtain X-rays of what pathways were severed by injecting opaque oil into the surgical area. The emphasis was placed on severing the thinking and feeling parts of the brain to create people whose emotional reactions were less intellectualized and whose intellectual reactions were less emotional. The complexity of the functioning of the brain in relationship to thinking and feeling and the role of the frontal lobes are not understood clearly even today. The frontal lobes do not seem to be involved in any particularly discrete motor, perceptual, or sensory function, but they are critical in how information is used. They are crucial for thinking because without them responses are made to events without reflection. There is no planning for the future. Damage to the motor-premotor component of the frontal lobes leaves symptoms like stroke with altered muscle tone, aphasia, and weakness. Damage to the prefrontal cortex causes disturbances in thinking and behavior. The planning and sequencing of complex behaviors may be disturbed as well as the ability to sustain behavioral outputs. Thus abstract thinking, attainment of future goals, creativity, ethical and moral components, feelings of autonomy and identity, initiative, organization of behavior over time and space, and reasoning are all believed to be associated with the frontal lobes.

Dr. Francois Lhermitte in Paris, in his studies of people who had suffered frontal lobe damage from tumors, accidents, or strokes, found that such people had an irrepressible urge to imitate what they saw. They were aware of their imitations and explained it by saying they felt that they had to do it. They were virtually totally dependent on their social and physical surroundings. Lhermitte called this an environmental dependency syndrome (EDS). Experiments using PET scans have shown evidence of the constant activity of the prefrontal and frontal areas of the brain. Even when doing nothing, the anterior prefrontal area displays a higher metabolism and regional blood flow than the rest of the brain (Restak, 1988).

Because prefrontal lobotomy required a trained surgeon and an extensive staff for surgery and recovery, Freeman refined a transorbital lobotomy procedure developed by Amarro Fiamberti in 1937. This procedure involved driving a trocar through the eye socket to reach the frontal lobes. Fiamberti had then injected alcohol or formalin to destroy brain cells, but Freeman cut the nerve fibers to have better control of the process, which actually did less damage than traditional psychosurgery. He did his first "icepick" surgery in

1946 after practicing first on cadavers. Freeman was not a surgeon, but this procedure allowed him and other non surgeons to perform psychosurgery and rapidly spread the use of the procedure. Watts was to oppose Freeman's belief in quick and simple lobotomy. He felt that any surgery affecting the brain was serious and should be done by a neurologist (Freeman and Watts, 1950).

Over the years interest in psychosurgery and changes in procedures continued. The First International Conference on Psychosurgery was held in 1948, and the Fifth conference was held in 1978. Elliot Valenstein, in his book *Great and Desperate Cures* (1986), examines how such a radical procedure as psychosurgery could become so widespread so rapidly and with so little scientific research support. "There was nothing compelling about any of his [Moniz's] arguments that should have persuaded a prudent man to attempt psychosurgery. It was not genius that enabled Moniz to see beyond the risks; rather, it was his willingness to take these risks" (p. 100). Moniz may also have given too much weight to behavior changes that reduced patient management problems (p. 117). Valenstein (1986, p. 170) sees this oversimplification of the complex processes involved as very dangerous.

Thus, ambitious physicians can contribute to the spread of a treatment. Economics also explained some of the popularity and rapid spread of psychosurgery. Public institutions were anxious to find treatments that decreased patient populations and were not too expensive to administer widely. Thus, the majority of early operations were performed on the populations of the state institutions. Between 1946 and 1949 there was a 10-fold increase in lobotomies. By 1949, 5,000 surgeries per year were being performed (56 percent in state institutions). The popular media also played an important role in the promotion and spread of the procedure (Valenstein, 1986).

The best results were reported with people suffering from "agitated depression." (Valenstein, 1986:120) Some patients' anxieties were alleviated, but some patients suffered negative personality changes. These adverse results led to major opposition to the procedure. Research by Erick Feuchtwanger in Germany of gunshot wound damage to the frontal lobe of the brain actually foreshadowed what could happen during psychosurgery. He found changes in mood and drive and deficits in judgment and the ability to understand and plan for the future (Teuber, 1964). These same kinds of outcomes were also seen later in Fetal Alcohol Syndrome children who suffered damage to the frontal lobes. Concerns were also raised that the prefrontal lobotomy interfered with research to find alternative treatments (Chorover, 1974).

Opposition to conducting this procedure became very strong in the United States and other countries. The Soviet Union prohibited psychosurgery in 1951, partially because Soviet leaders believed that it was in conflict with Pavlovian theory. Many states in the United States regulate the procedure. The introduction of psychoactive drugs in the mid-1950s sped the decline of psychosurgery. By 1970 only about 300 surgeries were performed in the United States, and new stereotaxic instruments, which allow precise measurements of three dimensional space, were used to make the surgery very specific (Rodgers, 1992). But there was increased debate over psychosurgery and its uses and potential uses (Chorover, 1974). Oregon and California developed very comprehensive regulations for the procedure in the 1970s, and in 1982 Oregon outlawed it. Although many states still allow psychosurgery, there have been very few procedures performed since the 1950s, and in many states, like California, years go by without any procedures being performed. Also in the 1970s, the National Commission for the Protection of Human Subjects of Biomedical and Behavioral Research was established to study questionable research practices. The commission issued a report which criticized any use of psychosurgery for social control or control of patients in institutions but concluded that some patients might be helped by psychosurgery if they were not responsive to other treatments (National Commission for the Protection of Human Subjects of Biomedical and Behavioral Research, 1977). This conclusion was based on various studies reported to the commission which viewed psychosurgery as helpful to some patients (Teuber, Corkin, and Twitchell, 1977). Although the American Medical Association supported the procedure and modern procedures are much safer than the earlier ones, many surgeons avoid performing the surgery. The few surgeons who continue to perform the surgery avoid publicity (Valenstein, 1980).

The argument was made that the price of the surgery was too high in terms of the irreversibleness of the surgery, the blunted emotional effect, and the personality changes caused by the procedure. Concern was also raised that the surgery could be used to control antisocial behavior and could be applied to political dissidents. It was viewed as a potential instrument of class and racial oppression or as the forerunner of an ultimate technocracy based on technological control of the mind (Kleinig, 1985). And, in fact, it has been used in questionable areas such as for treatment of drug dependence, alcoholism, and deviant sexual behavior. In addition, in India and Japan operations have been performed on the amygdaloid nucleus of the brain to control hyperactivity in children (Whitlock, 1987).

Increased controversy arose with publication in 1970 of the book *Violence and the Brain* (Mark and Ervin, 1970). The authors argued that violence was caused by brain pathology and that neurosurgery could eliminate much of the problem. Two years later there was a report that psychosurgery had been performed on three convicts in California (Aarons, 1972), and a year later Michigan funded research on evaluating psychosurgery for use on incarcerated violent sexual offenders (Chorover, 1973). However, these were isolated cases, as most professionals felt that psychosurgery should not be used on violent persons because it might make them less inhibited and more impulsive (Scoville,

1971).

Although procedures are still being carried out to a limited degree, they have largely been replaced because of consumer movement opposition, the development of more effective drugs, and improved behavioral therapies. The original psychosurgery procedures underwent many changes over the years. The modern techniques involve exact stereotactic procedures for directing electrodes, which place very small lesions in key areas of the brain. Techniques also include radio frequency waves, use of radioactive elements with a short half-life, and freezing using cryoprobes. On-line video monitors and X-rays are used routinely to carry out the procedures. The best results are reported with patients suffering from severe chronic anxiety, agitated depression with a high risk of suicide, and incapacitating obsessive compulsive disorders. The procedure is also used for intractable pain (Rodger, 1992). Most current practitioners of psychosurgery still do not think the operation helps schizophrenics (Whitlock, 1987).

New technologies have opened the way to examine former psychosurgery patients and gain new knowledge of their condition. Valenstein (1986, p. 249) describes the case of a woman who had two lobotomies in the 1940s. In 1980 at the National Institutes of Health she was examined with a PET scan. The test showed that her frontal lobes were large, nonfunctioning areas of dead brain tissue. Previously on the Luria-Nebraska Test to evaluate brain damage she had performed within normal range, with no sign of organic impairment. The PET scan, however, clearly showed the organic damage, which explained such facts as her greatly impaired sense of time.

PSYCHOLOGICAL THEORIES AND TREATMENTS

So far the focus has been on biological approaches to treatment based on the view that the brain's chemistry is malfunctioning in some way or there is anatomical damage to the brain. However, there are other views of mental disorder which lead to different treatment approaches. Some psychiatrists refuse to accept somatic therapies, refusing to accept the assertion that they have a solid scientific foundation and provide effective treatment. Some researchers believe that psychiatric symptoms come mainly from disturbances of the mind, including early childhood traumas. This psychotherapeutic approach includes many psychological theories: psychoanalytic, cognitive, humanistic existential, family systems, and social learning/behavioral. These approaches, which are oriented to removing symptoms by acting on the mind rather than on brain tissue, dominated American psychiatry for many years. This school of thought sees biochemical changes detected in schizophrenia or depression as consequences rather than causes of the disease.

Psychoanalytic therapy is based on the work of Sigmund Freud (1923). During the late nineteenth century Freud turned away from the use of hypnotism and developed a new method, which used interpretation or analysis of what a patient said or omitted saying while freely associating under instructions to report his/her thoughts without reservation. This became psychoanalysis, the most influential of the psychotherapies from the 1940s to the 1960s. Freud developed concepts regarding unconscious ideas, ideas inadmissible to consciousness, resistance, and the splitting of the mind. For example, Freud believed that the depressed individual was communicating grief similar to feelings associated with bereavement and that depression represented the unconscious and symbolic loss of a love relationship. This resulted in feelings of dependence and vulnerability.

With the rise of Nazism in Europe, many Freudian psychoanalysts came to the United States. These analysts, as well as some American ones, came to have much influence in the American Psychiatric Association. William Alanson White, an American psychiatrist and psychoanalyst, became president of the association in 1924. The rise of psychoanalysis was connected to its acceptance by university intellectuals and by university psychiatrists, who considered themselves to be more intellectual than other physicians (Shorter, 1987). Psychiatrists trained in the major psychiatric teaching hospitals were trained quickly in the psychoanalytic theory, even though only about 10 percent of psychiatrists became certified psychoanalysts. Psychoanalysis became popularized and sought after by the upper-and middle-income classes who could afford it. Much of the work of psychoanalysis was done with the nonpsychotic mental illnesses. Freud himself doubted that psychoanalysis could be effective with schizophrenia (Gay, 1988). Psychoanalysis tended to be done with a different client population and in a different setting than the organic approaches. Many other psychoanalytic theories developed over time.

Behavioralism/social learning led to a return to a biological focus. It was based on work by Watson (1925), Wolpe (1952), and Skinner (1953). Watson (1925) argued that psychology could do without the concept of Consciousness and the technique of introspection and should instead be focused on the objective study of the behavior of people, the same way that animal studies were done. The original aim was to use behavioralism to establish a scientific psychology of life in the home and workplace. This approach moved psychology toward a biological approach and opened the way for the use of technology. This scientific approach to psychology dominated American psychology from the 1920s to the 1950s.

Wolpe (1952) noted that if an animal was fed in the presence of an object that it had come to fear, the fear would diminish gradually. With humans he developed the procedure of systematic desensitization involving the development of a graded hierarchy of fears by the client. The therapist worked with the client, starting with the mildest fear and working up the hierarchy, and at the same time the client was encouraged to relax by using relaxation techniques. Skinner (1953) went on to develop the key concepts of reinforcement and punishment. The term *secondary gains* was developed to explain the side benefits that came from having a mental disability. Skinner also made famous the notion of shaping, controlling the rewards and punishments to shape behavior. The core concept of behaviorism is that people are biological machines and do not consciously act but react to stimuli. Behavior is the product of conditioning.

Liberman and Raskin (1971) applied this work to depression by asserting that people became and remained depressed because of the attached social rewards, such as sympathy and concern of others. Lewinsohn, Youngren, and Grosscup (1979) argued that people were depressed because of the reinforcement contingencies they experienced, and they felt that much of the problem was due to lack of positive reinforcement.

Biofeedback

Biofeedback became prominent in the late 1960s. In 1967 at the annual meeting of the Pavlovian Society of North America, Neal Miller (1968) introduced a technique that his colleague, Jay Towill, had first used, which involved immobilizing animals and then using electrodes placed in the "pleasure centers" in the brain for the purpose of operant conditioning to teach the animal to increase or lower blood pressure, heart rate, etc. Miller and Towill used D-tube curarine for paralysis of skeletal muscles to avoid the possibility that the animal was modifying its autonomic responses by voluntary activities such as breathing rate or muscle tension, and they also used placement of electrodes in the brain. This type of animal research has led to the animal rights movement, which has raised policy issues concerning the right to use animals for research purposes.

Research has led to various techniques aimed at enabling people to develop some voluntary control over physiological functions such as heart rate and blood pressure. Various electronic devices have been developed to provide the client with visual or auditory feedback on any modification occurring. The equipment—including transducers, amplifiers, and auditory and visual displays—serves as an artificial extension for parts of the biological system that do not have such conscious feedback. The client is then expected to learn from the feedback how to control the physiological function. Although how this process works within the individual is not understood clearly, one clear advantage of the approach is the active role of the client in determining the course of treatment (Yates, 1980).

Hypnosis

Hypnosis has been used in modern times by physicians and other medical professionals and by experimental psychologists. It has also been used by psychotherapists as an adjunct to other therapies. The term *hypnosis* was coined by James Braid, a physician and surgeon, in the 1800s when he was introduced to what the French called mesmerism. In the late 1800s there was a revival of interest in hypnotism, and experimental psychologists explored its nature and mechanisms. At that time, the French neurologist Jean Martin Charcot popularized hypnotism as a treatment. However, the modern era in the study of hypnotism can be traced to Clark L. Hull (1933) and his colleagues at Yale University in the 1930s. Hull asserted that hypnotism was a normal phenomenon that could be studied in the same way as other mental capacities, which vary from individual to individual. He made the first systematic attempt to apply modern psychological experimental and statistical methods to the study of hypnosis and suggestibility. His work showed that although hypnosis did not appear to transcend the limits of the normal, it was still possible through hypnotic suggestion to influence human performance, sometimes dramatically. Hull produced evidence of some increase in muscular capacity; alterations in the threshold of some sensory stimuli, whereby the stimulation needed to produce a conscious sensation was raised (for example, raising the threshold at which pain was felt); and some evidence that the memories of childhood might become more accessible. In the 1950s and 1960s standardized scales of hypnotic susceptibility were developed, including the Stanford scales (Hilgard, 1965).

Researchers have also studied hypnotic anesthesia. Experiments have shown that while a subject is under hypnosis, the nervous messages from the sense organs do reach the relevant areas of the cerebral cortex, where electrical responses normally arise (Halliday and Mason, 1964). It appears that the conscious sensory response undergoes some form of dissociation or suppression. An experiment of Hilgard's (1965) showed that a hypnotized subject with a profound loss of pain sense induced by suggestion, who denied feeling any pain, could admit to the pain through automatic writing, although he did not know what he had written. This hypnotic dissociation suggests that hypnotic anaesthesia is a true dissociative phenomena (Zangwill, 1987). This ability of hypnosis to control pain has been used by medical practitioners. By inducing hypnosis, they can use it rather than drugs to control pain or to reduce the dosage of drugs for pain control. Clients can also be trained to use self-hypnosis for control of chronic pain or for surgery rather than an anesthetic.

Hypnosis has also been studied in relationship to sleep. The electroencephalogram (EEG) has been used to show that hypnosis does not resemble any recognized states of sleep. The EEG does not recognize the hypnotized person as being in a state any different from wakefulness. It remains to be seen if more advanced technology can discriminate a difference. It is only in recent years that physiological correlates of dreaming have been established. Although there are currently no physiological or biochemical criteria of an altered state of consciousness in hypnosis, such criteria may yet be discovered (Zangwill, 1987).

Psychotherapy

Psychotherapy has developed in many different directions, providing for widely divergent approaches based on different theories. Frank (1973) has described psychotherapy as the type of social influence exerted by a socially sanctioned and trained healer with a person who is suffering and seeking relief through a defined series of contacts.

Individual psychotherapy may be based on the principles of many schools. Some therapists use only one approach, while other therapists are eclectic and mix and combine various approaches. Strict Freudian psychoanalysis has declined rapidly in the United States in favor of more direct and shorter forms of psychotherapy, some of which have been founded from psychoanalysis. Fisher and Greenberg (1985), after a review of the research, concluded that there was no evidence that psychoanalytic therapies resulted in better outcomes than less time-consuming approaches.

Psychotherapy Results. An English psychologist, H.J. Eysenck, in 1952 challenged the effectiveness of psychotherapy. He suggested that psychoneurotic difficulties tended to resolve spontaneously, regardless of treatment. He used data from insurance claims for psychological disability and discharge rates of neurotics from mental hospitals to claim that approximately two thirds of neurotics recovered without treatment (Eysenck, 1952). Bergin and Lambert (1978) challenged those figures and claimed the spontaneous recovery rate was nearer to 46 percent. According to Crowne (1987:62) "It seems probable, therefore, that one-third to one-half of neurotic patients who have no systematic psychotherapy improve symptomatically. A smaller percentage, perhaps one-quarter, show constructive personality changes."

These challenges brought about a more critical look at psychotherapy and stricter research regarding outcomes, which have shown that psychotherapy is an effective treatment for many people (Malan, 1973). However, estimates show that 3 to 6 percent of clients treated with dynamic or behavioral psychotherapy become worse (Strupp, 1978), so psychotherapy cannot be considered a benign treatment that if it does not work, will not cause harm. However, the type of psychotherapy used may not be important. Luborsky, Singer, and Luborsky (1975) concluded that roughly four fifths of patients get better regardless of the type of therapy (Adlerian, Freudian, family, behavioral, etc.) and that the elements held in common which caused change were a helping relationship with a therapist, suggestion, and abreaction (release of repressed emotions through a retelling of an experience). Torrey (1986) discusses that psychotherapy is known not just in Western cultures, but that curanderos, espiritistas, witch doctors, and medicine men and women perform a similar function. They use the same techniques and get about the same results. However, Luborsky and colleagues (1975) have found a major difference in terms of improved success rates when psychotherapy is administered with drugs.

In the 1970s and 1980s support for the use of psychotherapy with schizophrenic patients diminished markedly. This decline was encouraged by the growing focus on genetics and biology and the view that drug therapy made psychotherapeutic approaches obsolete. Wasylenki (1992), however, argues that new information supports reconsidering the use of psychosocial approaches, including psychotherapy. Although he acknowledges drug therapy as the basis of treatment for most schizophrenics, he urges that psychotherapy be used with drugs to maximize effects.

BLENDING THE BIOLOGICAL, PSYCHOLOGICAL, AND SOCIAL

Adolf Meyer established the main theoretical bridge between the organic and functional approaches. A neurologist and pathologist who also practiced psychiatry, he worked in the United States in the late 1800s and early 1900s. His psychobiological approach recognized the importance of biological factors in mental disorders but also focused on the whole person. He emphasized the importance of taking complete life histories, including early childhood and family; the use of play and work therapy to strengthen the healthy aspects of the person's personality; and the interconnectedness of psychiatry and the community. He stressed a therapeutic program of socialization. He became president of both the American Neurological Association and the American Psychiatric Association. Although he could see the advantages of combining both approaches, he was not able to overcome the conflict involving the two approaches, as they were based in competition over the same patient population (Valenstein, 1986).

Now many people who receive psychoactive drugs also receive other services. For example, Klasson (1989) describes how occupational therapists can serve as case managers for people with chronic schizophrenia and also provide them with needed rehabilitation. Various other professionals may also serve as case managers and/or service providers to sustain persons with long-term mental illness in psychosocial programs over long periods of time, during which they may also be receiving drug treatment. Supporters of chronically mentally ill persons have also turned increasingly to models which build the necessary infrastructure of support in the community. For example, metropolitan Toronto has a housing coalition which coordinates the efforts of housing agencies, consumers, and treatment facilities to provide housing for people with psychiatric illnesses. The coalition has been involved in housing policy, changes in municipal laws, development of programs, and development of housing stock (Trainor, Lurie, Ballantyne, and Long, 1987). The National Institute of Mental Health sponsored a 1980 survey of 1,471 chronically mentally ill persons in community support systems. This work indicated that there were clearly 10 established components to community support systems, and these involved many social system elements (Tessler, Bernstein, Rosen, and Goldman, 1982).

While mental health components are often overlooked when people are being treated for physical health problems, the reverse may also be true. Persons with chronic mental illness may receive inadequate medical care for nonpsychiatric illnesses. On the whole, they tend to have a poorer health care status. The medical problems of these individuals may lead to excessive morbidity and mortality. Their physical health care problems may also affect their ability to adjust to their psychiatric illness. The use of case managers is recommended as a way to help overcome problems with barriers to medical care (Schwab, Drake, and Burghardt, 1988).

Treatment Environment

Treatment environment may determine how much drug or nondrug treatment is required. For example, crowding on a psychiatric intensive care unit may lead to greater aggression, which may require more treatment (Drinkwater and Gudjonsson, 1989). In Sweden during a 25-week period, all incidents of aggressive behavior were recorded in a 19-bed psychiatric acute care unit using the Staff Observation Aggression Scale (Palmstierna and Wistedt, 1987). Palmstierna, Hutfeldt, and Wistedt (1991) concluded that an increased number of patients on the ward increased significantly the likelihood of aggressive behavior. This was especially true for patients with schizophrenia or schizophreniform disorder. They also found, consistent with other studies (Aiken, 1984; Pearson, Wilmot, and Padi, 1986), that much of the aggressive behavior was related to the patients' inability to have their immediate wishes met. They recommended that a ward milieu and treatment strategy that was as permissive as possible, with legal and diagnostic constraints, would likely reduce aggressive behavior or at the minimum change its pattern.

Family environment may also play a role in how much treatment is required. Most people with chronic psychiatric illness live with their families after hospital discharge (Goldman, 1982). Researchers and clinicians have for a long time associated the quality of family life with the course of many psychiatric disorders. Many studies have confirmed the association between relapse and family environment (Goldstein, 1988). There are, however, some studies which have found no association (Parker, Johnston, and Hayward, 1988). There are also other factors (such as severity of symptoms; patient functioning between acute episodes; and symptoms such as social withdrawal, poor role functioning, and lack of affect) which are thought to be influenced by environmental variables (Liberman, DeRisi, and Mueser, 1989).

An Australian study examined the relationship between negative symptoms and quality of life for patients with functional psychoses and their family environments. They found that a higher level of positive emotional expressions in the family predicted milder and fewer negative symptoms and a better quality of life at a six-month follow-up. The predictions were found to be independent of the initial severity of the psychopathology or the patient's earlier adjustment. Patients who had relatives who reported more family conflict at hospital admission and discharge displayed greater psychopathology at the six-month follow-up. Diagnosis did not predict significantly the level of negative symptoms or the quality of life at follow-up. The researchers recommended the use of the description of positive family attributes by therapists in working with families to build therapeutic alliances and to focus intervention on promotion of positive family interaction (Halford, Schweitzer, and Varghese, 1991). Another study by Sommers (1988) explored whether some quality of interaction between former patients and their social and physical environment resulted in differential levels of community adjustment in a study of 60 former state hospital patients with a schizophrenic diagnosis. Three indexes of posthospital adjustment were used: instrumental performance, social participation, and satisfaction overall. The findings suggested that the personal and community adjustment of chronically mentally ill persons depends significantly on their relations with relatives and friends. The trend to focus on biological causations for mental disorders has relieved many families of a sense of blame for the disorders which had been caused by earlier studies that emphasized family dysfunction; but these new studies, which point out the importance of family functioning in improving the functioning of people with mental disorders, should not be ignored.

TREATMENT OF DEVELOPMENTALLY DISABLED AND MENTALLY RETARDED PERSONS

The treatment environment also may impact upon the success or failure of working with people with developmental disabilities or mental retardation as well. After reviewing studies of the deinstitutionalization of people with developmental disabilities, Molony and Taplin (1988) concluded that positive effects on skills, behavior, level of activity, social interaction, and the general quality of life have generally been obtained by subjects who were relocated from institutions. In particular, an association was demonstrated between the normality of the environment and improvements in adaptive behaviors. Although the outcome for those with more severe maladaptive behaviors or who were more profoundly and multiply disabled was less positive, there was still some evidence that under certain conditions, they too could show improvements in their functioning when transferred to the community.

In a very limited number of cases, mental retardation in children may be halted or even cured by removing a source of internal or external poisoning before there is irreversible damage to the brain. This approach was mentioned earlier in discussing PKU and lead poisoning.

Disability caused by social factors such as malnutrition, infection, or poor stimulation are also addressed primarily through prevention. Once brain damage has occurred, in most cases it is irreversible. No drugs have been found to reverse this damage. As noted in the previous chapter, drugs can be used to address additional problems such as epilepsy, or (as in the case of dual diagnosis such as mental retardation/mental illness) psychoactive drugs may be used, but drugs are of limited value. Psychotherapy has also been used in working with people with mental retardation, but this approach has been limited. The most favored approaches have been the psychosocial and the biologically oriented behavior modification therapies.

Because the medical and biological models have not been able to address fully most cases of mental retardation, this area of mental disability has turned largely to social and educational approaches. This is one of the reasons why most proponents of this subset of mental disability have removed themselves from the mental health arena, which has remained more biologically and medically focused, and instead have established their own policy arena for persons with developmental disabilities.

7

Experimentation and the Future

Experimentation is the basis for the development of many of the drug and non-drug treatments for people with mental disabilities. People with mental disabilities have also served as subjects for research which has not involved their mental disabilities. Experimentation which involves human subjects or substances taken from human subjects has raised many questions. This chapter looks at some of the issues regarding experimentation and then briefly examines the future of biomedical research and mental health in relation to brain research, genetics, and the physical/mental health connection.

Over the years human subjects were used regularly in research exploring the causes and treatment of mental disorders. Gradually there was a growing realization that many experiments raised ethical issues about the way in which they were conducted or even whether they should have been conducted at all.

EXPERIMENTATION—A QUESTION OF ETHICS

In the nineteenth century research was frequently done which would be considered highly unethical today. General paresis (syphilis) was the cause of much mental illness in the nineteenth and early twentieth centuries. Franz Nissl in 1896 became able to diagnose general paresis on the basis of histopathological evidence. In 1897 Richard von Krafft-Ebing injected fluid from the sores of known syphilitics into general paralytic patients. Because these patients had no reaction to the injections, he concluded that they already had syphilis (Valenstein, 1986).

Even in the twentieth century endangering or ignoring the consent of the patient was not uncommon. Egas Moniz, in developing cerebral angiograms, endangered and damaged patients. In 1927 he began injecting a 70 percent solution of strontium bromide into the carotid artery and at times injected too much, leaving patients with neurological problems. Moniz and Pedro Almeida had their sixth patient die a few hours after the procedure. They then switched to a 25 percent solution of sodium iodide injected directly through the carotid artery through an incision in the neck. In pinching off the artery, they sometimes had negative results, including temporary paralysis of half the body, epileptic convulsions, and severe pain during the procedure. Moniz also used Thorostrast, a radioactive substance. At the time it was suspected of being unsafe; and within 10 years Thorostrast granulomas (nodules of inflamed tissue) were found in the brains of patients, and its use was discontinued (Valenstein, 1986).

Freeman recommended electroconvulsive shock rather than conventional anesthetic during lobotomies in state hospitals because an anesthesiologist was often not available. He also recommended ECT for difficult to handle patients because they could be brought to unconsciousness quickly and they usually did not remember their earlier resistance (Freeman, 1948). In 1938 Cerletti and Bini first tried their electroconvulsion technique on a human. A man who was wandering in a confused state at a train station and who was presumed to be a schizophrenic was sent to them by the police commissioner. After the first electric shock, the man did not lose conciousness. Hearing the doctors say they were going to repeat the procedure at a higher voltage, the patient said, "Not another one! It's deadly." Deciding that those were the only comprehensible words he had spoken, the doctors ignored him and did the second procedure. When the man awoke from it, he did not know what had happened (Cerletti:265 1956). These are but a few of the examples of ignoring the safety, consent, and expressed wishes of patients.

The theme of the 1990 American Psychiatric Association's annual conference was "The Research Allliance." Clinical treatment depends on research for improved treatments. However, research may also interfere with clinical practice and may cross ethical lines. Pinheiro (1992) describes how even something as seemingly simple as filling out data collection forms may create a problem. When state hospital psychiatrists filled out forms, it took time away from the limited time that was already spent on clinical care. As agents of the research, they also lost some of their spontaneity and creativity. This limitation of scope comes about because research can only deal with a small number of variables. Pinheiro also points out that since research is usually funded by government or foundations, there may be biased priorities, and problems with research may revolve around what research subjects are chosen.

Experimentation on Sexual Offenders

Lobotomy has been used on sexual offenders. For example, a man imprisoned in Sing Sing for sexually molesting children was treated by Ralph Banay, a psychiatrist at the prison psychiatric clinic. The prisoner was obsessed and anxious, so Banay decided a prefrontal lobotomy was justified. The surgery was performed in 1941 by a neurosurgeon. The prisoner was described six months later as no longer agitated or obsessed with sexual fantasies and able to resume his clerical work in the prison. The patient also seemed pleased with the results. Based on the research, Banay and Davidoff (1942) recommended the procedure as useful for some cases of sexual offenders.

The originally treated prisoner was released in 1942 and appeared in a Veterans Hospital in Chicago in 1944. He was unable to hold a job because he was undependable and had childish judgment. He had no insight into his behavior, was confused, had poor memory, and was often incontinent as well as unable to attend to bowel movements. He also had clearly resumed his sexual obsessions and attempts to molest. After a pneumoencephalogram, an electroencephalogram, and other examinations, Friedlander and Banay (1948) concluded that his dementia was a result of the lobotomy. Lobotomy did not change his thought processes, but only the intensity of the emotional involvement with some ideas. In this man's case the obsessional ideas were only muted for a short period of time, and he became unable to function in the community without support. Only a few other prisoners were ever lobotomized.

Sterilization is another approach that has been taken with sexual offenders, the developmentally disabled, and others with mental disabilities. As discussed earlier, part of the eugenics scare was the passage of sterilization laws. The Supreme Court has established that the individual's decision whether or not to have a child rests within her/his constitutionally protected zone of privacy (*Griswold v. Connecticut*, 381 U.S. 479, 1965). Since basic rights are infringed by involuntary sterilization, the state must show that sterilization laws are rationally related to and necessary to accomplish legitimate state goals. So while sterilization has become very restricted under most circumstances for people with mental disabilities, the one area in which it is still occasionally seen as viable is in regard to sexual offenders. But because of the constitutional safeguards, it would not be easy to justify such an approach now.

Periodically castration has been used as a punishment for a criminal offender. Although research shows that sexual assault is not about sex, the public may be accepting of approaches such as castration. In 1992 there were still attempts to take this approach. A judge in Houston, Texas, in March 1992 approved a child molester's request to be castrated surgically. The offender, who had been charged with raping a 13-year-old girl, volunteered to undergo castration after reading about the State District Judge's support for castration of some sex offenders. The charge of sexual assault carried a 5 to 99 years or life prison sentence and a fine of up to $100,000. The defendant was still serving a 10-year probation for pleading guilty to indecency with a seven-year-old girl. The defendant volunteered to undergo surgical removal of both testicles in return for being placed on 10 years probation. Although sexual drive would diminish because the testicles produce the hormone testosterone, the man still might be capable of erection. Also, obviously, the surgery would not change the psychodynamics of why the person offends. The judge refused to consider the use of drugs to suppress sex drive because after the 10-year probation the defendant could stop taking the injections. If the judge had ordered the surgery without the defendant volunteering, the Eighth Amendment (which pertains to cruel and unusual punishment) could have been raised. Many questions were unanswered about this case. If the man were returned to the community without psychological treatment, he would likely reoffend because the problem is more psychological than physiological. The true voluntariness of the consent could be questioned, and this might make it difficult to find a surgeon willing to carry it out. A community activist threatened to file a complaint against the judge and any medical personnel involved in the procedure. Arthur Caplan, director of the Center for Biomedical Ethics at the University of Minnesota, expressed the concern that allowing this type of action could lead to governments ordering other people to be sterilized for other crimes and social deviancy. He viewed the procedure as barbaric ("Surgical Castration . . .," 1992).

The defendant's family hired an attorney to get the castration decision overturned, and they met privately with the judge, saying that they did not believe the defendant was capable of making the castration decision. Opposition continued to grow from black activists, who claimed the procedure would have never been considered if the defendant were white. Other critics said that while the surgery would lower the man's sex drive, it would not prevent rape because rape is not a sexual desire but an impulse to violence. Two doctors who had said they would do the surgery both changed their minds. The judge, in a brief hearing, then withdrew his approval for the castration because a doctor could not be found to perform the operation ("Castration Deal Withdrawn . . .," 1992).

Sexual psychopath laws provide for long-term incarceration of a person determined to be a mentally disordered sex offender, sexually dangerous person, or sexual psychopath. Usually persons who come under these laws are committed to a hospital or psychiatric facility and are held there until the medical staff determines that they have been cured. Various reviews may be required to safeguard rights. Some laws provide for indeterminate incarceration. About half the states have sexual psychopath laws, which were passed based on the argument that they provide treatment of the sex offender while protecting the public. However, they were often passed after highly publicized sex crimes. One of the most serious problems with sexual psychopath laws is that it is difficult to define clearly which persons are subject to the law. Although such laws allow civil commitment through a hearing process, courts have realized their criminal-like nature, and the resulting incarceration involves a serious stigma (Smith and Meyer, 1987). In some states civil and criminal proceedings can both occur. Because of concerns that many sexual offenders cannot be rehabilitated, most states require sexual offenders to register with law enforcement officials for several years after their release.

In 1986, in *Allen v. Illinois* (196 S. Ct. 2988), the Supreme Court handed down a decision regarding the rights of those handled through sexual psychopath laws. The court emphasized the differences between civil and criminal proceedings. Allen claimed that his right to avoid self-incrimination had been violated because he had to submit to two psychiatric exams to determine him to be a sexually dangerous person. The court held that his case was civil even though the Illinois law required proof of a criminal sexual assault, provided a jury trial, established a "beyond a reasonable doubt" standard of proof, and permitted the person to be placed in a maximum-security prison. The court said that the right to avoid self-incrimination did not apply in civil cases.

Mental health professionals often play a major role in the legal system in evaluating and treating people charged with sex offenses. Treatment of sexual offenders remains a difficult area. The prognosis for people with impulse-ridden character disorders, including multiple sexual perversions, promiscuity, and polymorphous-perverse sexual trends, varies (Kernberg, 1975). However, it is believed that the more unstable and chaotic their behavior, the better the prognosis. The more stable the sexual deviation, the worse the prognosis. The prognosis is improved for those people who are able to maintain nonexploitive object relationships. Expressive psychotherapy is considered to work quite well unless there is an underlying narcissistic personality with a stable sexual deviation, in which case the prognosis is poor because such patients tend not to tolerate the psychoanalytic approach and often do poorly in any treatment (Chatham, 1989). Various aversive behavior modification approaches have also been taken. That approach has raised concerns about civil rights.

Research on Families

Research on schizophrenia in the mid-1950s focused on family interaction. Families agreed to participate in what they thought were scientific studies. They were not aware that they had been identified as the cause of the schizophrenia. Hundreds of families participated in laboratories of academic institutes and hospitals. Their verbal and nonverbal expressions were recorded by tape recorders and projectors. Their biographies were studied by interdisciplinary panels of doctors, psychologists, sociologists, and technicians. In one National

Institute of Mental Health study, families agreed to live in the hospital for six months to two years. Out of this research came the view of families producing a scapegoat, the schizophrenic person, through the process of double-bind. The father was spineless and passive, the mother was domineering, and the other children were unstimulating and disloyal (Sedgwick, 1982).

There is now a strong focus on the belief that chemical imbalances in the brain are solely responsible for mental disorders. While this has had many positive benefits and has alleviated much family distress of self-blame, Pinheiro (1992) warns that it can be used by families, professionals, and patients defensively to undermine good clinical care. He gives as an example a depressed man whose father was also depressed. If the patient's depression is labeled as genetically linked, other important information may be ignored, such as the experiences of the patient in growing up in such an environment. This leads to target symptoms which are disconnected from the past, a lack of patient history, and a lack of recognition of the social environment while treatment is focused on medication.

Research on Women

One of the major problems of women in regard to research is the lack of research using them as subjects. In the late 1980s pressure was applied to the National Institutes of Health (NIH) to adopt a policy calling for inclusion of women in all future clinical trials. Traditionally NIH funded research on laboratory rats that were almost invariably males because their physiology was simpler. This also applied to human research subjects. Women have usually been treated based on knowledge obtained relating to male subjects in research. Thus, differences regarding females have frequently remained unknown. This means, for example, that it is unknown whether greater or lesser amounts of drugs are required for treatment. Predominantly female diseases have also had difficulty in receiving research interest and funding.

The Congressional Women's Caucus in the early 1990s focused on this concern, in hearings which showed that policy to include women in research has been ignored by a predominantly male medical establishment, and that NIH had not rectified the situation. The fact that the small number of women in Congress had a caucus which addressed women's issues and that some women were on key committees brought pressure on the situation. One solution to this problem was the recruitment and placement of more women in private and public health organizations. This approach was taken by the Bush administration, with appointment of a woman to head NIH. Part of her agenda was to see that women subjects were included in research and that predominantly female diseases were researched.

One of the few areas in which research is increasingly examining women separately is alcoholism. There is growing recognition that women, for biological and environmental reasons, require different treatment.

Genetic Research

Biological and genetic research has also raised concerns of subjects of research. In the case *John Moore v. The Regents of the University of California* (763 P. 2d 479 Cal. App. 249 Cal. Rptr. 494, 1988) the court ruled that explicit consent was required for the use of cells. The plaintiff had argued that researchers commercially exploited products from cells that he had donated. Ownership issues have also arisen with DNA that is banked for testing. Some families have pooled their funds for the tests and have then refused access to others who have not contributed money. Banked DNA can become involved in family feuds and has been used as a bargaining chip in divorce and custody cases.

Wertz (1990) makes 10 recommendations regarding ownership of DNA. These include that all patients should sign consent agreements before blood is drawn which determines ownership and disposition; ownership of DNA should be familial and accessible to all blood relatives, regardless of financial contributions, for the purpose of learning their genetic status while the donor's anonymity is maintained; DNA banks should do follow-up to inform families of new developments in testing and treatment; DNA should be destroyed when there are no remaining living relatives; spouses should not have access to the DNA bank even with the patient's consent, but the party whose DNA is banked has a moral obligation to reveal all relevant information when having children is considered; all third-party institutions such as employers and insurance companies should be denied access even if they have the patient's consent; qualified researchers should have access but without identification of the patient; and family members have a moral obligation to help themselves and other generations by participating in research related to familial disease.

While these are excellent recommendations for establishing consent and protecting anonymity, there remains one area in which consent is not operational under these recommendations. There is no call for consent before DNA is made available to researchers. Although there is a recommendation for a moral obligation by families to participate in research, it would seem that this should not supersede actual consent by those whose DNA will be used in research.

Selection of Subjects

One issue involved in human research is how are subjects selected. Comparison groups are used widely in clinical research. But to carry out accurately this type of research, a normal population must be defined. Epidemiologic research has shown the prevalence of various psychiatric disorders in community samples (Robins, Helzer, Weissman, Orvaschel, Gruenberg, Burke, and Regier, 1984). When volunteers are drawn from the community to participate in biomedical research, some way must be found to distinguish those in the sample with psychiatric disorders from those without. There have been some attempts to assess candidates with interviews, questionnaires, and rating scales. Some studies have found a low rate of psychopathologic conditions, which were sustained in follow-up (Grinker and Werble, 1974). Other studies have consistently found high prevalence in volunteers (Gibbons, Davis, and Hedeker, 1990; Halbreich et al., 1989; Thaker et al., 1990).

One research group (which needed young, normal volunteers without any illness that affected the brain, anatomically or physiologically, for research which focused on the relationship of the brain and behavior in schizophrenia) followed a two-step procedure to select subjects. Their research required subjects who were willing to undergo neuroanatomic measures (magnetic resonance imaging), neurophysiologic procedures (positron emission tomography, single-photon emission-computed tomography, xenon 133 cerebral blood flow, computed electroencephalography-evoked potentials), and neurobehavioral assessment. In order to find the population, they advertised in several city and suburban newspapers for healthy people 18 to 45 years of age for paid research. They used a set of exclusion criteria in first a telephone screening and then a personal evaluation by a research psychiatrist. During the phone interview, information was provided on the goals of the research, the procedures, and the research protocols. Subjects uninterested excluded themselves. Individual and family histories were collected, and a review team by consensus decision selected subjects without medical, neurologic, or psychiatric history for interviews with a research psychiatrist. The psychiatric interview used the Structured Clinical Interview for *DSM-IIIR*: Non-Patient Version (Spitzer, William, and Gibbon, 1989) for a detailed clinical history and a semistructured clinical interview. Physical and neurologic exams, including lab work, were performed. Included subjects were then again informed of protocols, and informed consent was obtained. Of 1,670 respondents, 23.1 percent declined during the phone interview and 50.9 percent were excluded based on data obtained in the phone interview. Another 168 subjects were rated a low-priority status for not fitting currently needed sociodemographic characteristics for controls. This left 463 (27.7 percent) volunteers scheduled for the second review process.   Of those who passed telephone screening, approximately half were eventually excluded: 155 (49.7 percent) had a past or present medical, neurologic, or psychiatric history. This left 157 persons who could be studied as normal subjects. Of the 809 people excluded by telephone and personal interview, 40.5 percent were excluded because of personal psychiatric history. During participation in the studies, eight more subjects were identified as having a psychiatric diagnosis (Shtasel, Gur, Mozley, Richards, Taleff, Heimberg, Gallacher, and Gur, 1991).

This study shows the complexity of trying to find a "healthy, normal" volunteer group for research, and the difficulties of attracting a large enough pool of potential candidates to obtain the needed subjects after subjects' refusals based on informed consent and ruling out subjects who could invalidate the research.   The extent of the technological procedures which were required to conduct the described research also points out why subjects who are given informed consent based on detailed protocols may decide to forgo participation. This may be a growing problem, as the biologically based research of today calls for the use of technologies which may involve considerable time commitments and can include invasive procedures such as the injection of dyes with their potential risks.

Informed Consent

Over the last 30 years the doctrine of informed consent has established that patients and research subjects should be knowledgeable before they give consent to treatment or participate in research. This means that they should understand a description of the proposed treatment/research and should be aware of the risks, benefits, and alternatives.   The patient/subject must be competent to understand the information being given and the meaning of informed consent. To be valid, the consent must be voluntary. The courts are the final determiners of competency, but as a practical matter health care professionals and researchers must draw their own conclusions about competency in treatment decisions and selection of research subjects.

There are quantitative scales to help judge a person's cognitive capacity and capacity for daily living activities. There is also a new instrument for quantitative assessment of clinical competency.   The Hopkins Competency Assessment Test (HCAT) is available to help clinicians determine clinical competency, but it does not address legal competency. The instrument involves a brief essay describing informed consent and durable power of attorney, followed by six questions related to the essay. The essay is available at three grade levels (thirteenth, eighth, and sixth), while the questionnaire is written at the sixth-grade level.

This instrument was tested on subjects who were patients on a general medical ward and a general and geriatric psychiatry ward at John Hopkins Hospital. Forty-one subjects agreed to participate: 25 (61 percent) were psychiatric patients. Informed consent using the Hopkins Institutional Review Board procedures was obtained, and the subjects completed the Mini-Mental Status Examination (MMSE) of cognitive functioning. Clinical and demographic data were also collected. In 1990 for 12 days data were collected by two examiners. Subjects were given the thirteenth-grade version while the examiner also read it aloud. The questionnaire was then read, and if the subject scored eight or higher, the procedure ended. If the patient scored seven or less, the eighth-grade version was read and the questionnaire administered. If the subject scored eight or higher, the exam ended. If the subject scored seven or less, the sixth-grade version was read and the questionnaire administered. Within 24 hours of the HCAT exam, a forensic psychiatrist performed a clinical competency exam on each subject. The results of the HCAT and the MMSE were compared to the forensic psychiatrist's exam. Interestingly, similar ranges of scores were found in the medical patients and the psychiatric patients. The designation as a psychiatric or medical patient did not predict scores on the HCAT or the MMSE. The HCAT was found to be a reliable screening test for competency, as the scores from the instrument agreed with a forensic psychiatrist's opinion of clinical competency. The forensic psychiatrist identified as incompetent subjects who had scored less than four on the HCAT. More than 30 percent of the subjects were judged incompetent to make treatment decisions (Janofsky, McCarthy, and Folstein, 1992).

Reporting the Results of Research Studies

Whether and how results of research studies reach the public is an important issue. If the media focuses on a new technology or procedure, that may cause demand for the technology or procedure to accelerate greatly. This was the case with psychosurgery. Studies have shown that researchers whose reports show no effects or only adverse effects have difficulty in getting them accepted for presentation at medical meetings or for publication in medical journals (Dickersin, 1990; Koren, Graham, Shear, and Einarson, 1989;). This may mean that many authors do not even submit their research for publication (Rosenthal, 1984). However, once reports are published, positive reports may receive wider coverage in the media.

One study found the number, length, and quality of newspaper reports on positive medical research studies was greater than on negative studies (Koren and Klein, 1991). Out of 17 newspapers, which were identified from a base of 168 newspapers, 19 published reports were found on two studies, one with negative findings and one with positive findings. Nine reports were solely on the positive study, and 10 reports covered both studies. Where both studies were covered, the mean length given to the positive reports was significantly longer than for the negative reports. No reports covered the negative study only. The researchers concluded that since the public receives much of its medical information from newspapers, if bias against reporting negative results exists as indicated by the research, the public is likely to receive an unbalanced view of controversial health subjects. They also concluded that physicians would be influenced by this distorted reporting as well since they are also part of the general public and frequently receive initial information on new developments from the media. "The well-known media phrase that 'good news is no news' may be detrimental in the biomedical context, as it helps perpetuate a bias against negative studies" (Koren and Klein, 1991:1826). This points up the need for journalists to present balanced reports when covering controversial health topics, and it should serve as a cautionary note for consumers of media coverage. Valenstein (1986) also warns of the danger when desperate patients and families receive premature reports of cures which are promoted through the media.

Experimentation and the Antipsychiatric Movement

Ken Kesey first learned of LSD in 1960 through a veterans' hospital research project funded by the federal government. While a graduate student at Stanford, he went to Menlo Park and was paid $75 a day to take the drug. Soon he took a job in a psychiatric ward, where many drugs were available. He felt, after taking LSD, that the men in the psychiatric ward were not so crazy after all. After experiencing peyote and LSD, he wrote his antipsychiatric novel, *One Flew Over the Cuckoo's Nest* (Kesey, 1975). This was a reflection of an era of distrust of authority, concerns over evidence of government-sponsored experiments on unconsenting subjects, and concerns over social and political control through mind control. The antipsychiatric movement is still concerned with rights to refuse treatment and research and experimentation without proper, informed consent, and these concerns have led to guidelines to protect research subjects.

The National Commission for the Protection of Human Subjects of Biomedical and Behavioral Research

The National Commission for the Protection of Human Subjects of Biomedical and Behavioral Research was established in 1974 to study questionable research practices. The commission has issued guidelines on psychosurgery. The commission was charged with conducting a comprehensive investigation and study to identify the basic ethical principles which should govern the conduct of biomedical research involving human subjects; developing appropriate guidelines; and identifying the requirements for informed consent to participate in biomedical and behavioral research by institutionalized mentally handicapped persons (Public Law 93-348, Sect. 201-205, July 12, 1974; codified in Short Title Note to 42 U.S.C. Sect. 289.1, Suppl. IV, 1974). The Department of Health, Education, and Welfare had already established a guide for institutions on protection of human subjects (DHEW, 1971), and researchers involved with federal funding are required to meet guidelines to protect human subjects.

Animals and Research

Like many other scientific research fields, animals have been used in many research projects involving mental health issues. It has been considered acceptable to perform research on animals which would not be considered acceptable if performed on humans, and research on animals is often conducted as trials prior to conducting the research on humans. Although there are regulations concerning the maintenance and treatment of research animals aimed at reducing unnecessary suffering among such animals, there is still little control over the decision to use animals in such research or what animals are used. There is a growing animal rights movement which objects strenuously to the use of animals in research. Its proponents have increasingly brought the issue to the public's attention by media-attracting events. The more extreme proponents have engaged in illegal acts by breaking into laboratories and freeing research animals.

Animal research is particularly paradoxical in mental health research, because it would seem that the quest to create mentally healthy individuals and mentally healthy environments would be founded on an ethical and philosophical base in which it would be difficult to accept the abuse of either humans or animals. Yet at the same time there is recognition of the knowledge that has been gained from such research. This creates a moral and ethical dilemma. Also of concern are the mental health consequences to researchers who frequently use animals in their experiments. In addition, one must question the frivolous and repetitive animal research done by high school and college students for psychology classes.

In contrast to the typical lab research involving insertion of electrodes into animal brains or manipulation of animal behaviors, there is now a small but growing use of animals as co-therapists in psychotherapy. Animals appear to be particularly effective in working with children, the elderly, and mentally handicapped persons, who may be willing to relate to the animal before they are willing to relate to a person.

Organ Donation and the Mentally Disabled

Another concern raised is in regard to infants who are born so mentally disabled that they cannot survive, and when and whether organs from those infants should be used for transplant. In March of 1992 this issue attracted media attention when the parents of a baby girl born with anencephaly in Florida wished to donate the baby's vital organs to other children. The baby had a brain stem which automatically controlled her breathing and heartbeat, but she had no skull and no higher brain development. She was hospitalized in critical but stable condition and she continued to function physiologically. A 1988 Florida law did not allow her to be determined brain dead, as the brain stem was functioning. This meant that her vital organs could not be taken prior to her death.

Her parents wanted to have the child declared brain dead so her vital organs could be donated to other children before they deteriorated. However, a lower court and the Fourth District Court of Appeals in West Palm Beach ruled that state law did not allow the child to be declared brain dead while part of her brain functioned. The court did rule that nonvital organs, such as one kidney, could be removed. However, after looking for a match with the 8,000 to 9,000 patients registered and awaiting a kidney transplant, none was found ("Law Bars Dying Baby's Organs . . .," 1992).

This case again upholds the growing trend of court decisions that people with a mental disability cannot be treated differently. It also deals with the question of brain death, which increasingly is becoming the accepted means of determining death in the United States.

The traditional medical definition of death involved the permanent cessation of respiration and circulation. But because advances in medical technology have allowed machines to maintain these functions indefinitely, a new definition for death became necessary. Brain functioning has become a criterion for death because technology has not yet found a way to restore consciousness. In 1968 the Harvard criteria for brain death were established (Ad Hoc Committee, 1968). Kansas in 1970 was the first state to recognize brain-based criteria for death. In 1981 a Uniform Definition of Death Act was proposed (President's Commission, 1981) which has been approved by the American Medical Association, the American Bar Association, and the Uniform Law Commissioners. The President's Commission's recommendation is for total brain death including the brain stem. This is the issue which came into play in

Florida. There are those who feel that it is higher brain function that defines human beings and that cessation of the higher brain function should be the definition for death. Further brain research may help to change this definition in the future. However, there is the possibility of greater conflict. For example, there are now attempts to use cryopreservation to preserve the brains of dying persons and to reactivate them at another time. Although a focus on this type of issue is probably far in the future, mental health issues remain as conflicts arise over when someone should be considered dead and what measures should be used in maintaining that person. These conflicts can result in disempowerment of family members and family conflict.

THE FUTURE OF BIOMEDICAL TECHNOLOGY, RESEARCH, AND MENTAL HEALTH

Although, as the previous chapters indicate, biomedical technology and research have made it possible to treat some mental disorders successfully and prevent others, there remain many disorders which are not yet preventable and others for which treatment is limited. Three areas are primary to the future of biomedical technology, research, and mental health: a greater understanding of the functioning of the brain's mechanisms, genetics, and the physical/mental health connection.

Research on the Brain

Most of the complex features of the brain's organization are as yet incompletely understood and defined. The essential properties of the brain that enable it to allow for emotional, cognitive, and behavioral performance, which make up the symptoms of psychosis, are mostly unknown.

Beginning in the 1970s, new technologies allowed researchers to examine the living brain. Research focused on the differences between the brains of normal persons and those with schizophrenia and other mental disorders. PET scans showed differences in the distribution of blood flow to different regions of the brain and differences in the way in which the brains of schizophrenic and normal subjects functioned when doing tasks. EEG studies also indicated that there was slower activity in the frontal regions of the brains of schizophrenics. MRI was used to examine the brains of identical twins, one with and one without schizophrenia. Such studies have revealed enlarged ventricles and cortical atrophy in schizophrenics; brain volume which appears smaller in some areas associated with thinking, concentration, memory, and emotion; and cerebrospinal fluid which fills larger ventricles. Research has concluded that subtle anatomical changes are probably a characteristic of the disease (Suddath et al., 1990). These technologies have also been used to explore the brain in relationship to bipolar disorder, Alzheimer's disease, and addictions.

In the 1990s there is a strong focus on research of the brain and away from the social, interpersonal, and intrapsychic aspects of mental disorders. The interest in the brain's central role in mental disorders is supported by psychiatry, government, research, businesses, and families of patients. This focus has become the dominant force and places psychiatric patients strongly into the medical model. Biochemical alterations are at the forefront of treatment. Pinheiro (1992) points out that even though the focus on the hard sciences is legitimate, one should also be aware that this focus serves powerful economic interests, such as pharmaceutical companies, insurance companies, and the government. He also recognizes that there is a new generation of psychiatrists who have been trained to focus on the brain and to work with computers and databases. He sees the primacy of computers as due to American enthrallment with them and the greater ease of collection of data made possible by them. He sees a problem in the elimination of the need for slower and more difficult data collection which allows for examination of "the meaning and impact of these disorders in the context of the patient's psychosocial history" (p. 104).

Increased research on the brain continues to make available new information. In a letter to the *New England Journal of Medicine*, a Canadian researcher reported that from autopsies of 62 brains, she found that as men age, the size of their corpus callosum, the band of 300 plus nerves that connects the two hemispheres of the brain, gets smaller. The average man, 61 to 70 years old, had a corpus callosum 20 percent smaller than that of a male 25 to 50. There was no size change in women (Witelson, 1991). As discussed earlier in this book, much of the research on the brain has been on brain chemistry. However, some of this new biological research is focused on grafting cells into the brain.

Brain Grafts. Research has been conducted on grafting cells from various parts of the body into the brain to help people with Parkinson's disease, Huntington's disease, and injuries that damage small areas of the brain. The theory behind the research is that diseased or damaged brain cells can be replaced with new cells, which can take over the function of the damaged cells. The first brain grafts were attempted by German and French scientists in the 1920s and 1930s, who put bones, teeth, muscle, and other tissue into the brains of laboratory animals to find out if they would be rejected. Those studies proved that the brain is privileged from an immunological standpoint in that it does not reject grafted tissue. The first modern rat studies involving brain cell implants were completed in the late 1970s and early 1980s, when identical brain cells from fetal animals were transplanted into the brains of adult animals with Parkinsonian symptoms, which had been created by destroying brain cells with chemical injections, and when peripheral cells from other parts of the body, dopamine-producing adrenal cells, were transplanted into the brains of rats. What were sought were peripheral cells which produced the same chemicals used for communication between cells as those replaced in the brain. Cells destroyed by Parkinson's disease produce dopamine, which is also manufactured in the adrenal glands. After the rat studies, studies were done on monkeys because the monkey brain is closer to the human brain. Cells affected by Huntington's disease produce gamma-aminobutyric acid, acetylcholine, and certain peptides. Some of those chemicals are also produced by ganglia in various parts of the body, including the abdomen. Early studies ran into difficulties because of the small amount of tissue being put into a larger brain (McIntosh, 1982).

In recent years adrenal tissue transplants into the brain have been used for treating Parkinson's disease. Parkinson's involves a lack of dopamine in the brain and the adrenal cells from the adrenal glands produce dopamine. However, the American Academy of Neurology in 1988 warned that great caution should be used in expanding use of the procedure because the effectiveness of the procedure had not been established. As was mentioned earlier in discussing psychosurgery, there is a danger in procedures spreading rapidly without sufficient evidence of their efficacy.

One of the controversial issues in tissue transplant has been the use of fetal tissue for transplants. In April 1992 the Senate approved a measure that would lift a ban on federal spending for fetal tissue transplant research. The House, in July of 1991, had already passed its own version of the legislation. Fetal tissue transplantation would be used to continue research involving Alzheimer's, Parkinson's, spinal cord injury, and diabetes.

Genetics

At least half of all genes are related to mental functions, and at least one third of genetic diseases are manifested in the central nervous system. Molecular biological, biochemical, and cytological methods have been used to explore the relationship of genetics to the functioning of the brain. In the 1940s Oswald Avery recognized that recombinant deoxyribonucleic acid (DNA) was the chemical basis of heredity. Between 1971 and 1973 fundamental experiments were performed with DNA. This was followed by the cloning of the first insulin gene in 1977 and in 1982 by the approval by the Food and Drug Administration of the first genetically engineered insulin.

One of the concerns raised about biological research is the speed with which it is occurring, which means that it is very difficult for public opinion, societal values, and government regulation to keep up. In 1975 a conference was held at Asilomar in California. That conference was held in response to many concerns raised by researchers and others over potential hazards of research and technology. The conference resulted in a call by scientific leaders for a moratorium on certain kinds of experiments until their safety could be ensured through the result of paradigm experiments. The National Institutes of Health Recombinant DNA Advisory Committee (RAC) subsequently developed guidelines which are binding on NIH grantees. The committee members are scientists who judge the scientific merit of research proposals to the National Institutes of Health for experiments using DNA. Many research labs have voluntarily adopted the RAC guidelines. Biotechnology and research are also at the center of controversy because of their potential for commercialization.

The first step in demonstrating a genetic component to a disease is usually to demonstrate a linkage between the disease in multiply affected families and a polymorphic DNA marker. Linkage analysis is used to localize the genetic defect to a subchromosomal region of 2 to 10 centimeters. Several techniques have been developed to bridge the gap between genetic mapping and the identification of a genetic defect which either predisposes or causes a particular disorder. The knowledge that has been gained through exploration of the role of genetics in physical diseases, such as cystic fibrosis and hypertension, and the methods that have been developed to gain this knowledge may be transferable to learning more about mental disorders. Progress has already been made in relation to the role of genetics in Alzheimer's disease, schizophrenia, bipolar disorders (manic depression) (Heyman et al., 1983; Murray et al., 1986), and alcoholism. The chromosomal location of Huntington's disease, a neurodegenerative disorder characterized by psychological disturbance, has been located to within several hundred kilobases of the gene causing the disorder (Wasmuth et al., 1988).

The World Health Organization, in collaboration with the IPSEN Foundation, in 1989 conducted a critical review of the knowledge about the genetics of mental disorder, methods of genetic research into those disorders, epidemiology, and issues arising in genetic research (Bulyzhenkov, Christen, and Prilipko, 1990). That collaboration identified a number of issues which needed to be dealt with. One problem faced in genetic research on mental disabilities is that the number of families which can be used for research is low. Recommendations have been made for international collaboration, with the establishment of banks containing pedigrees and DNA material (Bertelson, 1990; Smith and Potkin, 1990). New applications in molecular genetics, such as gene amplification techniques (polymerase chain reaction), may provide powerful new tools for data banking genetic material (Mendlewicz, 1990). If complex etiology is involved, trait segregation will not be sufficient to determine the way susceptibility to the disease is inherited. As many mental disorders may fall into this situation, Clerget-Darpoux (1990) believes that additional information provided by research involving genetic markers may be useful in determining the role of one factor and in subdividing heterogeneous groups of patients into subgroups homogeneous for one factor. This, of course, would mean even more problems in terms of having sufficient research pools of subjects. Because of the issue of complexity, McGue and Gottesman (1990) see the challenge for research as not so much in finding multiplex families to be studied intensively, but rather the development of approaches to deal with complexities, heterogeneity, and environmental affects on human behavior. They suggest that coronary heart disease and diabetes may be appropriate models for designing linkage studies of schizophrenia. They also believe that research indicates that the targeted strategy of using the candidate gene approach (Gurling, 1986) may be useful. They suggest that the research indicates that likely sources for candidate genes would be single-gene effects upon correlates of schizophrenia such as D2 dopamine receptors, cerebral blood flow assessed by positron emission tomography, cerebral ventricle size, and smooth pursuit eye tracking. Williamson and Goate (1990) suggest that advances in technology leading to the easy identification of coding sequence are needed. Bloom (1990) emphasizes the need for research at the level of molecular genetic specifications of the brain through the detection and characterization of proteins, functions, and supracellular attributes. These kinds of molecular genetic research are expensive and require substantial funding.

Results which may be possible from genetic research include improved diagnostic classification and prediction of risks; more knowledge about the basic mechanisms of mental illness; new methods of treatment and prevention; and the possibility of repair of genetic defects (Bertelson, 1990). However, the possibility remains that major mental disorders are heterogeneous and multifactorial, which would limit greatly the practical use of knowledge gained and the possibilities for prevention and intervention. Even if this proves to be the case, the discovery of linkage in mental disorders would clarify the mode of genetic transmission, allow study of gene interaction with other factors in complex behavior, and might eventually lead to isolation, sequencing, and cloning of mutant genes for etiological and preventive purposes (Mendlewicz, 1990).

In 1991 doctors focused on a gene that is believed to cause Lou Gehrig's disease, amyotrophic lateral sclerosis (ALS). ALS strikes about 5,000 Americans every year. The disease destroys nerve cells in the brain and spinal cord, resulting in muscle wasting, paralysis, and usually death within five years. No one has known what causes it or how to stop or slow the process. New research by a team led by Dr. Teepu Sidique, now of Northwestern University, was described as the first major advance toward unraveling the cause of the disease, which was identified 122 years ago. Researchers have narrowed the location of the gene to a single small area of approximately 10 million bits out of the some three billion bits involved in the 23 human chromosomes. The researchers at Duke University and Massachusetts General Hospital pooled information on 510 members of 23 families in which the disease was thought to be inherited. Only 5 to 10 percent of cases are thought to run in families. The remaining 90 to 95 percent are believed to be a random type, perhaps associated with a toxin or some other damage as well as a faulty gene (Siddique et al., 1991).

Mutagens. The effect of mutagens has been seen in the increase in birth defects among parents who were exposed to mutagens in the workplace and also in increases in birth defects in the general population. Behavioral changes resulting from exposure to mutagens are being researched. The greatest interest lies in research on alcohol, other drugs, environmental pollution, and the effect on antioxidants, which may suppress free radical action in aging. Chemical, physical, and biological mutagens induce DNA changes during cell division. Environmental mutagens may damage DNA directly or indirectly, through their metabolites. Either can affect DNA repair. Mutations in gametes can increase the frequency of spontaneous abortions, birth defects, problems of metabolism, predisposition to faster aging, brain maldevelopment, and deficient repair of genetic damage. According to Sram, Binkova, and Gebhart (1990), the possible effects of mutagens on mental functions, expressed through behavioral change, have not been studied sufficiently. They have urged the World Health Organization to encourage studies in these areas.

Research is being explored on how to block invaders of the body. Thomas E. Wagner (1991) and a research team at Ohio University have reported that an infection from viruses of the type that cause AIDS, retroviruses, can be blocked by a new genetic sequence into chromosomes of fertilized mouse eggs to create a strain of rodents immune to a virus that causes leukemia in mice. A retrovirus invades cells, inserts its own gene pattern into the nucleus of the cell, and forces the host cell to make more virus particles. The new technique uses a transplanted gene to block the "sense," or normal sequence, of the virus gene. These are but a few examples of the rapid expansion of genetic research, which can lead to prevention of mental disabilities and physical diseases with mental health components.

The Human Genome Project. Congress has budgeted more than $3 billion for a 15-year project to attempt to identify the more than 100,000 genes in the human body. The Human Genome Project hopes that the research will lead to treatments and cures for thousands of hereditary diseases. The lead agencies are the National Institutes of Health and the Department of Energy. Most of the NIH funding goes to seven academic centers at universities such as the Massachusetts Institute of Technology and Washington University, while most of the Energy Department's funding goes to three national laboratories: Lawrence Berkeley, Lawrence Livermore, and Los Alamos. In 1992 approximately $160 million was spent on the project. The research groups that NIH and DOE and other agencies like the National Science Foundation have funded have generated over 70 million nucleotides. The quantities of accumulated sequences are doubling every two years. Each research group is responsible primarily for a single part of the project, such as mapping a single chromosome or group of chromosomes. The funding includes some 150 smaller grants to individual researchers who are mapping or sequencing smaller-scale work, such as identifying genetic markers for specific genes or building hardware for automated sequencing (Erickson, 1992).

There are an estimated three billion nucleotides, and of the human being's 100,000 genes about 5,000 have been deciphered partially. By 2005 the Human Genome Project researchers hope to have located the rest. Genes will be only about 2 percent of the entire data the researchers plan to locate. The short-term goal is to create genetic and physical maps of each chromosome. The genetic maps will reveal the approximate positions of genes and code them for various traits, with markers spaced at intervals to help scientists follow genes through family trees. This will enable scientists to see how often genes such as those involved in diseases or disorders appear near which markers (Shapiro, 1991). The physical maps will be ordered collections of small DNA fragments from a chromosome, which can be cloned or made to reproduce itself indefinitely. The fragments can then be used to cover the original chromosome. A third type of map will be a complete sequence map of the bases A,C,G,T, the four nucleotides: adenine, cytosine, guanine, and thymine, which compose genes. But that long-term goal will not be feasible until technology improves (Erickson, 1992).

One group of researchers' function is to join computer science to biology. They will decide how the output of the project will be made available to researchers and what methods will be followed to build up the software to store and manage the data. This informatics project will determine the kinds of questions researchers will be able to ask the database in the future (Erickson, 1992).

Confidentiality. As more is learned about the genetic makeup of people, there are more concerns about how the information is used. Scientists and others have expressed the fear that the information could be used to deprive people of insurance and jobs, that people's privacy could be invaded, and that discrimination and selective abortions would increase. In the mid-1980s Albert Gore (1985), Chairman of the House Subcommittee on Oversight and Investigations in the U.S. House of Representatives, identified three broad areas of concern in regard to biotechnology and public policy. The first dealt with the information that comes from research and technology. This included a concern about genetic screening in the workplace and the use of genetic information by insurance companies.

In 1992 legislation was introduced in Ohio to prohibit insurance companies from considering genetic histories when deciding whether to sell insurance policies. This legislation was drafted by Representative Mike Fox when one of his constituents came to him about her problem in obtaining disability insurance.

In 1990, Theresa Morelli at the age of 29, had applied for disability insurance with American United Life of Indianapolis. She was refused because her father has Huntington's disease and the insurance company believed she might also have it. There was no proof Ms. Morelli would get Huntington's disease. She had never taken the genetic test for the disease because of the $5,000 cost and because she was not yet ready to know the test results. Huntington's chorea is a very rare degenerative nerve disease that starts in middle life. Uncontrollable body movements gradually develop and are followed by mental deterioration. Occasionally mental deterioration comes first. So far there is no treatment to slow the progression of the disease and no cure.

In an interview, Representative Fox said that about 20 percent of insurance companies check genetic histories. He gave as his reason for supporting the legislation the view that it was easier to deal with the issue early rather than waiting for it to become a widespread practice by insurance companies ("Woman Fighting . . .," 1992).

The Physical/Mental Health Connection

Increasingly research is looking at the connection between physical and mental health. For example, the mental health component is under exploration in chronic fatigue syndrome. The moods of anger and depression have been implicated in the disease. Some researchers believe that people who have certain emotional makeups may be more predisposed to get the syndrome. There has been a focus on searching for a viral cause for the illness, and for a time the Epstein-Barr virus was believed to be associated with the disease. But that idea has largely been abandoned because most people's chronic fatigue syndrome is not associated with Epstein-Barr, although many other viruses are being looked at, including those in the herpes family, the retroviruses, and lyme disease. Fatigue is the most widely reported symptom and may be caused by many other disorders, such as autoimmune diseases (including autoimmune endocrine problems, autoimmune thyroidis, lupus, and rheumatoid arthritis) as well as chronic allergies and other conditions, and even yeasts such as *Candida albicans*. As immune systems become imbalanced and weakened, they are more vulnerable to viruses and allergies. The brain's chemistry is also affected so people become less tolerant of stress and more and more vulnerable to the "negative effects of sensory input" (Anderson and Berger, 1991:56).

One study reported in 1989 found that acyclovir, a drug used to treat

Epstein-Barr virus, was found to cause no more frequent improvement than a placebo. The study found the only factor linked clearly to improvement was mood. As people's moods improved, especially anger and depression, their fatigue also lessened. But it could not be determined whether their moods improved because they felt better or they felt better because their moods improved. This has led to the hypothesis that the symptoms may be caused by the influence of people's moods on their hormones and immune defenses. This is reinforcement for the belief that a person's psychological makeup may have an impact on the expression of diseases. It has also been noted that people with some personality types appear to be less likely to survive cancer or heart attacks ("Moods Implicated . . .," 1989).

Researchers are exploring the possibility of teaching the body to use its own natural defenses. This could lead to treatment of some of the most unresponsive chronic diseases and eventually could result in elimination of many of the currently used drugs and surgery. The research is based on the concepts of behavior modification developed by Pavlov. In 1982 researchers gave mice lupus, an immune system disease. Drug treatment was given along with a drink of saccharin-sweetened water. After the conditioning period, the drug treatment was stopped. The animals who continued to get the saccharin-sweetened water continued to fight off the effects of the lupus (McGrath, 1988). In another experiment, a drug that causes the body to produce more interferon to fight bone-marrow cancer was given to mice along with the strong smell of camphor. Of three groups, one continuing to get the drug, one receiving no treatment, and one sniffing camphor, the camphor-sniffing group did best (Ghanta, Hiramoto, Sdvason, and Spector, 1987). This research approach is continuing to seek a way to get the benefits of drugs without their toxic side-effects. The Russians in the 1960s conducted studies showing the ability of people to stimulate and depress their immune systems through conditioning. A study in which people have been able to raise their own natural killer-cell production through conditioning is underway in Europe. Studies in the 1960s showed that body temperature and blood pressure can be conditioned. The Army's Research Institute of Environmental Studies has conditioned people with Raynaud's syndrome, a condition that cuts circulation to the hands in cold weather, to overcome that problem. Studies have also shown that conditioning can stimulate the immune system to combat autoimmune diseases and cancer (McGrath, 1988).

How illness is dealt with by others may also have a significant impact for patients. Research shows that a cancer's severity plays less of a role in a patient's mental health than does how openly the disease is discussed. A study involving 52 children and young adults, ages 7 to 21, who had been free of cancer for two to seven years showed that children who could talk openly about the disease gained empathy and support from friends and family and avoided social isolation (Fritz, Williams, and Amylon, 1989). Having the support of peers or a close friend during treatment contributed to healthy adjustment. The incidence of clinical depression, at around 6 percent, was found to be no greater than among the general child population. However, there were children with negative mental health outcomes. One 12-year-old boy who was unable to talk about his illness withdrew from his friends and talked little to his doctors. After ending treatment, he suffered severe weight gain and left school at age 14. Survival rates are growing for cancer, with the fatality per 100,000 dropping from 8.3 in 1950 to 3.6 in 1985 (National Cancer Institute, 1989). With survival rates for children's cancer improving, psychological adjustment is of increasing importance. Direct communication, the way the patient talks with family, peers, and teachers, is the variable most predictive of psychological functioning in a survivor (Fritz, Williams, and Amylon, 1989).

Environmental Medicine. Environmental medicine is a new branch of medicine which involves an overview approach to evaluate illness. Its predecessor was holistic medicine. But there is a difference between the two: as the term *holistic* implies nontraditional and non-Western, while environmental medicine relies on diagnosis from Western medical technology and science but treatment can branch into many different approaches (Anderson and Berger, 1991). Environmental medicine is an integration of many disciplines, including endocrinology, environmental toxicology, immunology and allergy, internal medicine, neurology, nutritional biochemistry, and diagnostic procedures. Mainstream medicine focuses on the organ about which there is a complaint without much attention to interdependency; how the organ systems interact; or genetic, familial, or environmental aspects. Treatment is conservative, symptomatic relief focused and drug oriented. Environmental medicine tries to look at all factors that influence a person's life and health. It looks for other problems both psychological and physical. This includes childhood experiences involving emotional, psychological, and physical events; environmental influences and exposures; and genetic history (Anderson and Berger, 1991).

Another dramatically growing field of study over the last 10 years is psychoneuroimmunoendocrinology. This area of research deals with the inner communication between vital bioregulatory systems in the body. It is based on the theory that the central nervous system, the immune system, the endocrine system, and the psyche are interconnected and influence each other. They are inseparable. This would include psychoemotional problems leading to imbalances in the body's systems (for example, sexual, physical, or psychological abuse in children leading to dysfunctions in the immune, endocrine, or neurological systems, which may later appear as migraine headaches, seizures, etc). It is hypothesized that a traumatized person who experiences tremendous conflict, fear, or rage is affecting the circuits in the brain by constantly overstimulating some and understimulating others, which leads to an imbalance in electrochemical activity in the brain. Neurotransmitters are depleted or produced in excess, and receptors are either overstimulated or understimulated. "The hypothalamic and pituitary regulatory mechanisms that largely control the immune systems, as well as the autonomic nervous system and the endocrine glands, become dysfunctional and physical problems develop (Anderson and Berger, 1991:56)." This leads to disease. "Abnormal, bio-chemical products are produced in the body, such as allergic mediators like histamine, serotonin, insulin; mediators of inflammation, like some prostaglandins; or certain peptides that are secreted by the gastrointestinal systems" (Anderson and Berger, 1991:56). There are receptors in the brain for all of those. As the body creates abnormal substances, the brain is over- or under-stimulated, leading to psychological dysfunction and neurological disorders which may include anxiety and panic attacks, eating disorders, dementia, obsessive compulsive behavior, and rage. This may explain addictions such as drugs, alcohol, and food. People use these substances originally to numb emotional pain, but they may have neurochemistry that leads to addiction because certain receptors, such as the pleasure centers and the limbic system, are being overstimulated. Also, food allergies may produce chemical changes in the brain which may lead to addiction (Anderson and Berger, 1991).

Jeffrey Anderson believes that if the body is chronically dysfunctional and imbalanced and there are environmental influences, then psychotherapy to improve the emotional makeup is not enough. Other factors may have to be dealt with, such as eliminating toxins and rebuilding physically the right substrates. But he sees treatment programs, which are often complicated and demanding in terms of their physical components, as also requiring mental health support to deal with frustration, pain, and tedium. Supportive psychotherapy is needed while people change their attitudes and the way they lead their lives (Anderson and Berger, 1991).

Some researchers believe that as much as 90 percent of physical problems have a psychological component (Padus, 1986). Anderson believes that all illnesses have a psychoemotional component, but they are often ignored because of the costs involved in diagnosis and treatment. Symptomatic relief is a quick fix. Anderson sees health maintenance organizations (HMOs) and preferred provider organizations (PPOs) as not helping this situation, because they are focused economically. He sees the same problems with a national health care system: Although it would be more democratic in terms of access, the quality of care would not improve. He points to the American Academy of Allergy and Immunology, the mainstream allergists' professional organization, as being one of the worst examples of mainstream medicine because it is tied to the pharmaceutical industry and deals with allergies with simplistic skin tests and drugs. As allergy is increasingly seen as a complex disorder, the Academy has spent several million dollars in the last 10 years to lobby against the development of environmental medicine. To move away from this traditional approach, Anderson believes that what is necessary is a grassroots consumer movement to apply heavy political and economic pressure for change, and the media could be an aid to this process (Anderson and Berger, 1991).

CONCLUSIONS

A common theme and point of consensus in discussing public policy and biomedical research and technology has been the importance of education and participation (Panem, 1985). Because biomedical research and technology have significant impacts on mental health and well-being, it is essential that when the impacts of research and technology are discussed the mental health effects are part of that discussion. This book has highlighted some of the potential areas in which those impacts occur. All biomedical research and technology should consider those impacts, and funding sources and regulatory processes should require such consideration. In turn, biomedical research and technology have enormous impacts on mental health policy. Those impacts should be explored carefully when mental health policy is being made, so that they are not either ignored unrealistically or focused on to the exclusion of other approaches.

References

Aarons, L. (1972). "Brain Surgery Is Tested on Three California Convicts." *Washington Post* (February 25):1.

Abel, Ernest L. and Barbara A. Dintcheff. (1986). "Effects of Prenatal Alcohol Exposure on Behavior of Aged Rats." *Drug and Alcohol Dependence* 16(4):321-330.

Abel, Ernest L. and Robert J. Sokol. (1987). "Incidence of Fetal Alcohol Syndrome and Economic Impact of FAS-Related Abnormalities." *Drug and Alcohol Dependence* 19(1):51-70.

Abraham, L. (1988). "Women Face AIDS Dilemma." *Medicine News* 3:20-24.

Ad Hoc Committee of the Harvard Medical School to Examine the Definition of Brain Death. (1968). "A Definition of Irreversible Coma." *Journal of the American Medical Association* 205:337.

Aiken, G.J.M. (1984). "Assaults on Staff in Locked Ward." *Medicine, Science, and Law* 24:199-207.

"Alcoholism." (1990). *Journal of Studies on Alcohol* 51:101-103.

Alder, E. and A.A. Templeton. (1985). "Patient Reaction to Treatment." *Lancet* 1:168.

Althende, David. (1977). "Mental Illness and the News: The Eagleton Story." *Sociology and Social Research* 61 (2):138-155.

Amaro, Mortensia, Rupert Whitaker, Gerald Coffman, and Timothy Heeren. (1990). "Acculteration and Marijuana and Cocaine Use: Findings from HHANES 1982-84." *American Public Health Journal* 80 Suppl.:54-60.

American Civil Liberties Union (ACLU) Reproductive Freedom Project. (1990, February 1). "Initial Report on RFPs South Carolina Investigation." Washington, D.C.: ACLU.

American College of Obstetricians and Gynecologists. (1987). "Patient Choice." (October): 1-55.

American Indian Policy Review Commission. (1977). *The Final Report of the American Indian Policy Review Commission.* Washington, D.C.: Government Printing Office.

American Psychiatric Association. (1978). "Electroconvulsive Therapy." Task Force Report 14. Washington, D.C.: APA.

American Psychiatric Association (1980). *Diagnostic and Statistical Manual of Mental Disorders* (DSM III) (3rd ed.). (1980). Washington, D.C.: American Psychiatric Association.

American Psychiatric Association. (1987). *Diagnostic and Statistical Manual of Mental Disorders*. 3rd ed. (revised). Washington, D.C.: APA.

American Psychological Association (1988). Amicus Brief in *Riese V. St. Mary's Hospital*, No. 5004002, Supreme Court of the State of California.

American Public Health Association (APHA). (1989). "Amici Brief." *State of Florida v. Jennifer Clarise Johnson* (Case No. E89-890 CFA, Cir. Ct. 18th Judicial Cir., Seminole Co., July 13).

American Public Health Association (APHA). (1990). "Policy Statements." *The Nation's Health* (May-June):6-7.

Anderson, Jeffery and Susan Berger. (1991). "Physical Illness and Psychological Functioning: An Interview with Jeffrey Anderson, M.D." *The California Therapist* (January/February):54-59.

Andreason, N.C., J.C. Ernhardt, V.W. Swayze, R.J. Alliger, W.T.C. Yuh, G. Cohen, and S. Ziebell (1990). "Magnetic Resonance Imaging of the Brain in Schizophrenia." *Archives of General Psychiatry* 47:35-44.

Andrews, Lori B. (1984). *New Conceptions: A Consumer's Guide to the Newest Infertility Treatments*. New York: St. Martin's Press.

Andrews, M.C. (1985). "An Analysis of the Obstetric Outcome of 25 Consecutive Pregnancies Conceived In Vitro and Resulting in 100 Deliveries." *American Journal of Obstetrics and Gynecology* 154:848-854.

Angrist, B.M. and S. Gershon. (1971). "A Pilot Study of Pathogenic Mechanisms in Amphetamine Psychosis Utilizing Differential Effects of D- and L-Amphetamine." *Pharmakopsychiatrie* 4:64-75.

Annas, George. (1986). "Checkmating the Baby Doe Regulations." *Hastings Center Report* (August):20-24.

Annas, George. (1990). "Foreclosing the Use of Force: A.C. Revised." *Hastings Center Report* 20:27-29.

"Antishyness Drug." (1988). *Prevention* (December):64.

Applebaum, Paul S. (1992). "Controlling Prescription of Benzodiazepines." *Hospital and Community Psychiatry* 43(1):12-13.

Applebaum, P.S. and T.G. Gutheil. (1980). "The Boston State Hospital Case." *American Journal of Psychiatry* 137:720-723.

Appleton, T. (1986). "Caring for the IVF Patient—Counseling Care." In S. Fishel and E.M. Symonds, eds., *In Vitro Fertilization*. Oxford: IRL Press. Pp. 161-169.

Atwood, Joan D. and Robert Chester. (1987). *Treatment Techniques for Common Mental Disorders*. Northvale, New Jersey: Jason Aronson Inc.

Austin, Debra Luccero. (1988). "Prosecution Plan Draws Fire: A Cop in the Delivery Room?" *Chico Enterprise-Record* (November 3):1A,6A.

Back, Kurt W. and Robert Snowden. (1988). "The Anonymity of the Gamete Donor." *Journal of Psychosomatic Obstetrics and Gynecology* 9(3):191-198.

Balisy, Sam S. (1987). "Maternal Substance Abuse." *Southern California Law Review* 60:1209-1238.

Banay, R.S. and L. Davidoff. (1942). "Apparent Recovery of a Sex Psychopath After Lobotomy." *Journal of Criminal Psychopathology*. 4:59-66.

Baruch, Elaine Hoffman. (1988). "A Womb of His Own." In Elaine Hoffman Baruch, Amadeo F. D'Adamo, Jr., and Joni Seagor, eds., *Embryos, Ethics, and Women's Rights*. New York: Haworth Press. Pp. 135-139.

Bateson, G. (1956). "Towards a Theory of Schizophrenia." *Behavioral Science* 1:251-264.

Bay Area Consortium of College and University Prevention Programs (BACCUPP). (1990). "Drugs." Rohnert Park, California: Sonoma State University.

Bayles, Fred. (1988). "Murder Case of Teenager Called Attention to Ritalin." *Chico Enterprise Record* (October 17):5B.

Beeson, D. and M.S. Golbus. (1985). "Decision Making: Whether or Not to Have Prenatal Diagnosis and Abortion for X-linked Conditions." *American Journal of Medical Genetics*. 20:107-114.

Bell, Cynthia J. (1986). "Adoptive Pregnancy: Legal and Social Work Issues." *Child Welfare* 65(5):421-436.

Bender, H.A. (1977). "A Geneticist's Viewpoint Towards Sterilization." *Amicus* (February):45.

Benn, P.A., L.Y.F. Hsu, A. Carlson, and H.L. Tannenbaum. (1985). "The Centralized Prenatal Genetics Screening Program of New York City." *American Journal of Medical Genetics* 20:369-384.

Bennett, A.E. (1938). "Evaluation of Artifical Fever Therapy for Neuropsychiataric Disorders." *Archives of Neurology and Psychiatry*. 40:1141-1155.

Berger, David M., Kenneth F. Doody, Abraham Eisen, and Jack Shuber. (1986). "Psychological Patterns in Donor Insemination Couples." *Canadian Journal of Psychiatry* 31(9):818-823.

Bergin, A.E. and M.J. Lambert. (1978). "The Evaluation of Therapuetic Outcome." In A.E. Bergin and S.L. Garfield, eds., *Handbook of Psychotherapy and Behavior Change*. New York. Pp. 174-185.

Bertelson, A. (1990). "Diagnosis and Classification of Mental Disorders in Relation to Molecular Research." In V. Bulyzenhnokov, Y. Christen, and L. Prilipko, eds., *Genetic Approaches in the Prevention of Mental Disorders*. New York: Springer-Verlag.

"Bill Would Set Guidelines for Surrogate Use." (1992). *Chico Enterprise-Record* (February 29):A4.

Blank, Robert H. (1986). "Emerging Notions of Women's Rights and Responsibilities during Gestation." *Journal of Legal Medicine* 7(4):441-469.

Blank, Robert H. (1988). "The Challenge of Emergent Public Policy Issues in Genetic Counseling." Susie Ball, ed., *Strategies in Genetic Counseling: The Challenge of the Future.* New York: Human Sciences Press.

Blank, Robert H. (1990). *Regulating Reproduction.* New York: Columbia University.

Bleckwenn, W.J. (1930). "Production of Sleep and Rest in Psychotic Cases." *Archives of Neurology and Psychiatry* 24:365-372.

Bloom, F.E. (1990). "Strategies for Understanding the Role of Gene Defects in the Pathogenesis of Mental Disorders." In V. Bulyzehnkov, Y. Christen, and L. Prilipko, eds., *Genetic Approaches in the Prevention of Mental Disorders.* New York: Springer-Verlag.

Blum, H.P. (1983). "Adoptive Parents: Generative Conflict." *Psychoanalytic Study of the Child* 38:141-164.

Boat, T.F., M.J. Welsh, and A.L. Beaudet. (1989). "Cystic Fibrosis." In C.F. Scriver, A.L. Beaudet, W.S. Sly, and D. Yalle, eds., *The Metabolic Basis of Inherited Disease.* Vol II. New York: McGraw-Hill. Pp. 2460-2480.

Bockoven, J.S. (1956). "Moral Treatment in American Psychiatry." *Journal of Nervous Mental Disease* 124:167-194, 292-321.

Bonner, Tom. (1990). "Marijuana's Brain 'Button' Cloned." *Idaho Free Press-Caldwell Press Tribune* (August 20):9A.

Bonnicksen, Andrea L. (1989). *In Vitro Fertilization.* New York: Columbia University Press.

Bouricius, J.K. (1989). "Negative Symptoms and Emotions in Schizophrenia." *Schizophrenia Bulletin* 15(2):201-208.

Brakel, Samuel and Ronald Rock. (1971). *The Mentally Disabled and the Law.* Chicago: University of Chicago Press.

Brand, Handre J. (1987). "Complexity of Motivation For Artificial Insemination by Donor." *Psychological Reports* 60(3):951-955.

Brand, Handre J. (1989). "The Influence of Sex Differences on the Acceptance of Infertility." *Journal of Reproductive and Infant Psychology* 7(2):129-131.

Breggin, Peter. (1983). *Psychiatric Drugs: Hazards to the Brain.* New York: Springer-Verlag.

Brill, Henry and Robert Patton. (1962). "Clinical-Statistical Analysis of Population Changes in New York State Mental Hospitals Since Introduction of Psychotropic Drugs." *American Journal of Psychiatry* (July):33-38.

Brinich, P. (1980). "Potential Effects of Adoption on the Self and Object Relationships." *Psychoanalytic Study of the Child* 35:107-134.

"British Tell Hospital to Hold Surrogate Mother's Child." (1985). *The*

Bakersfield Californian (January 6):A1.

Brody, J.E. (1982). "Mother's Effect on Fetus Viewed." *New York Times* (February 16):8

Brown, L. and J. Brown, with S. Freeman. (1979). *Our Miracle Called Louise*. London: Paddington Press.

Brown, Phil. (1984). "The Right to Refuse Treatment and the Movement for Mental Health Reform." *Journal of Health Politics, Policy and Law* 9(2):291-313.

Bukstein, O.G., D.A. Brent, and Y. Kaminier. (1989). "Comorbidity of Substance Abuse and Other Psychiatric Disorders in Adolescents." *American Journal of Psychiatry* 146:1131-1141.

Bulyzehnkov, V., Y. Christen, and L. Prilipko, eds. (1990). *Genetic Approaches in the Prevention of Mental Disorders*. New York: Springer-Verlag.

Burton, Barbara A. (1985). "Contentious Issues of Infertility Therapy: A Consumer's View." Unpublished paper presented at the Australian Family Planning Conference (March).

Butler, J.M. and L.N. Rice. (1963). "Audience, Self-Actualization, and Drive Theory." In J.M. Wepman and R.W. Heine, eds., *Concepts of Personality*. Chicago: Aldine Atherton.

Callan, Victor J. and John F. Hennessey. (1988). "The Psychological Adjustment of Women Experiencing Infertility." *British Journal of Medical Psychology* 81(2):137-140.

Calloway, S.P., R.J. Dolan, R.J. Jacoby, and R. Levy. (1981). "ECT and Cerebral Atrophy: A Computed Tomographic Study." *Acta Psychiatrica Scandinavia* 64:442-445.

Castaneda, D. and R. Sommer. (1989). "Mental Health Professionals' Attitudes Toward the Family's Role in Care of the Mentally Ill." *Hospital and Community Psychiatry* 40:1195-1197.

"Castration Deal Withdrawn." (1992). *Chico Enterprise Record* (March 16):6A.

Centers for Disease Control. (1988). *Congenital Malformations Surveillance Report: January 1982-December 1985*. Atlanta: Department of Health and Human Services.

Cerletti, U. (1956). "Electroshock Therapy." In F. Martij-Ibanez, A.A. Sackler, M.D. Sackler, and R.R. Sackler, eds., *The Psychodynamic Therapies in Psychiatry*. New York: Hoeber-Harper Pp. 258-270.

Chasnoff, Ira, Harvey J. Landress, and Mark E. Barrett. (1990). "The Prevalence of Illicit-Drug or Alcohol Use During Pregnancy and Discrepancies in Mandatory Reporting in Pinellas County, Florida." *The New England Journal of Medicine* 3222(17):1202-1206.

Chatham, Patricia M. (1989). *Treatment of the Borderline Personality*.

Northvale, New Jersey: Jason Aronson Inc.

Chavkin, Wendy. (1990). "Drug Addiction and Pregnancy: Policy Crossroads." *American Journal of Public Health* 80(4):483-487.

Chavkin, Wendy, Cynthia R. Driver, and Pat Forman. (1989). "The Crisis in New York City's Perinatal Services." *New York State Journal of Medicine* 12:658-663.

Children's Defense Fund. (1977). *EPSDT: Does It Spell Health Care for Poor Children?* Washington, D.C.: Washington Research Project.

Chorover, Stephen L. (1973). "Big Brother and Psychotechnology." *Psychology Today* 7:43-54.

Chorover, Stephen L. (1974). "Psychosurgery: A Neuropsychological Perspective." *Boston University Law Review.* 54:231-248.

Clark, B.A., J.M. Bissonnette, S.B. Olsen, and R.E. Maginis. (1989). "Pregnancy Loss in a Small Chronic Villus Sampling Services." *American Journal of Obstetrics and Gynecology* 161(2):301-302.

Clark, G.H. and J.V. Vaccaro. (1987). "Burnout Among CMHC Psychiatrists and the Struggle to Survive." *Hospital and Community Psychiatry* 34:729-733.

Clayman, Charles B. (1988). *The American Medical Association Guide to Prescription and Over-the-Counter Drugs.* New York: Random House.

Clerget-Darpoux, F. (1990). "Genetic Epidemiology Strategies in Psychiatric Disease." In V. Bulyzehnkov, Y. Christen, and L. Prilipko, eds., *Genetic Approaches in the Prevention of Mental Disorders.* New York: Springer-Verlag.

Clewell, William H., M.L. Johnson, P.R. Meir, J.B. Newkirk; S.L. Zide; R. W. Hendee, W.A. Bowles, F. Hecht, D. O'Keefe, G.P. Henry, and R.M. Shikes (1982). "A Surgical Approach to the Treatment of Fetal Hydrocephalus." *New England Journal of Medicine* 306:1320-1325.

Clifton, Laurie. (1989). "Senior News: Medicating the Elderly Studied." *Chico Enterprise-Record* (March 3):1B.

Coffey, C. Edward, Richard D. Weiner, William Djang, Gary Figiel, Sheryl A.R. Soady, Linda Patterson, Peter D. Holdt, Charles E. Pritzer, and William E. Wilkinson. (1991). "Brain Anatomic Effects of Electroconvulsive Therapy: A Prospective Magnetic Resonance Imaging Study." *Archives of General Psychiatry* 48:1013-1021.

Cohen-Overbeek, T.E., W.C. Hop, M.D. Ouden, L. Pypers, M.G.J. Johoda, and J.W. Wladimiroff. (1990). "Spontaneous Abortion Rate and Advanced Maternal Age." *Lancet* 336:27-29.

Cole, Helene. (1990). "Chorionic Villus Sampling: A Resassessment." *Journal of the American Medical Association* 263(2):305-306.

Cole, J.O. (1964). "Phenothiazine Treatment in Acute Schizophrenia." *Archives of General Psychiatry* 10:246-261.

Cole, Richard W. (1979). "Rogers v. Okin: A Lawsuit to Guarantee Patients' Right to Refuse Anti-Psychotic Medication." *American Journal of Forensic Psychiatry* (July):131-135.

Coleman, L. (1978). "Problem Kids and Preventative Medicine: The Making of an Odd Couple." *American Journal of Orthopsychiatry* 48(1):56-70.

Cook, Rachel, S. Golombok, B. Mason, and J. Parsons. (1989). "Emotional, Marital and Sexual Functioning in Patients Embarking Upon IVF and AID Treatment for Infertility." *Special Issue: Psychology and Infertility* 7(2):87-93.

Coppen, A. (1971). "Indoleamines and Affective Disorders." *Journal of Psychiatric Research* 9:163-169.

Corea, Gena. (1985). *The Mother Machine*. New York: Harper & Row.

Corea, Gena. (1988). "What the King Can Not See." In Elaine Hoffman Baruch, Amadeo F. D'Adamo, Jr., and Joni Seager, eds., *Embryos, Ethics, and Women's Rights*. New York: Haworth Press. Pp. 77-93.

Corkin, S. (1980). "A Prospective Study of Cingulotomy." In E. Valenstein, ed., *The Psychosurgery Debate*. San Francisco: W.H. Freeman. Pp. 164-204.

Cotton, H.A. (1922). "The Etiology and Treatment of the So-Called Functional Psychoses." *American Journal of Psychiatry*. 2:157-210.

Cournos, Francine, Karen McKinnan, and Carole Adams. (1988). "A Comparison of Clinical and Judicial Procedures for Reviewing Requests for Involuntary Medication in New York." *Hospital and Community Psychiatry* 39(8):851-855.

"Court Invalidates Surrogate Contract, Upholds Award." (1988). *Chico Enterprise Record* (February 3):6A.

Cramer, D.W., A.M. Walker, and I. Schiff (1979). "Statistical Methods in Evaluating the Outcome of Infertility Therapy." *Fertility and Sterility* 21:80-86.

Creasy, R.K. (1984). "Preterm Labor and Delivery." In R.K. Creasy and R. Resnik, eds., *Maternal and Fetal Medicine: Principles and Practice*. Philadelphia: W.B. Saunders Co. Pp. 415-443.

Crowe, C. (1985). "Women Want It: In Vitro Fertilization and Women's Motivations for Participation." *Women's Studies International Forum* 8:57-62.

Crowne, Sidney. (1987). "Assessment of Psychotherapy: What Happens to Untreated Patients?" In Richard L. Gregory, ed., *The Oxford Companion to THE MIND*. New York: Oxford University Press. Pp. 661-663.

Dackis, Charles A. and Mark S. Gold. (1990). "Medical, Endocrinological, and Pharmacological Aspects of Cocaine Addiction." In Nora D. Volkow and Alan C. Swann, eds., *Cocaine in the Brain*. New Brunswick, New Jersey: Rutgers University Press.

D'Adamo, Amadeo F., Jr. (1988). "Reproductive Technologies: The Two Sides of the Glass Jar." In Elaine Hoffman Baruch, Amadeo F. D'Adamo, Jr., and Joni Seager, eds., *Embryos, Ethics, and Women's Rights*. New York: Haworth Press. Pp. 9-30.

Dam, A.M. and M. Dam. (1986). "Quantitative Neuropathology in Electrically Induced Generalized Convulsions." *Convulsive Therapy* 2:77-89.

Daniels, Ken R. (1989). "Semen Donors: Their Motivations and Attitudes to Their Off-Spring." *Psychology and Infertility* 7(2):121-127.

DeClue, Terry J., Jim Davis, Dawn M. Schocken, Ruth Kangas, and Steve A. Benford. (1991). "Erum Lipid Concentrations in Subjects with Pheynylketonuria and Their Families." *American Journal of Diseases of Children* 145:1266-1268.

Demyttenaere, Koen, Phillipe Knoninck, Piet Nijs, and Omer Steeno. (1988). "Anxiety and Conception Rate in Donor Insemination." *Journal of Psychosomatic Obstetrics and Gynaecology* 8(3):175-181.

Dennerstein, Lorraine, and Carol Morse. (1988). "A Review of Psychological and Social Aspects of In Vitro Fertilization." *Journal of Psychosomatic Obstetrics and Gynecology* 9(3):159-170.

Department of Health, Education, and Welfare. (1971). *The Institutional Guide to DHEW Policy on Protection of Human Subjects*. Washington, D.C.: Government Printing Office.

DeRisi, William and William Vega. (1983). "The Impact of Deinstitutionalization on California's State Hospital Population." *Hospital and Community Psychiatry* 34(2):140-145.

Deutsch, A. (1949). *The Shame of the States*. New York: Harcourt, Brace.

Dickersin, K. (1990). "The Existence of Publication Bias and Risk Factors for Its Occurrence." *Journal of the American Medical Association*. 263:1385-1389.

Dill, Ann and David Rochefort. (1989). "Coordination, Continuity and Centralized Control: A Policy Perspective on Service Strategies for the Chronic Mentally Ill." *Journal of Social Issues* 45(3):145-159.

"Discovery of Schizophrenia Key Could Lead to Advances."(1988). *Chico Enterprise-Record* (December 25):9C.

Doll, W. (1976). "Family Coping with the Mentally Ill." *Hospital and Community Psychiatry* 27(3):183-185.

Dollard, J. and N.E. Miller. (1950). *Personality and Psychotherapy*. New York: McGraw-Hill.

Domino, E.F. (1978). "Pharmacological Aspects of Psychotherapeutics." In Norman Rosenzweig and Hilda Griscom, eds., *Psychopharmacology and Psychotherapy: Synthesis or Antithesis?* New York: Human Services Press.

Dorris, Michael. (1989). *The Broken Cord*. New York: Harper Perennial.

Drinkwater, J. and G.H. Gudjonsson. (1989). "The Nature of Violence in

Psychiatric Hospitals." In K. Howells and C.R. Hollin, eds., *Clinical Approaches to Violence*. Chichester, England: Wiley.

Dugdale, R.L. (1908). *The Jukes*. New York: Putnam.

Dullea, Georgia. (1981). "Motherhood Without the Marriage." *The Bakersfield Californian* (December 3):C1, C6.

Eaton, W.W. (1980). *The Sociology of Mental Disorders*. New York: Praeger.

Edelman, Robert J., Kevin J. Connolly, and Jill Robson. (1989). "The Impact of Infertility and Infertility Investigation." *Journal of Reproductive and Infant Psychology* 7(2):113-119.

Edwards, R.G. and J.M. Purdy, eds. (1982). *Human Conception In Vitro: Proceedings of the First Barn Hall Meeting*. New York: Academic Press.

Egeland, B. (1979). "An at Risk Approach to the Study of Child Abusers." *American Journal of Orthopychiatry* 4:48-50.

Elkins, T.E., T.G. Stoval, S. Wilroy, and J.V. Dacus. (1986). "Attitudes of Mothers of Children with Down Syndrome Concerning Amniocentesis, Abortion, and Prenatal Genetic Counseling Techniques." *Obstetrics and Gynecology* 68:181-184.

Ellenberger, Henri F. (1970). *The Discovery of the Unconscious*. New York: Basic Books.

Erickson, Deborah. (1992). "Hacking the Genome." *Scientific American* 266(4):128-133, 136-137.

Erikson, Erik. (1959). *Identity and the Life Cycle*. New York: International Universities Press.

Escalona, S.K. (1974). "Intervention Programs for Children at Psychiatric Risk: The Contribution of Child Psychiatry and Developmental Theory." In E.J. Anthony and C. Koupernik, eds., *The Child in His Family: Children at Psychiatric Risk*. New York: John Wiley & Sons.

Espinoza, M.I. and J.T. Parer. (1991). "Mechanisms of Asphyxial Brain Damage, and Possible Pharmacologic Interventions, in the Fetus." *American Journal of Obstetrics and Gynecology* 164:1582-1591.

Evans, Daryl Paul. (1983). *The Lives of Mentally Retarded People*. Boulder, Colorado: Westview Press.

Eysenck, H.J. (1952). "The Effects of Psychotherapy: An Evaluation." *Journal of Consulting Psychology*. 16:319-324.

Faith, Gilroy and Roberta Steinbacher. (1983). "Preselection of Children's Sex: Technology Utilization v. Feminism." *Psychological Reports* 53(2): 671-676.

Farrall, M., H.Y. Law, and C.H. Rodeck. (1986). "First Trimester Prenatal Diagnosis of Cystic Fibrosis with Linked DNA Probes." *Lancet* 1:1402-1404.

Ferster, E. (1966). "Eliminating the Unfit: Is Sterilization the Answer?" *Ohio State Law Journal* 27:591-597.

"Fetus Operated on Outside of Womb." (1981). *The Bakersfield Californian* (November 16):A3.

Field, Martha A. (1989). "Controlling the Woman to Protect the Fetus." *Law Medicine and Health Care* 17(2):114-129.

Finch, Ellen S. (1985). "Deinstitutionalization: Mental Health and Mental Retardation Services." *Psychosocial Rehabilitation Journal* VIII (3):36-48.

Fink, M. (1984). "Meduna and the Origins of Convulsive Therapy." *American Journal of Psychiatry* 141:1034-1041.

Finnamore, Eric P. (1981). *"Jefferson V. Griffin Spaulding County Hospital Authority."* American Journal of Law and Medicine 9(1):83-101.

Fishel, S.B., R.G. Edwards, J.M. Purdy, P.C. Steptoe, J. Webster, E. Walters, J. Cohen, C. Fehilly, J. Hewitt, and G. Rowland. (1985). "Implantation, Abortion, and Birth after In Vitro Fertilization Using the Natural Menstrual Cycle or Follicular Stimulation with Clomiphene Citrate and Human Menopausal Gonadotrophin." *Journal of In Vitro Fertilization and Embryo Transfer* 2:123-131.

Fisher, Seymour and Roger Greenberg. (1985). *The Scientific Credibility of Freud's Theories and Therapy.* New York: Basic Books.

Fletcher, John C. (1983). "Emerging Ethical Issues in Fetal Therapy." In Kare Berg and Knut E. Tranoy, eds., *Research Ethics*. New York: Alan R. Liss. Pp 293-318.

Foucault, M. (1973). *Madness and Civilization.* New York: Random House.

Fox, W. (1978). *So Far Disordered in Mind: Insanity in California 1870-1930.* Berkeley: University of California.

France, R.D., K.R. Krishnan, J.L. Houpt, and A.A. Maltbie. (1984). "Differentitation of Depression from Chronic Pain with the Dexamethasone Suppression Test and DSM-III." *American Journal of Psychiatry* 141:1577-1579.

Francell, C.B., V. Conn, and D.P. Gray. (1988). "Families' Perceptions of Burden of Care for Chronic Mentally Ill Relatives." *Hospital and Community Psychiatry* 39:1296-1300.

Frank, J.D. (1973). *Persuasion and Healing: A Comparative Study of Psychotherapy.* Baltimore: Johns Hopkins Press.

Franklin, Deborah. (1991). "The Puzzle of Addiction: Who's Vulnerable and Why?" *The Washington Post* (March 26): 12-15.

Franks, P.D. (1981). "Psychological Evaluation of Surrogate Mother Programs." *American Journal of Psychiatry* 138:1378-1379.

Frazier, Shervert H. and Delores L. Parron. (1987). "The Federal Mental Health Agenda." In Leonard J. Duhl and Nicholas A. Cummings, eds., *The Future of Mental Health Services: Coping with Crisis*. New York: Springer-Verlago. Pp. 29-46.

Freedman, D. (1984). "Psychiatric Epidemiology Costs." *Archives of General*

Psychiatry 41:913-933.

Freeman, E.W., A.S. Boxer, K. Rickels, R. Tureck, and L. Mastroianni. (1985). "Psychological Evaluation and Support in a Program of In Vitro Fertilization and Embryo Transfer." *Fertility and Sterility* 43:48-53.

Freeman, John and K.B. Nelson. (1988). "Intrapartum Asphixia and Cerebral Palsy." *Pediatrics* 82(2):240-249.

Freeman, Walter. (1948). "Transorbital Lobotomy." *Lancet* 2:371-373.

Freeman, Walter and J.W. Watts. (1942). *Psychosurgery: Intelligence, Emotion, and Social Behavior Following Prefrontal Lobotomy for Mental Disorders.* Springfield, Illinois: Charles C. Crowne.

Freeman, Walter and J.W. Watts. (1950) *Psychosurgery: In Treatment of Mental Disorders and Intractable Pain.* Springfield, Illinois: Charles C. Crowne.

Freud, Sigmund. (1905). "Three Essays on the Theory of Sexuality." *Standard Edition.* Vol. 7. London: Hogarth Press.

Freud, Sigmund. (1923). "Two Encyclopedia Articles." *Standard Edition.* Vol. 18. London: Hogarth Press.

Friedlander, J.W. and R.S. Banay. (1948). "Psychosis Following Lobotomy in a Case of Sexual Psychopathy." *Archives of Neurology and Psychiatry* 59:302-321.

Friend, Tim. (1988). "Asphyxia Lawsuits May Be Unjustified." *USA Today* (August 30):D-1.

Fritz, Gregory K., Judith Williams, and Michael Amylon. (1989). "After Treatment Ends: Psychological Squellae in Pediatric Cancer Survivors." *American Journal of Orthopsychiatry* 58(4):552-561.

Fromm-Reichmann, F. (1948). "Notes on the Development of Treatment of Schizophrenics by Psychoanalytic Psychotherapy." *Psychiatry* 11:263-273.

Fuchs, Victor R. and Leslie Perrault. (1986). "Expenditures for Reproduction-Related Health Care." *Journal of the American Medical Association* 255:76-81.

Gadow, Kenneth D. and Alan G. Poling. (1988). *Pharmacotherapy and Mental Retardation.* New York: Taylor and Francis.

Gawin, F.H. (1988). "Chronic Neuropharmacology of Cocaine." *Journal of Clinical Psychiatry* 49(Feb. Suppl.):11-16.

Gawin, F.H. and E. Ellinwood. (1988). "Cocaine and Other Stimulants." *New England Journal of Medicine* 318:1173-1182.

Gay, Peter. (1988). *Freud: A Life for Our Time.* New York: W.W. Norton & Co.

Gearheart, B.R. and F.W. Litton. (1977). *The Trainable Retarded: A Foundations Approach.* St. Louis: C.V. Mosby.

Ghanta, Vithal K., Raymond Hiramoto, H. Brent Solvason, and N. Herbert Spector. (1987). "Influence of Conditioned Natural Immunity on Tumor

Growth." *Annals of the New York Academy of Sciences* 1946:637-646.

Gibbons, R.D., J.M. Davis, and D.R. Hedeker. (1990). "A Comment on the Selection of 'Health Controls' for Psychiatric Experiments." *Archives of General Psychiatry* 47:785-786.

Gilroy, Faith and Roberta Steinbacher. (1983). "Preselection of Child's Sex." *Psychological Reports* 53(2):671-676.

Given, J.E., G.S. Jones, and D.L. McMillen. (1985). "A Comparison of Personality Characteristics between In Vitro Fertilization Patients and Other Infertile Patients." *Journal of In Vitro Fertilization and Embryo Transfer* 2:49-54.

Glass, R.H. (1985). "Infertility." In S.S.C. Yen and R.B. Jaffe, eds., *Reproductive Endocrinology*. Philadelphia: W.B. Saunders. Pp. 575-576.

Glasser, William. (1981). *Stations of the Mind*. New York: Harper & Row.

Goddard, H.H. (1912). *The Kallikak Family: A Study in the Heredity of Feeble-mindedness*. New York: Macmillan.

Goffman, Erving. (1961). *Asylums*. New York: Doubleday Anchor.

Golbus, M.S., W.D. Loughman, C.J. Epstein, G. Halbasch, J.D. Stephens, and B.D. Hall. (1979). "Prenatal Diagnosis in 3,000 Amniocenteses." *New England Journal of Medicine* 300:157-163.

Goldman, H.H. (1982). "Mental Illness and Family Burden." *Hospital and Community Psychiatry* 33:557-560.

Goldstein, K. (1934). *The Organism*. Boston: Beacon Press.

Goldstein, M.J. (1988). "The Family and Psychopathology." *Annual Review of Psychology* 4:138-142.

Gore, Albert. (1985). "A Congressional Perspective." In Sandra Panem, ed., *Biotechnology: Implications for Public Policy*. Washington, D.C.: Brookings.

Gottlieb, Jacques S. and Charles E. Frohman. (1978). "Certain Biological Approaches to the Understanding of Schizophrenia." In Norman Rosenzweig and Hilda Griscom, eds., *Psychopharmacology and Psychotherapy: Synthesis or Antithesis?* New York: Human Services Press.

Graedon, Joe and Theresa Graedon. (1988). *50+: The Graedons' People's Pharmacy for Older Adults*. New York: Bantam Books.

Greenfield, Dorothy, H. DeCherney, and Michael P. Diamond. (1988). "Grief Reactions Following In-Vitro Fertilization. *Journal of Psychosomatic Obstretics and Gynaecology* 8(3):169-174.

Greenspan, S.I. (1981). *Psychopathology and Adaption in Infancy and Early Childhood*. New York: International Universities Press.

Greil, Arthur L. (1991). *Not Yet Pregnant: Infertile Couples in Contemporary America*. New Brunswick, New Jersey: Rutgers University Press.

Greil, Arthur L., T. A. Leitko, and K.L. Porter. (1988). "Infertility: His and Hers." *Gender and Society* 2:172-199.

Grinker, R.R. and B. Werble. (1974). "Mentally Healthy Young Men (Homoclites) 14 Year Later." *Archives of General Psychiatry* 30:701-704.

Grob, Gerald N. (1983). *Mental Illness and American Society, 1875-1940*. Princeton: Princeton University Press.

Grob, Gerald N. (1987). "The Forging of Mental Health Policy in America: World War II to New Frontier." *Journal of The History of Medicine and the Allied Sciences* 42(4):410-446.

Grobstein, Clifford. (1988). *Science and the Unborn*. New York: Basic Books, Inc.

Grobstein, Clifford, M. Flower, and J. Medelhoff. (1983). "External Human Fetilization: An Evaluation of Policy." *Science* 222:127-133.

Grossman, H.J. ed. (1973). *Manual for Terminology and Classification in Mental Retardation*. Washington, D.C.: American Association for Mental Deficiency.

Grossman, H.J. (1983). *Classification in Mental Retardation*. Washington, D.C.: American Association on Mental Deficiency.

Guendelman, Sylvia, Jeffrey B. Gould, Mark Hudes, and Brenda Esenaji. (1990). "Generational Differences in Perinatal Health Among the Mexican American Population: Findings from HHANES 1982-1984." *American Journal of Public Health* 80 Suppl.:61-65.

Gurling, H. (1986). "Candidate Genes and Favoured Loci: Strategies for Molecular Genetic Research into Schizophrenia, Manic Depression, Autism, Alcoholism and Alzheimer's Disease." *Psychiatric Development* 4:289-309.

Hafner, H. (1986). "The Risk of Violence in Psychotics." *Integrative Psychiatry* 4:138-142.

Halbreich, U., Y. Bakhai, K.B. Bacon, S. Goldstein, G.M. Asnis, J. Endicott, and J. Lesser. (1989). "The Normalcy of Self-proclaimed 'Normal Volunteers.'" *American Journal of Psychiatry* 146:1052-1055.

Halford, W. Kim, Robert D. Schweitzer, and Frank N. Varghese. (1991). "Effects of Family Environment on Negative Symptoms and Quality of Life of Psychotic Patients." *Hospital and Community Psychiatry* 42(12):1241-1247.

Hall, R.C.W. and J.R. Joffe. (1972). "Aberrant Response to Diazepam: A New Syndrome." *American Journal of Psychiatry* 129:738-742.

Halliday, A.M. and A.A. Mason. (1964). "The Effect of Hypnotic Anaethesia on Cortical Responses." *Journal of Neurology, Neurosurgery, and Psychology* 27:300-305.

Haney, Daniel Q. (1988). "Drug Helps 80 Percent of ADD Kids, But No One Knows Why." *Chico Enterprise-Record* (October 17):5B.

Harris, M. (1986). "Caring for the IVF Patient—Nursing Care." In S. Fishel and E.M. Symonds, eds., *In Vitro Fertilization*. Oxford: IRL Press. Pp.

155-160.

Harrison, Michael, R.A. Filly, J.T. Parer, M.J. Faer, J.B. Jacobson, and A.A. DeLorimier (1981). "Management of the Fetus with a Urinary Tract Malformation." *Journal of the American Medical Association* 246(6):635-639.

Haseltine, F.P., C. Mazure, W. De L'Aune, D. Greenfield, N. Laufer, B. Tarlalzis, M.L. Polan, E.E. Jones, R. Graebe, and F. Nero (1985). "Psychological Interviews in Screening Couples Undergoing *In Vitro* Fertilization." *Annals of the New York Academy of Sciences* 442:504-522.

Haugland, Gary, Carole Siegel, Mary Jane Alexander, and Marc Galanter. (1991). "A Survey of Hospitals in New York State Treating Psychiatric Patients with Chemical Abuse Disorders." *Hospital and Community Psychiatry* 42(12):1215-1220.

Haverkamp, A. and M. Orleans. (1982). "An Assessment of Electronic Fetal Monitoring." *Women and Health* 7(3,4):115-134.

Health and Welfare Canada. (1988). *Mental Health for Canadians*. Ottawa: Minister of Supply and Services.

"Health: Upjohn Defends Its Besieged Sleeping Pill." (1991). *Chico Enterprise-Record* (December 22):8E.

Heber, R.F. (1961). "A Manual on Terminology and Classification in Mental Retardation." *American Journal of Mental Deficiency* 66 (Monograph Suppl.):1-35.

Henefin, Mary Sue. (1988). "Introduction: Women's Health and the New Reproductive Technology." In Elaine Hoffman Baruch, Amadeo F. D'Adamo, Jr., and Joni Seager, eds., *Embryos, Ethics and Women's Rights*. New York: Haworth Press. Pp. 1-7.

Heyman, A., W.E. Wilkinson, and B.J. Hurwith. (1983). "Alzheimer's Disease: Genetic Aspects and Associated Clinical Disorders." *Annotated Neurology* 14:507-515.

Hilgard, E.R. (1965). *Hypnotic Susceptibility*. New York:.

Hobbs, N. (1975). *The Futures of Children*. San Francisco: Jossey-Bass.

Hobson, J. Allan. (1988). *The Dreaming Brain*. New York: Basic Books.

Hoffer, A. (1957). "Epinephrine Derivatives as Potential Schizophrenic Factors." *Journal of Clinical Experimental Psychopathology* 18:27-31.

Hoge, Steven, P.S. Appelbaum, T. Lawlor, J.C. Beck, R. Litman, A. Greer, T.G. Gutheil, and E. Kaplan. (1990). "A Prospective, Multi-Center Study of Patients' Refusal of Antipsychotic Medication." *Archives of General Psychiatry* 47(10):949-956.

Hollinger, J. (1985). "From Coitus to Commerce: Legal and Social Consequences of Noncoital Reproduction." *Journal of Law Reform* 18:865-872.

Hollister, Leo. (1978). "Psychopharmacology." In John C. Shershow, ed.,

Schizophrenia: Science and Practice. Cambridge: Harvard University Press.

Howitz, Nancy. (1989). "The Psychological Aspects of In-Vitro Fertilization." *Pre and Peri-Natal Psychology Journal* 4(1):43-50.

Hubbard, Ruth. (1988). "Eugenics New Tools, Old Ideas." In Elaine Hoffman Baruch, Amadeo F. D'Adamo, Jr., and Joni Seger, eds., *Embryos, Ethics, and Women's Rights.* New York: Haworth Press. Pp. 225-235.

Huber, P.W. (1987). "Biotechnology and the Regulation Hydra." *Technology Review* (November/December):57-65.

Hull, Clark L. (1933). *Hypnosis and Suggestibility: An Experimental Approach.* New York: Irvington.

Humphrey, Michael and Heather Humphrey. (1987). "Marital Relationships in Couples Seeking Donor Insemination." *Journal of Biosocial Science* 19(2):209-219.

Huxley, Aldous. (1963). *The Doors of Perception.* New York: Harper & Row.

"Infertility Doctor Accused of Fraud." (1992). *Chico Enterprise-Record* (February 10):6A.

Isaac, Rael Jean and Virginia C. Armat. (1990). *Madness in the Streets.* New York: The Free Press.

Jacobsen, Frederick M., Thomas A. Wehr, David A. Sack, Steven P. James, and Norman E. Rosenthal. (1987). "Seasonal Affective Disorder: A Review of the Syndrome and Its Public Health Implications." *American Journal of Public Health* 77(1):57-60.

Jain, L., C. Ferre, D. Vidyasagar, S. Nath, and D. Sheftel. (1991). "Cardiopulmonary Resuscitation of Apparently Stillborn Infants: Survival and Long-term Outcome." *Journal of Pediatrics* 118:778-782.

Janofsky, Jeffrey S., Richard J. McCarthy, and Marshal F. Folstein. (1992). "The Hopkins Competency Assessment Test: A Brief Method for Evaluating Patients' Capacity to Give Informed Consent." *Hospital and Community Psychiatry* 43(2):132-136,

Johnson, Dawn. (1986). "Creation of Fetal Rights." *The Yale Law Journal* 95:599-625.

Johnson, Myron A., Glenn E. Palomaki, and James E. Haddow. (1990). "Maternal Serum-a-Fetoprotein Levels in Pregnancies Among Black and White Women with Fetal Open Spina Bifida." *American Journal of Obstetrics and Gynecology* 162:328-331.

Johnston, Marie, Robert Shaw, and David Bird. (1987). "Test-tube Baby Procedures: Stress and Judgments Under Uncertainty." *Psychology and Health* 1(1):25-38.

Johnston, W.I.H., K. Oke, A. Speirs, G.A. Clarke, J. McBain, C. Bayly, J. Hunt, and G.N. Clarke. (1985). "Patient Selection For In Vitro Fertilization." *Annals of the New York Academy of Sciences* 442:523-532.

Joint Commission on Mental Illness and Health. (1961). *Action for Mental*

Health. New York: Basic Books.

Jones, B. (1990). "Schizophrenia Treatment Strategies in the 90s: A New Level of Sophisitcation of Pharmacotherapy." Unpublished paper presented at International Conference Schizophrenia 1990, Vancouver, B.C. (July).

Kanner, L. (1964). *A History of the Care and Study of the Mentally Retarded*. Springfield, Illinois: Charles C. Thomas.

Kaplan, Mark S. and Gary Marks. (1990). "Adverse Effects of Acculteration." *Social Science and Medicine* 31(2):1313-1319.

Kaufman, Edward and Jill P. McNaul. (1992). "Recent Developments in Understanding and Treating Drug Abuse and Dependence." *Hospital and Community Psychiatry* 43(3):223-236.

Kay, Stanley R., Lewis A. Opler, and Abraham Fiszbein. (1990). *Positive and Negative Syndrome Scale (PANSS)*. Toronto: Multi-Health Systems.

Kemeter, P., A. Eder, and M. Springer-Kremser. (1985). "Psychosocial Testing and Pretreatment of Women for In Vitro Fertilization." *Annals of the New York Academy of Sciences* 442:490-503.

Kemeter, P. (1988). "Studies on Psychosomatic Implications of Identity." *Human Reproduction* 3(3): 341-352.

Kemp, Donna R. (1978, September). *Civil Liberties of Institutionalized Mentally Retarded: Development and Implementation*. Unpublished Doctoral Dissertation. Moscow, Idaho: University of Idaho.

Kemp, Donna R. (1981, June). "Implementation of Rights in Institutions for Mentally Retarded." Published Occasional Papers. Waukegan, Illinois: National Association for Superindentents of Public Residential Facilities for the Mentally Retarded.

Kemp, Donna R. (1991). "Mental Health Crisis in California." *Journal of Mental Health Administration* 18(2):154-164.

Kemp, Donna R. (1992). "Comparative Mental Health Policy: Australia, New Zealand, and the U.S." *New England Journal of Human Services* X(4):13-23.

Kernberg, O.F. (1975). *Borderline Condition and Pathological Narcissism*. New York: Jason Aronson.

Kerr, Ann, Ruth Thompson, and Joel Jeffries. (1988). "Schizophrenia: *A Guide for Patients and Families*." Toronto: Clarke Institute of Psychiatry.

Kesey, Ken. (1975). *One Flew Over the Cuckoo's Nest*. New York: Viking.

Kety, Seymour S. (1978). "Current Research on the Biological Components of Mental Illness." In Norman Rosenzweig and Hilda Griscom, eds., *Psychopharmacology and Psychotherapy: Synthesis or Antithesis?* New York: Human Sciences Press.

Kety, Seymour S., R.B. Woodford, M.H. Harmel, F.A. Freyhan, K.E. Appel, and C.F. Schmidt. (1948). "Cerebral Blood Flow and Metabolism in Schizophrenia. The Effects of Barbiturate Semi-narcosis, Insulin Coma and

Electroshock." *American Journal of Psychiatry* 104:765-770.

Keye, William. (1982). "Strategy for Avoiding Iatrogenic Infertility." *Contemporary Obstetrics and Gynaecology* 19:185-195.

Khoury, Muin J. and Anne B. McClearn. (1990). Centers for Disease Control, unpublished data. Cited in Fatima Mili, Larry D. Edmonds, Muin J. Khoury, and Anne B. McClearn, 1991. "Prevalence of Birth Defects Among Low-Birth-Weight Infants." *American Journal of Diseases of Children*. 145:1313-1318.

Khoury, Muin J., J.D. Erickson, J.F. Cordero, and B.J. McCarthy. (1988). "Congenital Malformations and Intrauterine Growth Retardation." *Pediatrics* 82:83-90.

Kiely, John L. and Mervyn Susser. (1992). "Preterm Birth, Intrauterine Growth Retardation, and Perinatal Mortality." *American Journal of Public Health* 82(3):343-345.

Kiesler, C.A. and A.E. Sibulkin. (1987). *Mental Hospitalization: Myths and Facts About a National Crisis*. Beverly Hills: Sage.

Kiesler, Charles A. (1980). "Mental Health Policy as a Field of Inquiry for Psychology." *American Psychologist* 35:1066-1080.

Kiesler, Charles A. (1982). "Mental Hospitals and Alternative Care: Noninstitutionalization as Potential Public Policy for Mental Patients." *American Psychologist* 37:349-360.

Kiloh, L.G. (1982). "Electroconvulsive Therapy." In E.S. Paykel, ed., *Handbook of Affective Disorders*. New York: Guildford Press. Pp. 262-275.

Kirk, Stuart and Herb Kutchins. (1992). *The Selling of DSM: The Rhetoric of Science in Psychiatry*. Hawthorne, New York: Aldine de Gruyter.

Klasson, Elayne M. (1989). "A Model of the Occupational Therapist as Case Manager: Two Case Studies of Chronic Schizophrenic Patients Living in the Community." *Occupational Therapy in Mental Health* 9(1):63-90.

Kleinig, John. (1985). *Ethical Issues in Psychosurgery*. London: George Allen & Unwin.

Kolb, L. and V. Vogel. (1942). "The Use of Shock Therapy in 305 Mental Hospitals." *American Journal of Psychiatry* 99:90-100.

Kolder, Veronika, Janet Gallagher, and Michael T. Parsons. (1987). "Court Ordered Obstetrical Interventions." *The New England Journal of Medicine* 316:1192-1196.

Kopeloff, N. and G.H. Kirby. (1923). "Focal Infection and Mental Disease." *American Journal of Psychiatry* 3:149-197.

Koren, Gideon, K. Grahm, M. Shear, and T. Einarson (1989). "Bias Against the Null Hypothesis: The Reproductive Hazards of Cocaine." *Lancet* 2:1440-1442.

Koren, Gideon and Naomi Klein. (1991). "Bias Against Negative Studies in

Newspaper Reports of Medical Research." *The Journal of the American Medical Association* 266(13):1824-1826.

Kramer, M.S. (1987). "Determinants of Low Birth Weight: Methodological Assessment and Meta-analysis." *Bulletin of the World Health Organization* 65:663-737.

Krishef, Curtis H. (1972). "State Laws on Marriage and Sterilization of the Mentally Retarded." *Mental Retardation* (June):36-38.

Kuhar, Michael, Candace Pert, and Solomon Snyder. (1973). "Regional Distribution of Receptor Binding in Monkey and Human Brain." *Nature* 245(5426):447-450.

Kunz, Jeffrey R., ed. (1982). *The American Medical Association Family Medical Guide.* New York: Random House.

LaBrosse, E.H., J.D. Mann, and S.S. Kety. (1961). "The Physiological and Psychological Effects of Intravenously Administered Epinephrine and Its Metabolism in Normal Schizophrenic Men." *Journal of Psychiatric Research* 1:68-75.

Lakaski, Carl, Valerie Wilmot, Tom Lips, and Monica Brown. (1993). "Canada." In Donna Kemp, ed., *International Handbook of Mental Health Policy.* Westport, Connecticut: Greenwood Press. Pp.45-66.

Landers, Ann. (1990). "Column."(1992). *Chico Enterprise-Record* (November 6):2B.

"Law Bars Dying Baby's Organs from Donation." (1992). *Chico Enterprise-Record* (March 28):4C.

"Lawyer: Killer's 'Brain Shrinking.'" (1989). *Chico Enterprise-Record* (March 26):1B

"Lawyer: Surrogate Motherhood Is Selling Babies." (1986). *Chico Enterprise-Record* (September 28):1B.

Ledbetter, David H., A.D. Martin, Y. Verlinsky, E. Pergament, L. Jackson, T. Yang-Feng, S.A. Schonberg, F. Gilbert, J.M. Zachary, and M. Barr. (1990). "Cytogenetic Results of Chorionic Villus Sampling." *American Journal of Obstetrics and Gynecology* 162(3):495-501.

Lee, Maring and Bruce Shlain. (1985). *Acid Dreams: The CIA, LSD and the Sixties Rebellion.* New York: Grove Press.

Leeton, J., A.O. Trounson, and C. Wood. (1982). "IVF and ET: What It Is and How It Works." In W. Walters and P. Singers, eds., *Test-Tube Babies.* Melbourne: Oxford. Pp. 2-10.

Leiblum, Sandra R., Ekkehard Kemmann, and M.K. Lane. (1987). "The Psychological Concomitants of In Vitro Fertilization." *Journal of Psychosomatic Obstetrics and Gynecology* 6(3):165-178.

Lenzer, I.I., C.M. Hourihan, and C.L. Ryan. (1982). "Relation Between Behavioral and Physical Abnormalities Associated with Prenatal Exposure to Alcohol." *Perceptual and Motor Skills* 55(3, Pt. 1):903-912.

Lewinsohn, P.M., M.A. Youngren, and S.J. Grosscup. (1979). "Reinforcement and Depression." In R.A. Depue, ed., *The Psychobiology of the Depressive Disorders: Implications for the Effects of Stress*. New York: Academic.

Liberman, R.P. and D. E. Raskin. (1971). "Depression: A Behavioral Formulation." *Archives of General Psychiatry* 24(6):515-523.

Liberman, R.P., W.J. DeRisi, and K.T. Mueser. (1989). *Social Skills Training for Psychiatric Patients*. New York: Pergamon.

Lifton, Betty Jean. (1979). *Lost and Found the Adoption Experience*. New York: Dial.

Lifton, Betty Jean. (1988). "Brave New Baby in the Brave New World." In Elaine Hoffman Baruch, Amadeo F. D'Adamo, Jr., and Joni Seager, eds., *Embryos, Ethics, and Women's Rights*. New York: Haworth Press. Pp. 149-153.

Littleton, Christine A. (1988). "Choice in Definitions of Sexual Equality and Reproductive Choice." Unpublished paper presented at the Annual Meeting of the Western Political Science Association, San Francisco, CA (March 10-12).

Loevenhart, A.S., W.F. Lorenz, and R.M. Waters. (1929). "Cerebral Stimulation." *Journal of the American Medical Association* 92:880-883.

Lohr, J.B. and J.L. Cadet. (1987). "Neuropsychiatric Aspects of Brain Tumors." In R.E. Hales and S.C. Yudovsky, eds., *Neuropsychiatric Aspects of Brain Tumors*. Washington, D.C., American Psychiatric Press.

Lorber, Judith. (1988). "In Vitro Fertilization and Gender Politics." In Elaine Hoffman Baruch, Amadeo F. D'Adamo, Jr., and Joni Seager, eds., *Embryos, Ethics, and Women's Rights*. New York: Haworth Press. Pp. 117-133.

Losco, Joseph. (1989). "Fetal Abuse." *Western Political Quarterly* 42(2):265-286.

Love, H.D. (1973). *The Mentally Retarded Child and His Family*. Springfield, Illinois: Charles C. Thomas.

Lowman, Mary. (1990). "Overcoming the Mountain of Infertility." *Chico Enterprise-Record* (November 8):1B.

Luborsky, Lester, L. Singer, and L. Luborsky. (1975). "Comparative Studies of Psychotherapies." *Archives of General Psychiatry* 32:995-1008.

Lubs, M.L. and R.F. Falk. (1977). "Response to Prospective Genetic Counseling in Severe X-linked Disorders." In H.A. Lubs and F. de la Cruz, eds., *Genetic Counseling*. New York: Raven Press. Pp. 269-289.

Luby, Elliot D. and Robert Bielski. (1978). "Pharmacologic Management of Schizophrenics." In Norman Rosenzweig and Hilda Griscom, eds., *Psychopharmacology and Psychotherapy: Synthesis or Antithesis?* New York: Human Sciences Press.

Lundvall, H. (1915). "Blood Changes in Dementia Praecox and Artificial

Leucocytosis in Its Treatment." *American Journal of Clinical Medicine* 22:115.

Lydiard, R.B., E.F. Hosell, and M.T. Laraia. (1989). "Depression in Patients Receiving Lorazepam for Panic." *American Journal of Psychiatry* 146:629-631.

Macri, J.N. and R.R. Weiss. (1982). "Prenatal Serum Alpha-Fetoprotein Screening for Neural Tube Defects." *Obstetrics and Gynecology* 59(5):633.

Mahler, M.S., F. Pine, and A. Bergman. (1975). *The Psychological Birth of the Human Infant*. New York: Basic Books.

Maier, Gary J., Robert D. Miller, and Lou Roach. (1992). "The Real Cost of Clozapine: A Patient Buys Freedom." *Hospital and Community Pschiatry* 43(2):177-178.

Main, Denise M. and Michael T. Mennuti. (1986). "Neural Tube Defects: Issues in Prenatal Diagnosis and Counseling." *Obstetrics and Gynecology* 67(1):1-16.

Malan, O. (1973). "The Outcome Problem in Psychotherapy Research." *Archives of General Psychiatry* 29:719-729.

Malzberg, B. (1938). "Outcome of Insulin Treatment of One Thousand Patients with Dementia Praecox." *Psychiataric Quarterly* 12:528-553.

Mandel, M. (1975). "Electroconvulsive Therapy for Chronic Pain Associated with Depression." *American Journal of Psychiatry* 138:1-13.

Manual of the International Statistical Classification of Diseases, Injuries, and Cause of Death (Vol. 1). (1977). Geneva: World Health Organization.

Marbury, Marian C., S. Linn, and R. Monson. (1983). "The Association of Alcohol Consumption with Outcome of Pregnancy." *American Journal of Public Health* 73(10):1165-1168.

Mark, Mordechi, Ilan Modai, Dov Aizenber, Yechiel Heilbronn, and Avner Elizur. (1991). "Bipolar Disorder Associated with an Acoustic Neurinoma." *Hospital and Community Psychiatry* 42(12):1258-1259.

Mark, Vernon H. and Frank R. Ervin (1970). *Violence and the Brain*. New York: Harper & Row.

Markel, D.S., A.B. Young, and J.B. Penney. (1987). "At-risk Persons: Attitudes Toward Presymptomatic and Prenatal Testing of Huntington Disease in Michigan." *American Journal of Medical Genetics* 26:295-305.

Markides, Kyriakos S., Laura A. Ray, Christine A. Stroup-Benham, and Fernando Trevino. (1990). 'Acculturation and Alcohol Consumption in the Mexican American Population of the South-Western United States: Findings from HHANES 1982-84." *American Journal of Public Health* 80 Suppl.:42-46.

Marks, Gary, Melinda Garcia, and Julia Solis. (1990). "Health Risk Behaviors of Hispanics in the U.S.: Findings from HHANES, 1982-84." *American Journal of Public Health* 80 Suppl.:20-26.

Martin, Russell. (1986). *Matters Gray and White: A Neurologist, His Patients, and the Mysteries of the Brain.* New York: Henry Holt and Company.

Mascola, L. and M.E. Guinan. (1986). "Screening to Reduce Transmission of Sexually Transmitted Diseases in Semen Used for Artificial Insemination." *New England Journal of Medicine* 14(21):1354-1359.

Maslow, Abraham H. (1970). *Motivation and Personality.* 2nd ed. New York: Harper & Row.

Mazure, Caroline M., William Delune, and Alan H. DeCherney. (1988). "Two Methodological Issues in the Psychological Study of In Vitro Fertilization." *Journal of Psychosomatic Obstetrics and Gynecology* 9(1):17-21.

McBain, J.C. and A. Trounson. (1984). "Patient Management-Treatment Cycle." In Carl Wood and Alan Trounson, eds., *Clinical In Vitro Fertilization.* New York: Springer-Verlag. Pp. 49-65.

McClelland, H.A., A.V. Metcalfe, T.A. Kerr, D. Dutta, and P. Watson. (1991). "Facial Dyskinesia: A 16-Year Follow-up Study." *British Journal of Psychiatry* 158:691-696.

McCormic, Richard K. (1981). "To Save or Let Die: The Dilemma of Modern Medicine." In Thomas A. Mappes and Jane S. Zembaty, eds., *Biomedical Ethics.* New York: McGraw-Hill, 383-387.

McCormick, M.J., M.E. Rylance, W.E. Mackenzie, and T. Newton. (1990). "Patients' Attitudes Following Choronic Villus Sampling." *Prenatal Diagnosis* 10:253-255.

McGrath, Mike. (1988). "Training the Body to Cure Itself." *Prevention* (December):44-47.

McGue, M. and I Gottesman. (1990). "Genetic Linkage in Schizophrenia: Perspectives from Genetic Epidemilogy." In V. Bulyzhenkov, Y. Christen, and L. Prilipko, eds., *Genetic Approaches in the Prevention of Mental Disorders.* New York: Springer-Verlag.

McIntosh, Hugh. (1982). "Grafts Offer Hope for Brain Disease Victims." *The Bakersfield Californian* (March 21):C1.

McShane, Patricia M. (1988). "In Vitro Fertilization, GIFT and Related Technologies—Hope in a Test Tube." In Elaine Hoffman Baruch, Amadeo F. D'Adamo, Jr., and Joni Seager, eds., *Embryos, Ethics, and Women's Rights.* New York: The Haworth Press. Pp. 31-46.

Meldrum, B.S. (1986). "Neuropathological Consequences of Chemically and Electrically Induced Seizures." *Annals of the New York Academy of Science* 462:186-193.

Mendlewicz, J. (1990). "New Genetic Strategies in Neuropsychiatric Disorders." In V. Bulyzhenkov, Y. Christen, and L. Prilipko, eds., *Genetic Approaches in the Prevention of Mental Disorders.* New York: Springer-Verlag.

Merrick, Janna C. (1988). "Biomedical Ethics and the Treatment of

Handicapped Newborns.'' Unpublished paper presented at Annual Meeting of the Western Political Science Association, San Francisco.

Merrick, Janna C. (1990). "Maternal-Fetal Conflict: Adversaries or Allies?'' Unpublished Paper presented at Annual Meeting of the American Political Science Association, San Francisco.

Meryask, D.L. and D. Abuelo. (1988). "Counseling Needs and Attitudes Toward Prenatal Diagnosis and Abortion in Fragile-X Families.'' *Clinical Genetics* 33:349-355.

Miall, C.E. (1986). "The Stigma of Involuntary Childlessness.'' *Social Problems* 33:268-282.

Micioni, G., L. Jeker, M. Zeeb, and A. Canpana. (1987). "Doubtful and Negative Psychological Indications for AID.'' *Journal of Psychosomatic Obstetrics and Gynecology* 6(2):89-99.

Mikesell, S.G. and R. Falk. (1985). "Low Marital Distress Reported by In Vitro Fertilization Participants.'' Unpublished paper presented at Annual Meeting, American Fertility Society, Chicago.

Mili, Fatima, Larry D. Edmonds, Muin J. Khoury, and Anne B. McClearn. (1991). "Prevalence of Birth Defects Among Low-Birth-Weight Infants'' *American Journal of Diseases of Children* 145:1313-1318.

Miller, Neal E. (1968). "Paper Presented at the Annual Meeting of the Pavlovian Society of North America.'' *Conditioned Reflex* 3:129-135.

Millstein, V. I. Small. (1985). "Electroconvulsive Therapy: Attitudes and Experience.'' *Convulsive Therapy* 1:89-100.

Minkoff, K. (1978). "A Map of Chronic Mental Patients.'' In J.A. Talbott, ed., *The Chronic Mental Patient*. Washington, D.C.: American Psychiatric Association.

"Missouri Parents Can't Sue Doctor.'' (1988). *Chico Enterprise-Record* (October 11):8A.

Mitchell, J. (1988). "What About the Mothers of HIV Infected Babies?'' *NAN Multi-Cultural Notes on AIDS Education and Service* 1:1-2.

Moccia, John A. (1983). "The Desperate Alternative.'' *Federal Probation* (June):70-72.

Molony, Helen and John Taplin. (1988). "Deinstitutionalization of People with Developmental Disabilities.'' *Australian and New Zealand Journal of Developmental Disabilities* 14(2):109-122.

"Moods Implicated in 'Yuppie Disease.''' (1989). *Chico Enterprise-Record* (January 29):6B.

Morris, Grant H. (1978). "Conservatorship for the Gravely Disabled.'' *Journal of Law and Psychiatry* 1:403-409.

Moskop, John C. and Rita A. Saldania. (1986). "The Baby Doe Rule.'' *Hastings Center Report*: 16(2): 8-14.

Moss, Nancy and Paul A. Hensleigh. (1988). "Substance Use by Hispanic and

White non-Hispanic Pregnant Adolescents: A Preliminary Study." *Journal of Youth and Adolescents* 17(6):531-541.

Murphy, Joan. (1990). "Fetal Protection v. Women's Jobs: Case Is Before Supreme Court." *The Nation's Health* (November):1, 3.

Murphy, Joan. (1991). "Federal Agencies Gearing Up for New Efforts Against Lead." *The Nation's Health* (May-June):1, 23.

Murray, R., P. McGuffin, and A.M. Reveley. (1986). "Genetics of Schizophrenia." *Psychiatric Clinics of North America* 9:3-16.

Mushin, D.N., M.C. Beruieda-Hanson, and J.C. Spensley. (1986). "In Vitro Fertilization Children: Early Psycho-social Development." *Journal of In Vitro Fertilization and Embryo Transfer* 3:247-252.

Nadler, H.L. (1986). "Amniocentesis." *World Book Encyclopedia* 1:414.

National Advisory Mental Health Council (NAMHC). (1990). *National Plan for Research on Child and Adolescent Mental Disorders.* Washington, D.C.: National Institute of Mental Health.

National Association for Perinatal Addiction Research and Education (NAPARE). (1990). "NAPARE Policy Statement Number 1" Chicago, Illinois: Author.

National Cancer Institute. (1989). Cited in Karen Schwartz. "Talking About Cancer Helps Mental Health." *Chico Enterprise-Record* (January 28):1B.

National Center for Health Statistics. (1991). *Health, United States.* 1990. Hyattsville, Maryland: Public Health Service.

National Commission for the Protection of Human Subjects of Biomedical and Behavioral Research. (1977). *Report and Recommendations: Psychosurgery.* Washington, D.C.: Government Printing Office. Department of Health, Education and Welfare, Pub. No. 05 77-0002.

National Institute of Mental Health (NIMH). (1986). *Mental Health, United States. 1986.* R.W. Manderscheid and M.A. Sonnenschein, eds., DHHS Pub. Washington, D.C.: Superintendent of Documents, Government Printing Office.

National Institute of Mental Health (NIMH). (1990). *Mental Health, United States. 1990.* R.W. Manderscheid and M.A. Sonnenschein, eds., DHHS Pub. No. (ADM) 90-1708. Washington, D.C.: Superintendent of Documents, Government Printing Office.

National Institute of Mental Health (NIMH). (1992). Unpublished estimate. Washington, D.C.: Statistical Research Branch. In Peggy R. Barker, Ronald W. Manderscheid, Gerry E. Henderslot, Susan S. Jack, Charlotte A. Schoenbon, and Ingrid Goldstrom, "Serious Mental Illness and Disability in the Adult Household Population: United States, 1989." *Advance Data* 218 (September 16). Washington, D.C.: National Center for Health Statistics, Center for Disease Control.

National Institute on Drug Abuse (NIDA). (1987). *National Household Survey on Drug Abuse: Population Estimate 1985*. Washington, D.C.: Government Printing Office.

National Institute on Drug Abuse (NIDA). (1989). *NIDA Capsules: Drug Abuse and Pregnancy*. Washington, D.C.: Department of Health and Human Services (June).

Needleman, Sima K. (1987). "Infertility and In Vitro Fertilization: The Social Worker's Role." *Health and Social Work* 12(2):135-143.

Nelson, Karin B. and Alan Leviton. (1991). "How Much of Neonatal Encephalopathy is Due to Birth Asphyxia?" *American Journal of Diseases of Children* 145:1325-1331.

Nelson, Lawrence J. and Nancy Milliken. (1988). "Compelled Medical Treatment of Pregnant Women." *Journal of the American Medical Association* 259(7):1060-1066.

Newacheck, Paul W. and William R. Taylor. (1992). "Childhood Chronic Illness: Prevalence, Severity and Impact." *American Journal of Public Health* 83(3):364-371.

Newman, Robert G. (1977). *Methadone Treatment in Narcotic Addiciton*. New York: Academic Press Inc.

Nolan, Kathleen. (1990). "Protecting Fetuses from Prenatal Hazards." *Criminal Justice Ethics* 9(1):13-23.

O'Brien, P. Ch., A. R. Childness, and I. O. Arndt. (1988). "Pharmacological and Behavioral Treatments of Cocaine Dependence." *Journal of Clincial Psychiatary* 49:17-22.

O'Connor, D. Michael. (1986). "1986 Electroconvulsive Therapy (ECT) Report." Sacramento: Department of Mental Health.

Office of Technology Assessment (OTA). (1987). *OTA Proposal: Infectibility Prevention and Treatment*. Washington, D.C.: OTA.

Office of the Inspector General, HHS. (1987). *Infant Care Review Committee Under the Baby Doe Program*. Washington, D.C.: Government Printing Office.

Ogg, Elizabeth. (1973). "Securing the Legal Rights of Retarded Persons." 10 (Public Affairs Pamphlet No. 492).

Oster, Gerry, Daniel Huse, Shelley A. Adams, Joseph Imbimbo, and Mason W. Russell. (1990). "Benzodiazephine Tranquilizers and the Risk of Accidental Injury." *American Journal of Public Health* 80(12):1467-1470.

Padus, Emrika. (1986). *The Complete Guide to Your Emotions and Your Health*. Emmaus, Pennsylvania: Rodale Press.

Palmstierna, Tom, Bernard Hutfeldt, and Borje Wistedt. (1991). "The Relationship of Crowding and Aggressive Behavior on a Psychiatric Intensive Care Unit." *Hospital and Community Psychiatry* 42(12):1237-1240.

Palmstierna, Tom and Borje Wistedt, (1987). "Staff Observation Aggression

Scale, (SOAS): Presentation and Evaluation." *Acta Psychiatrica Scandinavica* 76:657-663.

Panem, Sandra, ed. (1985). *Biotechnology: Implications for Public Policy.* Washington, D.C.: Brookings Institution.

Parker, G., P. Johnston, and L. Hayward. (1988). "Parental Expressed Emotion as a Predictor of Schizophrenic Relapse." *Archives of General Psychiatry* 45:806-813.

Parker, P.J. (1984). "Surrogate Motherhood Psychiatric Screening." *Bulletin of the American Academy of Psychiatry and the Law* 12:21-39.

Paul, G.L. and R.J. Lentz. (1977). *Psychosocial Treatment of Chronic Mental Patients.* Cambridge: Harvard University Press.

"Peak Ages for Developing Mental Illness Are Childhood, Adolescence." (1990). *The Nation's Health* (November):7.

Pearson, M., E. Wilmot, and M. Padi. (1986). "A Study of Violent Behavior Among In-patients in a Psychiatric Hospital." *British Journal of Psychiatry* 149:232-235.

Perry, John. (1987). "A Unified Theory of Substitute Consent." *Mental and Physical Disability Law Reporter* 11(6):378-385, 441.

Perske, R. (1973). "About Sexual Development." *Mental Retardation* 11:3-10.

Petrila, John P. and Robert L. Sadoff. (1992). "Confidentiality and the Family as Caregiver." *Hospital and Community Psychiatry* 43(2):136-139.

Pies, Ronald W. (1988). "Atypical Depression." In Joe P. Tupin, Richard I. Shadeer, and David S. Harnett, eds., *Handbook of Clinical Psychopharmacology.* Northvale, New Jersey: Jason Aronson. Pp. 329-356.

Pinheiro, Marcio V. (1992). "The Selling of Clinical Psychiatry in America." *Hospital and Community Psychiatry* 43(2):102-104.

Plog, Stanley C. and Miles B. Santomous. (1980). *The Year 2000 and Mental Retardation.* New York: Plenum Press.

Plutchek, Robert and B. Toksoy. (1991). "Computers in Psychotherapy: An Overview." *Computers in Human Behavior* 7(1-2):33-44.

Potter, Ann E. and Patricia K. Knaub. (1988). "Single Motherhood By Choice: A Parenting Alternative." *Lifestyles* 9(3):240-249.

President's Commission for the Study of Ethical Problems in Medicine and Biomedical and Behavioral Research. (1982). *Splicing Life: A Report on the Social and Ethical Issues of Genetic Engineering with Human Beings.* Washington, D.C.: Government Printing Office.

President's Commission for the Study of Ethical Problems in Medicine and Biomedical and Behavioral Research. (1981). *Defining Death.* Washington, D.C.: Government Printing Office.

Randall, C., B. Mandelbaum, and T. Kelly. (1984). "Letter from Three General Secretaries to President Carter." In National Council of Churches of Christ, ed., *Genetic Engineering: Social and Ethical Consequences*. New York: Plenum Press. Pp. 47-49.

Rapp, Rayna. (1988). "Moral Pioneers: Women, Men and Fetuses on a Frontier of Reproductive Technology." In Elaine Hoffman Baruch, Amadeo F. D'Adamo, Jr., and Joni Seager, eds., *Embryos, Ethics and Women's Rights*. New York: Haworth Press. Pp. 101-116.

Reading, Anthony, Li C. Chang, and John F. Kerin. (1989). "Psychological State and Coping Styles Across an IVF Treatment Cycle." *Journal of Reproductive and Infant Psychology* 7(2):95-103.

Regier, D.A., J.K. Myers, M. Kramer, L.N. Robins, D.G. Blazer, R.L. Hough, W.W. Eaton, and B.Z. Locke. (1984). "The NIMH Epidemiologic Cathment Area Program: Historical Context, Major Objectives, and Study Population Characteristics." *Archives of General Psychiatry* 41:934-941.

Restak, Richard. (1988). *The Mind*. New York: Bantam Books.

Rhoden, Nancy (1986). "The Judge in the Delivery Room." *California Law Review* 74(6):951-2030.

Rhoden, Nancy. (1987). "Cesareans and Samaritans." *Law, Medicine, and Health Care* 15(3):118-125.

Robertson, John A. (1983). "Procreative Liberty and The Control of Conception, Pregnancy, and Childbirth." *Virginia Law Review* 69(3):405-464.

Robertson, John A. (1988). "Procreative Liberty Embryo, and Collaborative Reproduction: A Legal Perspective." In Elaine Hoffman Baruch, Amado F. D'Adamo, Jr., and Joni Seager, eds., *Embryos, Ethics, and Women's Rights*. New York: Haworth Press. Pp. 179-195.

Robins, L.N., J.E. Helzer, M. Weissman, H. Orvaschel, E. Gruenberg, J.D. Burke, and D.A. Regier. (1984). "Lifetime Prevalence of Specific Psychiatric Disorders on Three Sites." *Archives of General Psychiatry* 41:949-958.

Robinson-Haynes, Ellen. (1990). "Methadone: Godsend and Controversy." *Chico Enterprise-Record* (October 21):A19.

Robinson-Haynes, Ellen. (1986). "Boycott Baby Girls? Sex Selection Troubles Ethicists." *The Sacramento Bee* 260 (August 11):A1.

Rodgers, Joann Ellison. (1992). *Psychosurgery*. New York: Harper Collins.

Rogers, Carl. (1951). *Client-Centered Therapy*. London: Constable.

Rollnick, B. (1984). "The National Society of Genetic Counselors." *Birth Defects* 20:3-7.

Rosefeld, A. (1982). 'The Patient in the Womb." *Science* 82:18-23.

Rosendahl, Henrik and Seppo N. Kivine. (1989). "Antenatal Detection of Congenital Malformations by Routine Ultrasonography." *Obstetrics and Gynecology* 73(6):947-995.

Rosenthal, N.D., C.J. Carpenter, S.P. James, B.L. Parry, S.L.B. Rogers, and

T.A. Wehr. (1986). "Seasonal Affective Disorder in Children and Adolescents." *American Journal of Psychiatry* 143:356-358.

Rosenthal, R. (1984). *Meta-analysis Procedures for Social Research.* Beverly Hills: Sage.

Rostain, A. (1986). "Deciding to Forgo Life-Sustaining Treatment in the Intesive Care Nursery." *Perspectives in Biology and Medicine* 30(1):1117-1135.

Rothenberg, Karen H. (1988). "Baby M, the Surrogacy Contract, and the Health Care Professional." *Law, Medicine and Health Care* 16(1-2):113-120.

Rothman, Barbara Katz. (1986). *The Tentative Pregnancy.* New York: Viking.

Russel, W.L. (1932). "The Presidential Address: The Place of the American Psychiatric Association in Modern Psychiatric Organization and Progress" *American Journal of Psychiatry* 12:1-18.

Ryan, H.W., F.B. Merrill, and G.E. Scott. (1968). "Increase in Suicidal Thoughts and Tendencies." *Journal of the American Medical Association* 203:135-137.

Sagan, Leonard A. (1987). *The Health of Nations.* New York: Basic Books.

Saharelli, Joseph J. (1985). "Genesis Retold: Legal Issues Raised by the Cryopreservation of Preimplantation Human Embryos." *Syracuse Law Review* 26:1021-1053.

Salvia, J. and F.E. Ysseldyke. (1981). *Assessment in Special and Remedial Education.* Boston: Houghton Mifflin.

Sarah, Rebecca. (1988). "Power, Certainty, and the Fear of Death." In Elaine Hoffman Baruch, Amadeo F. D'Adamo, Jr., and Joni Seager, eds., *Embryos, Ethics and Women's Rights.* New York: Haworth Press. Pp. 59-71.

Sauer, Mark V., L.J. Paulson, and R.A. Lobo. (1990). "A Preliminary Report on Oocyte Donation Extending Reproductive Potential to Women Over 40." *New England Journal of Medicine* 25;323(17):1157-1160.

Saunders, D.M., M. Matthews, and P.A.L. Lancaster. (1987). "The Australian Register, Current Research and Future Role (A Preliminary Report)." Unpublished paper presented at Fifth World Congress on In Vitro Fertilization and Embryo Transfer, Norfolk, Virginia.

Schechter, M.D. (1967). "Panel: Psychoanalytic Theory as It Relates to Adoption." *Journal of the American Psychoanalytic Association* 15:695-708.

Scheffler, Richard. (1987). "The Economics of Mental Health Care in a Changing Economic and Health Care Environment." In Leonard J. Duhl and Nicholas A. Cummings, eds., *The Future of Mental Health Services: Coping with Crisis.* New York: Springer Publishing Co. Pp. 47-54.

"Schizophrenia Signs Found in Infants." (1991). *Chico Enterprise-Record*

(March 22):8D.

Schneier, F.R. and S.G. Siris (1987). "A Review of Psychoactive Substance Use and Abuse in Schizophrenia; Patterns of Drug Choice." *Journal of Nervous and Mental Disease* 175: 641-642.

Schuker, Eleanor. (1988). "Psychological Effects of New Reproductive Technologies." In Elaine Hoffman Baruch, Amadeo F. D'Adamo, Jr., and Joni Seager, eds., *Embryos, Ethics, and Women's Rights*. New York: Haworth Press. Pp. 141-147.

Schwab, Brenda, Robert E. Drake, and Elisabeth Burghardt. (1988). "Health Care of the Chronically Mentally Ill: The Culture Broker Model." *Community Mental Health Journal* 24(3):174-184.

Schwan, Kassie. (1988). *The Infertility Maze*. Chicago, Illinois: Contemporary Books.

Schwartz, Harold I. (1992). "An Empirical Review of the Impact of Triplicate Prescription of Benzodiazepines." *Hospital and Community Psychiatry* 43(4):382-385.

Schwartz, Richard. (1991). "Heavy Marijuana Use and Recent Memory Impairment." *Psychiatric Annals* 21(2):80-82.

Scoville, W.B. (1971). "The Effect of Surgical Lesions of the Brain on Psyche and Behavior in Man." In A. Winter, ed., *The Surgical Control of Behavior*. Springfield, Illinois: Charles C. Thomas.

Scriver, Charles R. (1985). "Population Screening: Report of a Workshop." *Progress in Clinical and Biological Research*. 163B:89-152.

Sedgwick, Peter. (1982). *Psycho Politics*. New York: Harper & Row.

Sells, C.J. and F.C. Bennett. (1977). "Prevention of Mental Retardation: The Role of Medicine." *American Journal of Mental Deficiency* 82:120-125.

Shannon, Thomas A. (1988). "In Vitro Fertilization: Ethical Issues." In Elaine Hoffman Baruch, Amadeo F. D'Adamo, Jr., and Joni Seager, eds., *Embryos, Ethics, and Women's Rights*. New York: Haworth Press Pp. 155-165.

Shapiro, Robert (1991). *The Human Blueprint*. New York: St. Martin's Press.

Shaw, Paula, Marie Johnston, and Robert Shaw. (1988). "Counseling Needs, Emotional and Relationship Problems in Couples Awaiting IVF." *Journal of Psychosomatic Obstetrics and Gynaecology* 9(3):171-180.

Shaywitz, S.E. and B.A. Shaywitz. (1990). "Increased Medication Use in Attention Deficit Hyperactivity Disorder: Regressive or Appropriate?" *Journal of the American Medical Association* 259:2270-2271.

Shevory, Thomas C. (1990). "Through a Glass Darkly: Law, Politics, and Frozen Human Embryos." Unpublished paper presented at Annual Meeting of the American Political Science Association, San Francisco.

Shorter, Edward. (1987). *The Health Century*. Doubleday: New York.

Shostak, A.B. and G. Mclouth. (1984). *Men and Abortion*. New York: Praeger.

Shrednick, A. (1983). "Emotional Support Programs for In Vitro Fertilization." *Fertility and Sterility* 40:704.

Shtasel, Derri L., Requel E. Gur, David Mozley, Jeffrey Richards, Margaret M. Taleff, Carolyn Heimberg, Fiona Gallacher, and Reuben Gur. (1991). "Volunteers for Biomedical Research: Recruitment and Screening of Normal Controls." *Archives of General Psychiatry* 115(11):1022-1025.

Siddique, Teepu, D.A. Figlewicz, and M.A. Pericak-Vance. (1991). "Linkage of the Gene Causing Familial Amyotrophic Lateral Sclerosis to Chromosome 21 and Evidence of Genetic Locus." *New England Journal of Medicine* 4:325(1):71.

Simon, Carol Ann. (1978). "Parental Liability for Prenatal Injury." *Columbia Journal of Law and Social Relations* 14:47-90.

Simpson, Herb M. (1986). "Epidemiology of Road Accidents Involving Marijuana." *Alcohol, Drugs and Driving Abstracts and Reviews* 2(3-4):15-30.

Skinner, B.F. (1953). *Science and Human Behavior.* New York: Macmillan.

Smith, Blake D. and Carl Salzman. (1991). "Do Benzodiazepines Cause Depression?" *Hospital and Community Psychiatry* 42(11):1101-1102.

Smith, M. and S. Potkin. (1990). "Development of an Infrastructure for Molecular Genetic Analysis in Psychiatry." In V. Bulyzhenkov, Y. Christen, and L. Prilipko, eds., *Genetic Approaches in the Prevention of Mental Disorders.* New York: Springer-Verlag.

Smith, Steven R. and Robert G. Meyer. (1987). *Law, Behavior, and Mental Health: Policy and Practice.* New York: New York University Press.

Sokoloff, Burton Z. (1987). "Alternative Methods of Reproductive Effects on the Child." *Clinical Pediatrics* 26(1):11-17.

Solanto, M.V. and E.H. Wender. (1989). "Does Methylphenidate Constrict Cognitive Functioning?" *Journal of the American Academy of Child and Adolescent Psychiatry* 28(6):897-902.

Sommers, Ira. (1988). "Social and Geographic Correlates of the Community Adjustment of the Chronically Mentally Ill." *Administration and Policy in Mental Health* 16(1):25-39.

Sorosky, Arthur, Annette Baran, and Reuben Pannor. (1978). *The Adoption Triangle.* New York: Anchor Press/Doubleday.

Sovner, R. (1986). "Limiting Factors in the Use of DSM-III for Mentally Ill/Mentally Retarded Persons. *Psychopharmacology Bulletin* 22:1055-1059.

Sovner, R. (1987). "Behavioral Psychopharmacology." In J. Stark, F.J. Menolascino, M. Albarielli, and V. Gray, eds., *Mental Retardation and Mental Health* New York: Springer-Verlag.

Sovner, R. (1988). "Five Myths About Psychotropic Drug Therapy and Mentally Retarded Persons." *Psychiatric Aspects of Mental Retardation Review* 7(5):39-32.

Sperling, Dan. (1988). "Treating Pre-Menstrul Syndrome." *USA Today* (September 1):4D.

"Sperm Bank Announces First Baby." (1982). *The Bakersfield California* (June 23):A2.

Spitz, R. (1965). *The First Year of Life*. New York: International Universities Press.

Spitzer, R.L., J. Endicott, and E. Robins. (1978). "Research Diagnostic Criteria: Rationale and Reliability." *Archives of General Psychiatry* 35:773-782.

Spitzer, R.L., J.B.W. William, and M. Gibbon. (1989). *Structured Clinical Interview for DSM-III-R: Non-Patient Version (SCID-NP)*. New York: New York State Psychiatric Institute.

Sram, R.J., B. Binkova, and A. Gebhart. (1990). "Impact of Environmental Mutagens on Mental Health." In V. Bulyzhenkov, Y. Christen, and L. Prilipko, eds., *Genetic Approaches in the Prevention of Mental Disorders*. New York: Springer-Verlag.

St. John, Paige. (1992). "Scientists Can't Give Answers to Great Lakes Women." *Chico Enterprise-Record* (February 11):6A.

Stahl, S. (1990). "Novel Pharmacological Approaches for the Treatment of Schizophrenia." Unpublished paper presented at International Conference of Schizophrenia 1990, Vancouver, B.C. (July).

Stahlman, Mildred. (1989). "Implications of Research and High Technology for Neonatal Intensive Care." *Journal of the American Medical Association* 261:1791.

Staples, Robert. (1990). "Substance Abuse and the Black Family Crisis." *Western Journal of Black Studies* 14(4):196-204.

State of California (1990). *Governor's Budget Summary*. Sacramento, California: State Printing Office.

Stedman, Donald J. (1971). "Mental Retardation Programs: A Report to the Secretary's Committee on Mental Retardation." Washington, D.C.: Department of Health, Education, and Welfare.

Stephenson, P.S. (1975). "The Hyperkinetic Child: Some Misleading Assumptions." *The Journal of the Canadian Medical Association* 113(8):764, 767-769.

Stern, D.M. (1985). *The Interpersonal World of the Infant*. New York: Basic Books.

Stringer, L.A. (1973). "Children at Risk." *Elementary School Journal* 73(8):364-373.

Strobel, G. (1987). "Strobel: 'I Have Acted in Good Faith.'" *The Scientist* (October):11-12.

Stroud, Marion and Evelyn Sutton. (1988). *Expanding Options for Older Adults with Development Disabilities*. Baltimore: Brooks Publishing Co.

Strupp, H.H. (1978). "Psychotherapy Research and Practice: An Overview." In A.E. Bargin and S. Garfield, eds., *Handbook of Psychotherapy and Behavior Change*. New York: John Wiley & Sons.

Suddath, Richard, George Christison, E. Fuller Torrey, Manuel Casanova, and Daniel Weinberger. (1990). "Anatomical Abnormalities in the Brains of Monozygotic Twins Discordant for Schizophrenia." *The New England Journal of Medicine* 322(12):789-794.

Surber, Robert W., Martha Shumway, Richard Shadoan, and William A. Margreaves. (1986). "Effects of Fiscal Retrenchment and Public Mental Health Services for the Chronic Mentally Ill." *Community Mental Health Journal* 22(3):215-229.

"Surgical Castration Ok'd for Child Molester." (1992). *Chico Enterprise-Record* (March 7):3A.

"Surrogate Mother Gets Share of Custody." (1991). *Chico Enterprise-Record* (September 27):5A.

Szasz, Thomas. (1970). *The Manufacture of Madness*. New York: Harper & Row.

Taitz, L.S. (1980). "Effects of Growth and Development of Social Psychological, and Environmental Factors." *Child Abuse and Neglect* 4:55-65.

Talbott, J.H. and K.J. Tillotson. (1941). "The Effects of Cold on Mental Disorders." *Diseases of the Nervous System* 2:116-126.

Tardive Dyskinesia/Tardive Dystonia National Association. (1990). "Tardive Dyskinesia: Questions and Answers." Draft Two. Seattle: Author.

Taube, Carl A. and Howard H. Goldman. (1989). "State Strategies to Restructure Psychiatric Hospitals: A Selective Review." *Inquiry* 26(2):146-156.

Taylor, P.J. (1986). "The Risk of Violence in Psychotics." *Integrative Psychiatry* 4:12-24.

Teicher, Martin, Carol Glad, and Jonathan O. Cole. (1990). "Emergence of Intense Suicidal Preoccupation." *American Journal of Psychiatry* 147(2):207-210

Tessler, Richard C., Alice G. Bernstein, Beatrice M. Rosen, and Howard H. Goldman. (1982). "The Chronically Mentally Ill in Community Support Systems." *Hospital and Community Psychiatry* 33(3):202-211.

"Test Tube Fertilization Extends Baby Making Years." (1990). *Chico Enterprise-Record* (October 25):2A.

Teuber, H.L., S.H. Corkin, and T.E. Twitchell. (1977). "Study of Cingulotomy in Man: A Summary." In W.H. Sweet, S. Obrador, and J.G. Martin-Rodriguez, eds., *Neurosurgical Treatment in Psychiatry, Pain, and Epilepsy*. Baltimore: University Park Press.

Teuber, J.L. (1964). "The Riddle of Frontal Lobe Function in Man." In J.M.

Warren and K. Akert, eds., *The Frontal Granular Cortex and Behavior*. New York: McGraw-Hill. Pp. 415-416.

Thaker, G.K., M. Moran, A. Lahti, H. Adami, and C. Tammings. (1990). "Psychiatric Morbidity in Research Volunteers." *Archives of General Psychiatry*. 47:785-786.

Thornton, John F., Mary V. Seeman, Elizabeth D. Plummer, and J. Joel Jeffries. (1985). "Schizophrenia: The Medications." Clarke Institute of Psychiatry, Department of Psychiatry, University of Toronto. Ontario, Canada: Merrell Pharmaceuticals, Professional Services Department.

Toman, Walter. (1988). *Family Therapy and Sibling Position*. Northvale, New Jersey: Jason Aronson Inc.

Torrey, E. Fuller. (1986). *Witchdoctors and Psychiatrists*. New York: Harper & Row.

Torrey, E. Fuller. (1990). *Nowhere to Go: The Tragic Odyssey of the Homeless Mentally Ill*. New York: Harper & Row.

Torrey, E. Fuller, Karen Erdman, Sidney M. Wolfe, and Laurie M. Flynn. (1990). *Care of the Seriously Mentally Ill: A Rating of State Programs*. Washington, D.C.: Public Citizen Health Research Group and National Alliance for the Mentally Ill.

Toufexis, Anastasia. (1990a). "From the Asylum to Anarchy." *Time* (October):58-59.

Toufexis, Anastasia. (1990b). "Medicine; Warning About a Miracle Drug." *Time* (July 30):54.

Tourney, Garfield. (1978). "Introduction: Psychopharmacology and Psychotherapy." In Norman Rosenzweig and Hilda Griscom, eds., *Psychopharmacology and Psychotherapy: Synthesis or Antithesis?* New York: Human Sciences Press.

Trainor, John N., Steve Lurie, Ronald Ballantyne, and Dennis Long. (1987). "The Supportive Housing Coalition: A Model for Advocacy and Program Development." *Canadian Journal of Community Mental Health* 6(2):93-106.

Treece, C. and E. Khantzian. (1986). "Psychodynamic Factors in the Development of Drug Dependence." *Psychiatric Clinics of North America* 9:399-412.

Treffert, Harold. (1989). "The Obviously Ill Patient in Need of Treatment: A Fourth Standard for Civil Commitment." *Hospital and Community Psychiatry* (March):262-267.

Tushnet, Mark. (1984). "An Essay on Rights." *Texas Law Review* 62:1363-1403.

Ubell, Earl. (1983). "Should Death Be a Patient's Choice? *Parade Magazine* (February 9):24-28.

"Ultrasound Tells Tot's Sex." (1983). *The Bakersfield Californian* (October

20):A12.

Valenstein, Elliot S., ed. (1980). *The Psychosurgery Debate: Scientific, Legal and Ethical Perspectives*. San Francisco: W.H. Freeman and Company.

Valenstein, Elliot S. (1986). *Great and Desperate Cures: The Rise and Decline of Psychosurgery and Other Radical Treatments for Mental Illness*. New York: Basic Books.

Van de Vate, C. (1990, August). "Prevention." Unpublished paper presented at the International Society for Mentally Handicapped World Congress Paris, France.

Van Valkenburg, C. and G. Winokur. (1979). "Depression Spectrum Disease." *Psychiatric Clinics of North America* 2:469-482.

Vannucci, R.C. (1990). "Current and Potentially New Management Strategies for Perinatal Hypoxi-ischemic Encephalopathy." *Pediatrics* 85:961-968.

Verdun-Jones, Simon N. (1988). "The Right to Refuse Treatment: Recent Developments in Canadian Jurisprudence." *International Journal of Law and Psychiatry* 11(1):51-60.

Verlinsky, Y. and E. Pergament. (1986). "Genetic Analysis of Human Embryos Prior to Implantation." *Journal of In Vitro Fertilization and Embryo Transfer* 3:80-85.

Vitello, Stanley J. (1981). "Mental Retardation Law in 1980: A Review." *Education and Training of the Mentally Retarded* (October):222-224.

Wagner, Thomas E. (1991). *Proceedings of the National Academy of Science*. Cited in "Scientists Attack Virus at Genetic Level." *Chico Enterprise-Record* (May 16):6F.

Wald, Patricia M. and Paul R. Friedman. (1979). "The Politics of Mental Health Advocacy in the United States." In Paul R. Friedman, ed., *Legal Rights of Mentally Disabled Persons*. New York: Practicing Law Institute.

Walrond-Skinner, Sue. (1986). *Dictionary of Psychotherapy*. New York: Routledge & Kegan Paul.

Ward, Mary Jane. (1946). *The Snake Pit*. New York: Random House.

Warnock, Mary. (1985). *A Question of Life: The Warnock Report on Human Fertilization and Embryology*. Oxford: Blackwell.

Wasmuth, J.J., J. Hewitt, B. Smith, D. Allard, J.L. Haines, D. Skarecky, E.Parlow, and M.R. Hayden. (1988). "A Highly Polymorphic Locus Very Tightly Linked to the Huntington's Disease Gene." *Nature* 332:734-736.

Wasylenki, Donald A. (1992). "Psychotherapy of Schizophrenia Revisited." *Hospital and Community Psychiatry* 43(2):123-127.

Watson, J.B. (1925). *Behaviorism*. London: Routledge & Kegan Paul.

Watzalwick, Paul, Janet Melmick Beavin, and Don D. Jackson. (1968). *Pragnatics of Human Communication*. New York: W.W. Norton.

Wehr, Thomas A. and Normal E. Rosenthal. (1989). "Seasonality and Affective Illness." *American Journal of Psychiatry* 146(7):827-839.

Weil, William B. (1986). "The Baby Doe Regulations: Another View of Change." *Hastings Center Report* (August):31-32.

Weiner, R.D. (1984). "Does ECT Cause Brain Damage?" *Behavioral Brain Science* 7:1-53.

Weissman, M.M., E.S. Gershon, K.K. Kidd, B.A. Prusoff, J.F. Leckman, E. Dibble, J. Hamovit, W.D. Thompson, D.L. Pauls., and J.J. Guroff (1985). "Psychiatric Disorders in the Relatives of Probands with Affective Disorders." *Archives of General Psychiatry* 41:13-21.

Wertz, D.C. (1990). "Ethical Issues in the Application of Knowledge from Molecular Genetics to Mental Disorders." In V. Bulyzhenkov, Y. Christen, and L. Prilipko, eds., *Genetic Approaches in the Prevention of Mental Disorders*. New York: Springer-Verlag.

Wertz, Dorothy, Janet M. Rosenfield, Sally R. Janes, and Richard W. Erbe. (1991). "Attitudes Toward Abortion Among Parents of Children with Cystic Fibrosis." *American Journal of Public Health* 81(8):992-996.

West, E.D. and P.J. Daily. (1959). "Effect of Iproniazid in Depressive Syndromes." *British Medical Journal* 1:1491-1494.

Whitbeck, Caroline. (1988). "Fetal Imaging and Fetal Monitoring: Finding the Ethical Issues." In Elaine Hoffman Baruch, Amadeo F. D'Adamo, Jr., and Joni Seager, eds., *Embryos, Ethics, and Women's Rights*. New York: Haworth Press. Pp. 47-57.

White, W.D. and W. Wolfensberger. (1969). "The Evolution of Dehumanization in our Institutions." *Mental Retardation* 7:3-10.

Whitlock, F.A. (1987). "Psychosurgery." In Richard Gregory, ed., *The Oxford Companion to the MIND*. New York: Oxford University Press. Pp. 660-661.

Wiesner, Paul J. (1979). "Dear Colleague" Letter. Report no. 1979-642-979/6346. Washington, D.C.: Goverment Printing Office.

Willer, B.S., J.C. Intagliata, and A.C. Atkinson. (1979). "Crisis for Families of Mentally Retarded Persons Including the Crisis of Deinstitutionalization." *British Journal of Mental Subnormality* 25(1):38-49.

Willet, Walter C. (1992). "Folic Acid and Neural Tube Defect: Can't We Come to Closure?" *American Journal of Public Health* 82(5):666-668.

Williamson, Carl P., Roger A. Weiner, William T.C. Yuh, and Monzer Abu-Yousef. (1989). "Magnetic Resonance Imaging of Anomalous Fetuses." *Obstetrics and Gynecology* 73(6):952-957.

Williamson, R. and A.M. Goate. (1990). "The Identification of Genes which Cause or Predispose to Mental Illness." In V. Bulyzhenkov, Y. Christen, and L. Prilipko, eds., *Genetic Approaches in the Prevention of Mental Disorders*. New York: Springer-Verlag.

Wilstein, Steve. (1987). "Study Links Drugs, Birth Trauma to Later Problems." *Idaho Statesman* (June 7-11):4A.

Wing, J. (1978). *Reasoning About Madness*. New York: Oxford University Press.

Witelson, Sandra. (1991). "Letter: Sex Differences in Neuroanatomical Changes with Aging." *New England Journal of Medicine* 18;325(3):211-212.

Wolpe, J. (1952). "Experimental Neuroses as Learned Behavior." *British Journal of Psychology* 43:243-252.

"Woman Fighting Insurance Companies." (1992). *Chico Enterprise-Record* (March 10):4C.

"Woman Gives Her Twin Reproductive Organs." (1984). *The Bakersfield California* (October 26):1A.

"Woman's 'Attacked Personality' Says She Didn't Know What Sex Was." (1990). *Chico-Enterprise Record* (November 8):2E.

World Health Organization (WHO). (1946). "Preamble." *Constitution*. Geneva: Author.

Wurmbrand, Marci Joy. (1986). "Frozen Embryos." *Southern California Law Review* 59:1099-1100.

Yates, A.J. (1980). *Biofeedback and the Modification of Behavior*. New York: John Wiley & Sons.

Young, Jeffery T., Joseph D. Bloom, Larry R. Faulkner, Jeffrey L. Rogers, and P.K. Pati. (1987). "Treatment Refusal Among Forensic Inpatients." *Bulletin of the American Academy of Psychiatry and the Law* 15(1):5-13.

Yovich, J.L., J.D. Stanger, and D. Kay. (1984). "In-Vitro Fertilization of Oocytes from Women with Serum Antisperm Antibodies." *Lancet* 18(1):369-370.

Yovich, J.L., T.S. Parry, N.P. French, and A.A. Grauaug. (1986). "Developmental Assessment of Twenty In Vitro Fertilization (IVF) Infants at Their First Birthday." *Journal of In Vitro Fertilization and Embryo Transfer* 3:253-257.

Zangwill, O.L. (1987). "Experimental Hypnosis and Kraepelin." In Richard L. Gregory, ed., *The Oxford Companion to THE MIND*. New York: Oxford University Press. Pp. 328-330, 414.

Index

About the Author

DONNA R. KEMP is Professor of Political Science and Public Administration at California State University, Chico. She is the editor of *International Handbook on Mental Health Policy* (Greenwood, 1993) and the author of *Mental Health in the Workplace* (Quorum, 1994).

ISBN 0-275-94812-9

HARDCOVER BAR CODE